THE INDUSTRIAL AND COMMERCIAL WORKERS' UNION OF AFRICA

The Industrial and Commercial Workers' Union of Africa

P. L. WICKINS

1978
Oxford University Press
Cape Town

Oxford University Press
OXFORD LONDON GLASGOW
NEW YORK TORONTO MELBOURNE WELLINGTON
IBADAN NAIROBI DAR ES SALAAM CAPE TOWN
KUALA LUMPUR SINGAPORE JAKARTA HONG KONG TOKYO
DELHI BOMBAY CALCUTTA MADRAS KARACHI

ISBN 0 19 570124 0

The author gratefully acknowledges the financial assistance of the University of Cape Town towards the publication of this book

Set in 10 on 12pt and 8 on 10pt Times Roman

Printed by Citadel Press, Lansdowne, Cape
Published by Oxford University Press, Harrington House, Barrack Street, Cape Town 8001

τὸ παρὸν γὰρ αἰεὶ βαρὺ τοῖς ὑπηκόοις

Thucydides I 77.5

Subject peoples always find
the present time most hard to bear.

Contents

Illustrations

Preface

Students of African nationalism in South Africa have long been aware of the significance of the Industrial and Commercial Workers' Union of Africa, the ICU, and are familiar with the account given by the late Professor Edward Roux in his book, *Time Longer than Rope: A History of the Black Man's Struggle for Freedom*, first published in 1949 (2nd edn. Madison, 1964). The first one to tell the story, however, was not he, but Vera Brittain, whose *Testament of Friendship* (London, 1940), a biography of Winifred Holtby, appeared nine years before. The information in that book was derived partly from Arthur Creech Jones and, more particularly, W. G. Ballinger, who was appointed Adviser to the union in 1928. Though of value for the light it throws upon the Adviser himself and the White sympathizers with the ICU, it is tendentious and not free from error. Later writers have disregarded Vera Brittain and preferred to use – or abuse – *Time Longer than Rope*. This has, indeed, much to commend it. While he disapproved of the policy the leaders followed and had little regard for the White liberals who patronized them, Roux was sympathetic towards the union and had an unsentimental affection for Clements Kadalie and Allison Champion, the dominant figures. Drawing largely upon personal knowledge and upon newspapers (including some later issues of the ICU paper, *The Workers' Herald*), he painted a lively and generally objective and accurate picture. The principal weakness of the Roux account is its perfunctory treatment of the early period of the ICU's history, the years before the opening of its offices in Johannesburg. Furthermore, the author's emotional involvement in the cause of the oppressed led him to exaggerate the significance of the movement and vest its failure with a tragic pathos disproportionate to its real opportunity for bringing about change in South Africa.

The most comprehensive, accurate, and impartial history that has so far come out was undoubtedly intended for the specialist. Sheridan W. Johns III has written two papers, one published as an article in *Race* ('The birth of non-white trade unionism in South Africa') in October 1967, dealing with the foundation and early years of the ICU, and the second ('Trade union, political pressure group or mass movement? The Industrial and Commercial Workers' Union of Africa') included in a collection of papers edited by R. I. Rotberg and A. A. Mazrui, *Protest and Power in Black Africa* (New York, 1970). Dr Johns made use of, among other sources, a typescript copy of Kadalie's autobiography, the Library of Congress file of *The Workers' Herald*, the Creech Jones – Kadalie correspondence in the Winifred Holtby Collection at Kingston-upon-Hull and a number of important mimeographed documents in the possession of the

Program of African Studies, Northwestern University. The second of his papers is the fuller and better documented. Between the publication of Dr Johns's first article and the appearance of his second there was published the Kadalie autobiography, *My Life and the ICU: The Autobiography of a Black Trade Unionist in South Africa* (London, 1970). This, while doing less than justice to Kadalie's intelligence and tending to omit whatever redounds little to his credit, presents a truthful – though partial and, in places, slightly garbled – story. It is a helpful, though not indispensable, source book.

The account presented here makes use of archival material hitherto untouched, principally the Ballinger and Forman Collections. The Ballinger Collection, somewhat eccentrically divided between the Universities of Cape Town and the Witwatersrand, is made up of the papers of the late W. G. Ballinger and such documents as were preserved by Mrs Ethelreda Lewis and Miss Winifred Holtby (the main South African and English patrons of the ICU) and handed over to him. It contains little relating to the period prior to Mrs Lewis's association with the union (1926). The Forman Collection (in the University of Cape Town) is composed of the papers of the late A. W. G. Champion. The information derived from these two collections has been supplemented by a study of other, less important, manuscript collections and of all available extant copies of *The Workers' Herald*, first published in 1923. The earlier and more obscure period of the ICU's history required considerably more research. The material exploited comes chiefly from the South African state archives in Cape Town and Pretoria, from the papers of the Cape Federation of Labour Unions (lodged at the University of the Witwatersrand) and from contemporary newspapers.

I have benefited much from the advice of Professors H. M. Robertson of the University of Cape Town, L. C. Duly of the University of Nebraska, and T. R. H. Davenport of Rhodes University. My debt to Professor Robertson is particularly deep. I owe also a debt of gratitude to those survivors from the events recorded in these pages who, when interviewed, bore with patience my prolonged and persistent questioning. I refer to the late W. G. Ballinger, who gave me every assistance in the search for material, Mr J. Gomas, Mr H. Selby Msimang, and the late A. W. G. Champion. Among others who helped me in a variety of ways and to whom I express my thanks I must especially mention Mrs S. Forman for permission to use the Forman Collection, and the following: Mr J. R. Altman, Dr J. E. Atkinson, Mr Budd, Dr E. Brookes, Mrs A. M. Cunningham, Miss J. Curtis, Mr C. R. Diamond, Mrs R. A. B. Eave, Miss D. M. Hartwell, Mr J. Henry, Miss T. Hutchinson, Associate Professor M. Kooy, Mr E. H. McCann, Professor S. B. Ncgobo, Mr G. Quinn, the late Mrs W. Roux, Mrs L. Sacks, Dr C. C. Saunders, Professor G. A. Shepperson, Mrs P. Stevens, Mrs A. Thom, Mrs C. Thorne, Dr D. Ticktin, Associate Professor S. T. van der Horst, Mr J. Wainer and Associate Professor D. Welsh. I am grateful also to the South African Institute of Race Relations and to the staffs of the following libraries and archives: Cape Archives (Cape Town), Central Archives

(Pretoria), Cory Library (Grahamstown), Hiddingh Hall Library and J. W. Jagger Library (University of Cape Town), Johannesburg Public Library, Kingston-upon-Hull Central Library, Library of Congress Photoduplication Service, Natal Society Library (Pietermaritzburg), New York Public Library Photoduplication Service, South African Library (Cape Town), and the Library of the University of the Witwatersrand.

Publication has been made possible only by the generosity of the University of Cape Town. Study leave permitted uninterrupted work on the metamorphosis from thesis to book and a subsidy contributed substantially to the costs of publication.

The maps were prepared by Mr K. A. Behr of the Cartographic Section of the University of Cape Town. The spelling of place-names conforms to modern usage. In other respects, however, the nomenclature of the period has been retained, e.g. Basutoland, not Lesotho.

Mr P. J. de Jager, Deputy Director of Library Services, University of South Africa, Mrs L. J. de Wet, Curator of the Africana Museum, Johannesburg Public Library, Mrs J. Le Grange of the Africana Museum, and Miss J. F. Duggan, Librarian of the Killie Campbell Africana Library, University of Natal, were very helpful in the provision of illustrations. I must, moreover, thank Mr de Jager for the useful information he gave me on the contents of the University of South Africa's Champion Papers, of which I was ignorant at the time of writing this book. In a similar fashion I am indebted to Mr R. Moorsom, who directed my attention to the ICU Collection of the University of the Witwatersrand. My final debt is to Miss G. Pretorius of Oxford University Press, Cape Town.

CHAPTER 1

The Background, 1919

The first question that comes to mind is what earthly reason is there that there should be a different union for Natives and a different union for non-Natives?

(A. W. G. Champion, 1943)

It can scarcely be disputed that the industrial labour movement in South Africa, originating as an off-shoot of British trade unionism, developed in a unique way. Nowhere else did a labour movement become so rigidly divided on racial lines, a reflection of a distribution of employment and a differential access to skills that relegated the Black worker to unskilled employment. Yet this was not always so. There was a time when, in the older settled parts of the Cape of Good Hope, in particular the Cape Peninsula, but also the Eastern Province of the Cape, the Coloured people, many of them descendants of slaves, provided most of the skills that were required. It was only from the latter part of the last century that the European immigrant encroached upon the skilled trades to any great degree, and a White monopoly of skills was far from complete at the time of the formation in 1919 of the trade union that is the subject of this book. In the building industry in Cape Town in the 1920s, for example, the proportion of Coloured artisans varied from 50 per cent of the carpenters to 95 per cent of the plasterers.[1] Similarly there was a preponderance of Coloured workers in tailoring, leather working, and furniture making.[2] In Natal a similar position was enjoyed by Indian immigrants and their descendants. Although these, entering the country in the 19th century as indentured labourers, constituted a more alien and less favoured element than the Cape Coloured people, they undertook, on expiry of their indentures, skilled and semi-skilled work.[3] The number of Africans acquiring industrial skills was negligible in both the Cape Province and Natal.

Elsewhere – in the northern Cape, in the Transvaal, and in the Orange Free State (where, indeed, Indians were not permitted to take up residence) – European clashed with African in competition for employment, and, in this confrontation, the European sought the exclusive right to practise industrial skills. In diamond mining at Kimberley, then in gold mining on the Witwatersrand, far and away the most important economic activity in the country, White artisans performed most of the skilled work and were determined to use their power as trade unionists and voters in order to keep Blacks out. White trade unionists combined an inherited or recently acquired racial prejudice with the sectional interest of an 'in-group' that was set on maintaining a privileged position against the 'out-group' and in defiance of employers who, it was suspected, would not scruple to cut down the market price of labour to a bare subsistence level. In the Transvaal, the Chamber of Mines, anxious not to antagonize the 'in-group', placated it by offering a colour bar in the gold mining industry. At that time it was a question of excluding not Africans from reserved occupations but the Chinese indentured workmen whom the mine owners wanted to import in default of adequate African recruitment. The Transvaal Labour Importation Ordinance of 1904 confined the Chinese to unskilled work, or rather listed a considerable number of occupations from which they were shut out, and which had a future significance in that, after the last Chinese had left, they continued to be regarded as White preserves.[4] Although a feeling grew up among those mine managers and engineers who rated greater efficiency and decreased costs above racial solidarity, that skilled work should be opened to Blacks, the necessity of continuing to defer to White opinion reinforced the legislative colour bar. In the Transvaal, and in the Orange Free State too, with the passing of the Mines and Works Act of 1911, 'coloured persons' were not permitted, by regulations issued under that Act, to hold certificates of competency to perform specified tasks on the mines, and such certificates granted to these persons in Natal and the Cape Province were not valid in the two other provinces. The area of employment reserved for White men was subsequently enlarged by informal agreements between management and White labour.

After the 1914–18 War, and more especially after 1924, when the South African Labour Party and the National Party formed a coalition government, it was the practice and attitudes of the bulk of the northern White workers that came to prevail throughout the entire country. For the subordinate racial groups it became increasingly difficult to escape from unskilled work, most of which the ruling race looked upon only with contempt, designating it 'kaffir work'. This deep-rooted aversion to work associated with Blacks was felt by none more strongly than the group whose economic circumstances were closest to those of the 'Kaffirs', the so-called poor Whites. Their role in South African history between the wars was of great importance, and the political power they disposed of accounted in large measure for the racial division of the proletariat. As they moved into the towns in search of the subsistence the land could no longer give them, they came into competition for the better type of unskilled employment with Blacks who were in a similar plight. They found in the skilled immigrants from Europe an ally against cheaper Black labour. It was unfortunate for racial harmony that the White working class was able to satisfy its aspirations through political action and therefore did not need a class solidarity that transcended racial loyalty.

Given the difference in South Africa between the inland and the coastal provinces (especially the Cape Province) in the spread of skills among the Black labour force, it is hardly surprising that there has been a geographical dichotomy in the trade union movement. While the racial tolerance of the White worker in the Cape should not be exaggerated, he generally accepted the principle of the open trade union. Almost all of the dozen and a half trade unions in Cape Town at the end of World War I were multi-racial,[5] and almost all of them were grouped together in the Cape Federation of Labour Unions (or Trades), which had no colour bar, but was bound by its constitution to 'secure a thorough organisation of all workers, skilled and unskilled, irrespective of race, colour, creed or sex.[6] The position in the Federation of Trades at Port Elizabeth was much the same.[7] The South African Industrial Federation, on the other hand, like its constituent unions, practised, at least in the Transvaal, where its main strength lay, rigid discrimination, however much its leaders denied colour prejudice and appealed to the specious principle of equal pay for equal work, regardless of the colour of the worker – the so-called rate for the job – which had the effect of excluding Black and Coloured workers from skilled work because most employers, being themselves White, would prefer to employ Whites if compelled to pay all their workers at the same rate. In the Transvaal, indeed, Coloured workers were denied both the privileges of trade union membership and the rewards of 'scabbing'.[8]

Another peculiarity of the South African situation was that the formation of unions for unskilled labour, difficult enough in homogeneous societies, meant organizing a class not only underprivileged in economic terms, but also discriminated against on grounds of race. The obstacles to the unionization of the unskilled are formidable anywhere. A trade union exists to extort from employers a better bargain for its members than they would be able to make individually, and a union can make a better bargain only if it represents at least a very substantial proportion of the workers possessing the skill which employers require. The fewer the workers disposing of the skill, the easier it is to form a union and the stronger its bargaining position. Unskilled workers are the most numerous class of workers and, moreover, the poorest and worst educated. Not only is it difficult to persuade those in employment to enter a union (unless they are feeling particularly aggrieved), but also, in the early stages of industrialization, there are, in urban slums and overpopulated countryside, vast reserves of unemployed labour from which fresh recruits can be drawn to replace those who demand wages higher than the market price and who seek remedy in organization. Only when the excess labour that saturates the market has been mopped up, can such workers hope to lay claim to any great bargaining power, a situation reached late in the process of industrialization. 'There is, in fact,' as the Webbs put it, 'for unspecialised manual labour a practically unlimited "reserve army" made up of the temporarily unemployed members of every other class. As these form a perpetually shifting body, and the occupation of "general labouring" needs no apprenticeship, no combination however co-extensive it might be with the labourers actually employed at any one time, could deprive the employer of the alternative of engaging an entirely new gang.'[9] It is scarcely to be wondered at that even in highly industrialized societies the workers of the 'sweated trades' prove incapable of their own upliftment and must look, for an antidote to their helplessness, to protective legislation.

In South Africa, in this respect also apparently unique, a shortage of labour emerged early in the process of industrialization; and, paradoxically in a country where underemployed labour resources abounded, Chinese labour had to be imported into the Transvaal for the gold mines and Indian labour into Natal for the sugar plantations. This premature labour shortage arose, however, only in mining and European agriculture. Until artificial legal restraints were introduced there was rarely any shortage of unskilled labour for the docks, domestic service, municipal employment, construction, stores and factories. The point was that conditions of employment in mining and commercial agriculture were so distasteful that sufficient labour could not be attracted from subsistence farming, which could accommodate large numbers of underemployed peasants preferring the harsh poverty of the tribal land to the austerities of employment in mines or on White farms. Where there is communal land tenure, and poverty and ambition are not sharp enough spurs to a quest for industrial employment that offers meagre rewards, public authorities anxious to furnish agriculture or industry with labour must exert some kind of compulsion. In South Africa taxation was a powerful weapon used to induce Blacks to seek paid employment.[10] In such circumstances, where men are driven rather than drawn into employment, a shortage of labour is no more likely to promote trade unionism than is a surplus of labour forced from the land by the introduction of capitalistic agriculture.

Another obstacle to the unionization of the unskilled is the reluctance of country dwellers coming into towns in search of employment, to reconcile themselves to permanent urban residence. Where communal land holding persists the rural migrant has an even greater inducement to keep open his line of retreat to his village, frequently returning there for longer or shorter periods or, eventually, for good. Although growing towns may be embarrassed by the number of peasants offering themselves for employment, those who make up this surplus labour have not neccessarily cut their ties with the land. Discontinuity of employment, so often to be found with unskilled work, is made more pronounced by absences in the country, and hinders the task of organizing industrial labour. Furthermore, the combination of urban employment with peasant farming means that the former tends to be regarded simply as a supplement to the proceeds of the latter. Since the migrant labourer can fall back upon the income from his rural holding and has, moreover, the habit of interrupting his period of employment, he is more likely to look for a remedy for low wages in a different job than in industrial organization. Low wages themselves make union dues, however small, heavy to bear. In the early period of industrialization in South Africa employers distinguished between the partially assimilated and the wholly unassimilated Black, referring to the latter as the 'raw (or blanket) Kaffir'. The newcomer from the country, illiterate, speaking no European language and thrust into an alien society with strange customs, was an unlikely recruit to an institution so typical of industrial society as a trade union. Not only was he indifferent to trade unionism, but his mere presence, his willingness to accept whatever wage he was offered, undermined the bargaining position of the growing class of so-called detribalized Blacks.[11]

By the First World War the trend towards a permanent Black urban population was apparent, a trend which the 1921 census, revealing as it did a striking increase in the number of Black women living in towns, made blindingly clear. There can be little doubt that this trend would have been even more marked had not the instability of the urban labour force been fostered by the operation of the contract labour system that had evolved in the gold and coal mining industries, partly because labour, at least at the price employers were willing to pay, could not be obtained by any other means, partly because of the attitude of the White miners' unions, which, by preventing the employment of Blacks in skilled tasks, took away any incentive to the mining companies to build up a stable labour force, partly because of the reluctance of most of these companies to make provision for long-service married workers, partly because of the hostility of public authorities and White public opinion to the permanent urbanization of tribal Blacks. In the contract system there was no place for collective bargaining and withdrawal of labour by trade unions. The mining companies, purchasing labour at a predetermined price in large quantities, depressed its market price and thus performed precisely the opposite function to that of trade unions, which seek to raise the market price through their power of controlling the supply of labour and, by restricting it in the short- or long-run, extorting a better bargain. Each Black miner made his individual bargain – or rather gave his individual consent to a pre-arranged agreement – either with one of the recruiting agencies or with the mine to which he applied for employment, selling himself for an extended period of service for a remuneration that was uniform throughout the industry.[12] Then he and his fellows were housed in compounds, partially cut off from the outside world, an undigested lump in the belly of industrial society. Not only were they temporary immigrants from their permanent homes, but many of them came from beyond the political boundaries of South Africa and so were doubly alien. In such conditions the normal functioning of trade union organization was practically impossible and even concerted action difficult. In 1913 Black miners, roused by their grievances and stimulated by the example of their militant White fellow-workers, did take action together, but this was not the result of, nor did it lead to, unionization. It was not that they were unaware of the advantages of combination, and there was some talk among Blacks in 1913 of forming a union.[13] If none was formed, it was because the difficulties were so immense.

Such Black aspirations received no encouragement from the Government, which, indeed, displayed considerable mistrust even towards White combination, a mistrust that occasionally was transmuted into open hostility, as in

1914 when trade union leaders were deported, and in 1922, when there was a general strike and bloodshed on the Witwatersrand. The Riotous Assemblies and Criminal Law Amendment Act of 1914, which directly outlawed striking among employees engaged in a public service, and indirectly restrained the use of the strike weapon by curtailing the right of assembly, prohibiting intimidation and inhibiting picketing, was aimed against Whites rather than Blacks.[14] Africans were not forbidden to form combinations and these would not have been without means of supporting their members or of prosecuting their own delinquent officials.[15] Though suspicious of Black organizations, which were generally assumed to be subversive or likely to become so, the public authorities seem to have taken the view that trade unionism was irrelevant to the Black labour force. While not making Black unions illegal, they made, for dealing with problems of labour relations, arrangements which did not envisage the possibility of their existence. African mine workers came under the Native Labour Regulation Act of 1911, which obviated, in theory, the need for trade unions by providing machinery for the examination and redress of grievances and rendered them, if they were established, impotent by forbidding strikes in proclaimed labour districts.[16] Since the 'inspectors of native labourers' appointed under the Act were granted the power 'to enter any compound or other place occupied by native labourers, and to arrest any native suspected of contravening any regulations',[17] it may be assumed that safeguarding the employers' interests had a prior claim on their services. Outside these labour areas the situation of Black labour was affected by a body of legislation passed at a time when Black trade unions were unthought of, legislation composed of the various Masters and Servants Acts, going back to the Masters, Servants and Apprentices Ordinance of the Cape Colony (1841). These laws, by making breach of contract between employer and employee a criminal offence, not a civil wrong, in effect deprived the workman of his right to strike.[18] Of greater importance was the Cape Colony's Masters and Servants Act of 1856. Although this did not differentiate between the races and was apparently intended to enforce contracts between White, as well as non-White, servants and their masters, in fact its application did become restricted to contracts between White masters and non-White servants, and similar legislation in the Orange Free State and Natal was certainly discriminatory.[19] Needless to say, it was the servant whose side of the contract was enforced by the courts with the greater alacrity. Yet, although the laws were harshly administered in the interests of labour discipline, they did offer a function to any potential labour organization, since it was possible for a union to take up the cause of a victimized employee and pursue the defaulting employer into the courts; which, indeed, was one of the very things done by the ICU.

Another aspect of state intervention in South Africa that hindered trade union development should be noticed viz., restraints placed upon the mobility of African labour, *ad hoc* arrangements that varied from colony to colony in the interests of reducing vagrancy and facilitating the establishment of law and order. The various Ordinances and Acts that introduced them or altered them were loosely known as the Pass Laws. They were more strictly administered in the inland provinces than in the Cape of Good Hope, where the law of 1867, which had simplified existing legislation of this nature, fell into disuse in the latter part of the 19th century,[20] and in Natal, where a law of 1884 requiring Africans to obtain a pass before entering or leaving the colony was not very effectively enforced. In the Orange Free State and the Transvaal, before their annexation by Great Britain, Blacks on the move were required to have passes. Other rules were more particularly concerned with urban residence. In the inland provinces the right of Blacks to take up residence in towns was more severely controlled than in Natal, where, however, in Durban and Pietermaritzburg the registration of 'native servants and servants belonging to uncivilized races' was laid down, or in the Cape, where there was no restriction upon movement into towns, though in Cape Town and Port Elizabeth Blacks, unless specially exempted, were required (in theory rather than in practice) to reside either in a location or on their employers' premises.[21] Coloured people in the Cape were not affected.

A third aspect of public policy was exemplified by those provisions of the Masters and Servants Acts which sought to guarantee certain rights to the employee, that is the paternalism which was by no means free of discriminatory intent, nor untinged with racial prejudice, but which, nevertheless, represented a paradoxical strain in White racial attitude. Public authorities in South Africa, state and municipal, and great employers were not always indifferent to the welfare of Black workers, but sometimes insisted upon or furnished model accommodation and medical services, though obviously never entirely for disinterested motives. For the mining industry the Native Labour Regulation Act of 1911, in addition to those clauses which sought to stop trade union activity, aimed also at preventing abuses in the recruitment of labour for the gold mines, established minimum standards of accommodation, food, and medical facilities, and made provision for compensation for injuries. Although such paternalism should not be overrated, since Blacks in mine compounds and most urban locations lived in bleak and uncomfortable conditions, benefits and services stemming from paternalistic attitudes did diminish the need and demand for trade unions and no doubt helped to inhibit their development in the mining industry. Trade unions flourish upon a mixed diet of opportunity and grievance, and they do best when plenty of men are at work and willing to part with the subscriptions and when there is little competition for jobs, yet when prices are rising faster than wages, thus providing a most obvious grievance. The extent to which grievances are anticipated by a kindly government will sweeten more or less the acerbity of labour militancy.

It would be naive, however, to suppose that the chief hazard facing Black trade unions was that of being killed with kindness. The obstacles to organization were harsh and forbidding and the chances, in the early years of industrialization, of their being surmounted, seemed slim. Yet, in Cape Town, where the ICU was founded in 1919, circumstances for a short time just after the war were peculiarly favourable. Apart from the influence of the war itself and of Black participation in it, which must have contributed to the growth of self-confidence and self-assertiveness, economic conditions were propitious. The South African economy was booming. The upward swing that began in 1915 was reaching its peak, a prosperity that owed much to industrialization stimulated by the war, which had made imported manufactures difficult to obtain and expensive to buy. Industrial output and employment increased,[22] and, in Cape Town and the Western Province of the Cape as a whole, one of the areas where industrial development was especially marked, unskilled labour was for the moment in short supply.[23] At the same time there were grievances: wages were low and the price of basic foodstuffs soaring. The wartime boom was mainly a price boom,[24] and complaints about the cost of living were widespread and strident amongst Whites as well as Blacks.

A major grievance in Cape Town (as elsewhere) among the poor of all races was overcrowded and, in some cases, expensive housing. There were two locations for Blacks, both run by the Government, the Docks Location for single men and the much larger one at Ndabeni for both married and single. The former was for men working at the docks and in 1918 held 750.[25] The latter, built in 1902 when there was an outbreak of plague, and originally accommodating 700, by the end of the war, had a population of about 3 500,[26] which was something like 1 500 in excess of what it could reasonably hold.[27] Hundreds of Blacks, unable or unwilling to find accommodation in the locations, found dear and precarious lodging in the slums of the town.[28]

Blacks resident in Cape Town lived among the Coloured people. The two communities were not nearly so remote from each other as were, for example, Indians and Africans in Natal. There was a certain amount of intermarriage. Both Clements Kadalie, the leader of the ICU, and his brother Robert married Coloured women. It is true that in some respects the situation of those of mixed race was better than that of Blacks, for, generally speaking, their task of adjustment to a White-dominated society was a much less formidable one, since they had close cultural ties with Whites, spoke either Afrikaans or English or both, and had a higher degree of literacy, while their admission into the skilled trades and craft unions was an accepted practice. Nevertheless, like Blacks, many Coloured workers had been forced off the land by rural impoverishment and compelled to take up unskilled employment in the towns. The two groups had sufficient common interest to make co-operation feasible, and the possibility existed of forming a general union in which Blacks could find support and encouragement from a people better equipped to wrest from the prevalent economic system whatever advantages accrued to organization. It was from the Coloured community that the ICU drew a substantial part of its early supporters. In later years Clements Kadalie paid tribute to them. 'Tribal and colour prejudice had to be buried and it is a credit to the Coloured people of Cape Town who, for the first time in the annals of this country, joined the great pilgrimage towards the land of promise. They joined the new movement and disregarded colour prejudice. And they supplied the sinews of war.'[29]

Notes

1. Secretary of the Cape Peninsula Building Trade Joint Board, *Cape Times* 29 July 1922.
2. South African Trades Union Congress, Minutes of meeting of the National Executive Council with the Executives of the affiliated unions, 15 January 1928 (B/UCT).
3. Union of South Africa, *Report of the Economic Commission, January 1914* (U.G. 12–1914), para. 58–59.
4. I am indebted to Professor H. M. Robertson for letting me read his unpublished paper on the origins and economic effects of the colour bar in South Africa.
5. The Co-operative Masons' Society had a colour bar, which it owed to the pressure of its Transvaal members, as it was not restricted to the Cape (*Cape Times* 21 April 1919).
6. Constitution of the Cape Federation (T.U.C.S.A. Papers).
7. Union of South Africa, *Report of the Commissioners Appointed to Enquire into the Causes of, and Consequences at, the Native Disturbances at Port Elizabeth on the 23rd October 1920* (Annexure 143–1921), para. 11–12.
8. Cf. the building workers' strike of February, 1919 (Union of South Africa, *Annual Report of the Department of Justice for the Calendar Year 1919*, U.G. 35–1920, p. 45; *Cape Times* 24 March 1919).
9. Webb, S. and B. 2nd ed. 1898; *Industrial Democracy*, London, 758.
10. Most obviously the ten shillings labour tax provided for by the Glen Grey Act of the Cape of Good Hope (1894).
11. A growing body of literature has tried to detect signs of 'worker consciousness' very early in the process of rural migration in response to the development of wage labour. See for example, van Onselen, Charles, 1976, *Chibaro: African Mine Labour in Southern Rhodesia*, London. The existence of primitive proletarian discontent and spontaneous acts of defiance cannot be disputed, and the history of the I.C.U. itself amply illustrates this. It remains true, however, that first generation urban immigrants are not suitable material for a proper labour movement. It would be easy to show that even in countries much more advanced industrially than South Africa, new town dwellers did not fully accept the implications of their migration.
12. van der Horst, S. T., 1942, *Native Labour in South Africa*, Cape Town 193–97, 199ff; Robertson, H. M., 'One hundred and fifty years of economic contact between black and white', Part II, *The South African Journal of Economics, III*, 1, 1935, 18–19.
13. Union of South Africa, *Report of the Economic Commission, January 1914*, para. 95.
14. Kahn, E., The right to strike in South Africa: An historical analysis, *South African Journal of Economics, XI*, 1, 1943, 27–28, 33.
15. That the law tolerated African trade unions may be inferred from the Native Affairs Act of 1920, which provided for the convening of conferences to which might be invited, among others, delegates from 'any association or union purporting to represent any native . . . economic interest' (Union of South Africa, *Act 23 of 1920*, para. 16, sub-section 1). A

number of officials were successfully prosecuted by the I.C.U. In 1924 Morris Alexander asked the Minister of Justice in the House of Assembly 'whether there is anything to prevent coloured and native workers from forming trade unions in the same way as other sections of workers'. The answer was: 'So far as I am aware there is nothing' (Union of South Africa, *Debates of the House of Assembly*, 2 September 1924).

16. A district was proclaimed a 'labour district' if it contained a large number of employed Blacks. The labour districts in 1911 were mostly in the Transvaal and the Orange Free State. There was one in the Cape (Union of South Africa, *Official Year Book, No. 5–1922*, 434).
17. Union of South Africa, *Act 15 of 1911*, para. 18–19.
18. Doxey, G. V., 1961, *The Industrial Colour Bar in South Africa*, Cape Town, 128–29.
19. van der Horst, op. cit., 36–8; Union of South Africa, *Report of the Economic and Wage Commission* (U.G. 14–1926), para. 138; Kahn, E., loc. cit., 26.
20. A permit was necessary to enter or leave the Transkei.
21. In the labour districts proclaimed under the Native Labour Regulation Act of 1911 and in urban areas in the Transvaal, proclaimed under the Urban Areas Pass Act of 1909, passes had to be carried. Urban residence in the Cape was governed by the Native Reserve Locations Act of 1902. See Union of South Africa, *Second Report of the Select Committee on Native Affairs, 1st June, 1914* (S.C. 8–1914), Appendix A – 'Pass Laws', and Davenport, T. R. H., 1971, *The Beginnings of Urban Segregation in South Africa: the Natives (Urban Areas) Act of 1923 and its Background*, Grahamstown, 1–6.
22. Schumann, C. G. W., 1938, *Structural Changes and Business Cycles in South Africa, 1806–1936*, London, 168, 244–5.
23. *Cape Times* 23 December 1918; Union of South Africa, *Annual Report of the Department of Justice for the Calendar Year 1919*, 58.
24. Schumann, op. cit., 245.
25. They lived twenty-eight to a hut and paid six shillings a month each (*Cape Times* 19 December 1919).
26. *Cape Times* 21 June 1919.
27. Cape Archives: Résumé of Minutes of Proceedings of Council, City of Cape Town, Agendas, Reports and Résumés Book, Volume 1, Parcel 86, Item 161, 27 February 1919.
28. *The Cape Argus* 11 February 1920; *Umteteli wa Bantu* 19 May 1923.
29. Manifesto of 9 July 1928 (B/UCT).

CHAPTER 2

The Foundation of the ICU and the Cape Town Dock Strike, 1919-1920

We are building up a union
With which we hope to save the land,
ICU are its initials;
In its ranks we take our stand.

Union means an all-in movement,
None outside to scab upon us;
With folded arms we'll stand like statues
Sing our songs, but make no rumpus.
from an ICU poem, *c* 1925

The Industrial and Commercial Workers' Union of Africa, the ICU, began as a result of a chance encounter in Cape Town shortly before the end of World War I in 1918, between Clements Kadalie and a White trade unionist and part-time, somewhat unsuccessful, politician, Albert Batty, who ran his own cutlery business in the city. They got into conversation after Kadalie had protested at being pushed off the pavement by a White policeman, and a friendship grew up.[1] It was an opportune meeting for Batty, who, clearly appreciating his worth, found a place for Kadalie in his plans for encouraging trade unionism among Blacks.[2] Already, in the middle of 1918, he had founded a general, multi-racial union at Simonstown, some thirty kilometres south of Cape Town, a union which, in its early months, was called the Industrial and Commercial Union.[3] It very soon became the union of the semi-skilled and unskilled workers employed in the Admiralty dockyard and its name came to be simply the Industrial Workers' Union (IWU).[4] In January 1919, the ICU itself was founded – known too as the Industrial and Commercial Union – with the aim of organizing dock labour. Kadalie was elected its first Secretary.

At least two other White trade unionists – Englishmen like him – were associated with Batty in the formation of the ICU: F. Rayner, who also helped to found the Simonstown IWU, and J. H. Dean. Batty soon withdrew into the background and Rayner too pursued other interests,[5] but Dean (described in December 1919, as the 'Hon. Organiser' of the ICU,[6] was intimately concerned with the ICU throughout the whole of 1919 and later.

Though started through the efforts of the same men at much the same time, the ICU and the IWU soon followed divergent paths. While the IWU was taken under the wing of the Cape Federation of Labour Unions,[7] the ICU was never affiliated to it.[8] The different relationship established between the ICU and the Cape Federation may have developed because the ICU, being the product of the first attempt to form a labour union in a field of employment where Blacks were numerous, represented such a new and radical departure from existing trade union practice in Cape Town that it was difficult for the Federation to accommodate itself to it. Another, and more likely, explanation is that the ICU was too closely associated with Batty's political ambitions. After having been an unsuccessful candidate on behalf of the South African Labour Party in the general election of October 1915, Batty, together with Dean, Rayner, and other friends, had broken away to form the Democratic Labour Party, a splinter group confined to Cape Town, and, in competition with an official Labour candidate, stood for the new party in a by-election in December 1918, in which he was assisted by Kadalie. The origin of the schism lay in the unwillingness of Batty and other Cape socialists to tolerate the Labour Party's reluctance to give a genuine welcome to Coloured people in the labour movement, both political and industrial, and in its desire to extend the franchise arrangements of the Cape, which gave the vote to certain classes of Blacks, as well as to people of mixed blood, to the other provinces of the Union of South Africa. The DLP also advocated universal free education.[9] Clements Kadalie seems to imply in his autobiography that Batty was something of an opportunist, a view not unnaturally shared by his former Labour Party colleagues, who styled him 'a political chameleon. He had wooed every party, and found a home nowhere, and as far as his Labour prestige was concerned, he represented a party of one, viz. Batty.'[10] Yet he seemed popular enough among the Coloured voters,[11] and he did better in the election than his Labour Party opponent.[12]

Few references to the ICU are to be found in the Cape Town newspapers and elsewhere during the first months of its existence; fewer still the references to Clements Kadalie. He was young and inexperienced, an alien who had been in South Africa less than a year when he was chosen to be the ICU's first Secretary, perhaps simply because he was a Black of some education. His home was in Nyasaland, in the vicinity of Bandawe, a United Free Church of Scotland mission station, and he was born in or before 1896,[13] the second son of Musa and the grandson of the paramount chief of the Atonga tribe.[14] Musa intended his two elder sons, Robert and Clements, for the ministry, but died too soon (in 1904) to carry out his intention, and Clements's education became the responsibility of his mother and two of his uncles, both teachers. At the end of 1907 he entered Livingstonia College as a boarder, to begin his secondary education and teacher training, which he completed in 1912.[15] Although the level of education he attained was not high and his early letters – such few as survive – display an imperfect grasp of English and no little pomposity, his later letters and speeches certainly shed their Africanisms and became far more fluent and vigorous than would be supposed from the wooden and irritatingly self-congratulatory style affected in his autobiography. As a product of Scottish missionary education, he used biblical allusions freely, but in his public utterances he was opportunistic and inconsistent in his references to Christianity. 'Mr Kadalie,' said A. W. G. Champion, his later colleague, 'is not a Christian believer, but he is well read in scripture.'[16] This scepticism, which lasted until late in life, was publicly declared in 1928. 'Personally,' he said, 'I do not subscribe to any religious doctrine in the generally accepted sense of the term. In the words of Ingersoll, "The world is my country, to do good is my religion," and it seems to me that my life can be more usefully employed in endeavouring to improve the lot of my fellow-creatures here than in bothering about a chimerical life above.'[17]

The young Kadalie began his brief teaching career at the beginning of 1913. It lasted until early in 1915, when he left home 'in quest of a higher civilised life', sought first of all in Mozambique.[18] Like so many mission-trained expatriates of the Nyasa diaspora he was consumed with ambition and, filled as he was with a generous measure of self-confidence, was never reticent about his talents and achievements. The saga of his employment, even in the teaching profession, seems to have been tempestuous, punctuated with quarrels and frequent victimization springing from malice and jealousy. From the time he left home until he became the paid Secretary of the ICU at the beginning of 1920,[19] he went through a dozen jobs, mostly as a clerk – in Portuguese East Africa (where he stayed only a month), at various places in Southern Rhodesia (where he lived from 1915 to 1918), and in Cape Town[20] – and had his longest period of unbroken service at a gold mine at Shamva, where he stayed a year. In Southern Rhodesia he tried to enlist in the King's African Rifles and applied for repatriation to a Native Commissioner, who told him to join instead the Rhodesian Native Regiment, a pioneer unit, which was 'poorly equipped and did not even wear boots'.[21] This was as near as he got to joining the army, which, however, did not prevent him from claiming in a speech in May 1928, to have been, during the war, a 'law-abiding citizen who in 1914, when the Nationalists were in rebellion, was overseas fighting for the Empire.'[22]

Kadalie left Southern Rhodesia in February 1918, going straight to Cape Town, only breaking his journey for a short stay with a cousin in Kimberley. In Cape Town he was reunited with his brother Robert. 'When we reached his house,' Clements wrote in his autobiography, 'at the top of Waterkant Street, my brother's wife, a Coloured woman, said to him after she had shaken hands with me, "Look here, Robert, there is something in this boy and you will see". Quietly I pondered over her remarks.'[23]

In January of the following year the Nyasa immigrant became the unpaid Secretary of the newly-formed ICU. It was only one of a number of bodies competing for Black support in post-war Cape Town, where churches (conventional and Ethiopian), political groups, quasi-political labour organizations, and even genuine trade unions jostled one another. If Kadalie rose to the top, it was because he had exceptional talent. 'Clements Kadalie,' wrote another colleague, H. D. Tyamzashe, 'is one of the quickest learners amongst Natives who I have come in contact with. Tell him a thing and he will never forget it.'[24] With that quick intelligence, however, went 'arrogance, extravagance and obstinacy'.[25] Undoubtedly his outstanding talent was his ability to fire the crowds that came to listen to his speeches. These were very lengthy, very rapidly and energetically delivered, very vivid, often amusing, usually abusive, and always in English.[26] None of the vernacular languages of South Africa was familiar to him, no great disadvantage at Cape Town, where he addressed crowds composed of not only Blacks of a variety of tribes, but also Coloured people. Kadalie was distinguished from his rivals for popular support by his capacity to command the loyalty of both non-White racial groups. It was not merely a question of his oratory: in his personal relationships, his charm, when he chose to display it – he was equally capable of petulance and ill-temper – was compelling. Vain, unheroic, extravagant, and bon vivant, he was yet generous, frank, even naive, and without malice or greed. He was certainly no intellectual. The only book for which there is irrefutable evidence that he read and was impressed by, was a novel by Heaton Nicholls, *Bayette*, and this he recommended in 1927 to his colleagues,[27] presumably because he identified himself with its Black hero.[28] Yet, however meagre his intellectual contribution to the South African labour movement, his powers of leadership, the strength and attraction of his personality are beyond doubt, though these are not conveyed by the posed photographs that survive of him, in which, round-faced and astonishingly youthful in appearance, he displays few signs of his personal magnetism. Eagerness, quick intelligence, panache are more apparent than the capacity to sway, direct, and administer that was clearly his. This, then, was the young Kadalie, an immigrant who had never in his life done manual work, had never been employed in a factory, whose background was petty bourgeois, not proletarian, rural,not urban, professional or semi-professional, not industrial. Yet from that unpropitious background he emerged as South Africa's first Black labour leader.

Hindsight lends a spurious prominence to the early ICU, whereas it was just one of several organizations trying to draw in unskilled Black and Coloured workers.[29] Of importance for the ICU was the general union known as the Industrial Workers of Africa, started in Johannesburg in 1917 under the aegis of the International Socialist League, a precursor of the Communist Party of South Africa. The leaders were H. Kraai and R. Cetyiwe, who came down from Johannesburg in the course of 1919 and took up residence in Cape Town, in or before August.[30] The IWA, which was exclusively Black and had worked in Johannesburg in collaboration with the Transvaal section of the South African Native National Congress, the Transvaal Native Congress, similarly in Cape Town worked with the Cape Native Congress,[31] with which, however, it did not enter a formal relationship until May 1920.[32] It was a somewhat surprising partnership, for, whereas the IWA certainly began, even if it did not continue, as a militant body seeking a profound change in South African society, Congress was as a rule a conservative and moderate body, appealing to both the westernized élite and the tribal chiefs. Typically the President of the Cape Congress, Z. R. Mahabane, was a minister, a Wesleyan.[33] Before the advent of the ICU and the IWA, Congress seems to have been the chief channel for the communication of Black grievances.[34]

Relations between the ICU, on the one hand, and the IWA and the Cape NC, on the other, were evidently somewhat cool. To an extent the ICU and the IWA competed for membership, because the latter was also recruiting among dock labourers. More of the ICU's members were Coloured than Black,[35] but it did apparently attract a number of Blacks who were dissatisfied with Congress.[36] Congress, in turn, was suspicious of the intrusion of the alien Kadalie.[37] Discussions were held in August 1919, between the ICU and the IWA on the possibility of an amalgamation, but without immediate result and the two continued to operate separately. A major stumbling block to unification was the tie between the ICU and the DLP and the Cape Federation, for the IWA wanted nothing to do with Whites, did not even want to tolerate their presence at meetings, an attitude engendered in the harsh racial climate of the Transvaal.[38] The ICU's connection with the White labour movement also made co-operation with the Cape Congress and with the principal Coloured pressure group, the African Political (later People's) Organization, difficult. The APO's leader, Dr Abdurahman, while being alive to their faults, consistently supported the Unionists (and subsequently the South African Party), and there was little love lost between him and the DLP.[39] Congress, too, recommended voters to support the Unionists in the general election of March 1920.[40]

Alone among the unaffiliated general unions, the ICU received an invitation to attend the first conference of the Cape Federation of Labour Unions held in Cape Town in April 1919, being represented by its chairman, Joe Paulse, and J. H. Dean (who also spoke for the Operative Bakers' Union). F. Rayner (for the Bioscope Union) and A. F. Batty (for the Amalgamated Society of Engineers) also attended. Paulse raised the question of low wages for unskilled workers and stressed the need for an adequate minimum wage. Batty, Dean, and Rayner urged the removal of the trade union colour bar wherever it existed.[41]

Kadalie did not attend, or did not speak at, the Federation's conference. His first recorded public appearance was in November 1919, when he shared a platform with Dean and Paulse, as well as Dr Abdurahman, and gave vent to some strong sentiments.[42] He began by urging the solidarity of Black and Coloured workers against the capitalist and the White worker, and he went on to counsel defiance of the Government. 'Constitutional means were of no avail. Coloured people had begged and appealed to the Government long enough.'[43]

By November the ICU which, since its foundation in January had begun to call itself the Industrial and Commercial Workers' Union of South Africa instead of the Industrial and Commercial Union, had a reported membership of a thousand, mostly labourers on the docks and railways.[44] The docks and railways were undoubtedly a propitious field for industrial organization, employing together the largest single Black labour force in Cape Town, which worked partly for the state South African Railways and Harbours Administration and partly for a few shipping and stevedoring firms. Coloured and Black worked side by side, operating the railways and loading, unloading, and bunkering the ships. By the end of the war there was profound dissatisfaction with wages. For the dock labourers employed by SAR & H these had risen, notably through the payment of a war bonus from February 1918, but they still lagged behind the growing cost of living. The plight of the Black and Coloured railway workers, whose case had received some support from the White National Union of Railway and Harbour Servants (NURHS), was worse. They complained that they had not even received a war bonus, though one had been promised them, or, at least, had received it long after it had been promised. The dock workers, apart from Blacks on contract to SAR & H, were for the most part casual labourers. Very full weeks with plenty of overtime alternated with weeks when work was hard to come by, perhaps only two or three days a week, all depending upon the number of ships coming in and upon the supplies of bunkering coal available. In the latter part of 1919 the docks were by no means busy.[45]

Agitation for a wage increase predated the formation of the ICU. Twice in 1918 the dock workers put in an application to the private employers for a rise, to no avail, being threatened on the second occasion, in December 1918, with dismissal and replacement by fresh labour from the territories – the tribal lands. In September 1919, the ICU took up the wage issue, requesting, without success, the private employers (but evidently not SAR & H) to pay their labourers seven shillings and sixpence a day instead of the current four shillings. A further demand – also to the private employers – was made on 9 December, this time for eight and six for labourers and twelve and six for foremen, a demand supported by the Secretary of the Federation of Trades, Robert Stuart.[46] Then, just over a week later, a strike was precipitated that was not wholly connected with the pay dispute.

The dock strike of December 1919, which made the ICU's name, was not, any more than the formation of the union itself, an isolated event, but rather the most important of a series of industrial disputes involving Black labour.[47] What is more, it drew strength from the encouragement and support, not only of such regular supporters as Dean, who was chairman of the strike committee, and Rayner, who was its treasurer,[48] but also of other trade unions and of a substantial segment of public opinion. The chances of success depended largely upon the attitude and policy of the Cape Federation and the NURHS, since the ICU entered upon the strike with the backing of both. One of its aims – and this was where the interests of the other unions lay – was to bring to an end the export of foodstuffs, in the belief that prices were high because so much was being sent out of the country, a belief that gained widespread currency in the later months of 1919. While to suggest that the high prices could be explained wholly in terms of excessive exporting and profiteering (the two being associated in the public mind) was an over-simplification in an inflationary situation, there was an element of truth in it. It seems to be beyond doubt that certain agricultural products were being exported when there was insufficient for domestic consumption at a price within reach of the poorer classes.[49] Despite an exceptionally severe drought in the Eastern Province of the Cape and elsewhere in South Africa in the winter of 1919, which sent up the price of maize, staple diet of the African people, the Government, sensitive to the interests of White producers and insensitive to repeated warnings of dearth, but lacking precise information upon the size of national production and internal requirements, continued to permit considerable exports.[50]

At some point during the course of November the idea struck labour leaders that something could be done to bring food exports to a halt. The first move appears to have come from the Cape Town dockers, who later that same month protested against loading a ship with beef for export.[51] Whether this protest was spontaneous and gave the idea to the Cape Federation of putting an embargo upon exports, or whether Dean and Stuart had already discussed this line of action, is not clear. At all events, on 27 November a meeting of the Federation's Executive decided to ask its affiliated unions not to handle exports of foodstuffs, though Stuart was privately convinced that this would not bring down the cost of living.[52] Then, on 3 December, the Executive of the NURHS, which was not affiliated to the Cape Federation, also resolved to tell its members not to handle such exports. In its response to trade union protest and public indignation the Government acted in an indecisive and ambiguous way. Aware of the strength of public feeling, but unwilling to appear to give way to pressure, it gave an undertaking to restrict the export of foodstuffs to those of which there was 'a genuine surplus' and it ceased to issue permits for the export of meat and maize, which was continuing only because the permits previously issued had not yet been executed. It failed, however, to make clear what its policy was, and there was public suspicion about how it was defining 'genuine surplus.'[53]

Although the ICU was not a member of the Cape Federation, it was clear that nothing could be done without its co-operation, and some consultation took place before or after the meeting of the Federation's Executive on 27 November. The IWA was also consulted.[54] Both unions agreed to co-operate in preventing the export of foodstuffs. This was what the strike was about. On 6 December 1919, Clements Kadalie wrote to the Secretary of the Federation, explaining that at a meeting of his union, held the previous night, 'the following resolution was unanimously adopted. "That this Union asserts itself to put into operation the resolution passed by the Federation of Trades as to not handling 'Foodstuff' [*sic*] for exportation in the first instance of the next shipment and leaves the matter into the hands of the Committee to give such information to the members in the Docks." It was in a magnificent spirit that this resolution was adopted and the members alledged [*sic*] themselves to be loyal to this Union.'[55] Nothing was said about a demand for higher wages. Looking back in 1922, Kadalie declared that the dock strike had been 'not for wages but to save the whole country from starvation, when even the white workers were afraid to tackle the national duty.'[56] It is apparent that no explicit undertaking was sought from, or given by, the White trade unions to support the ICU's wage claim, and, even though this was from the beginning coupled with the aim of ending food exports, there was considerable misunderstanding between the ICU and White supporters about what the purpose of the strike was. Even Dean seems to have been somewhat hazy. When the strike was already some days old, he was saying, 'When the export of food is stopped, then will be the time to see precisely how far the strike is a protest against exportation, and how much for increase of wage.' At the end of the strike, when accusations and recriminations were being bandied about, the railway union repudiated any suggestion that it had committed itself to backing the Black workers in the matter of wages; and this was certainly a subordinate issue of no great interest for all the White trade unionists who applauded the striking dock workers.[57]

The dock employers at last announced a pay increase on Saturday 13 December, the Railways and Harbours Administration making an offer of an additional shilling a day, while the private firms offered to increase their daily rate from four shillings to six.[58] The Government's offer was repeated by the Port Goods Superintendent on the following Monday evening, at a meeting held in the Docks Location, and as far as the authorities were concerned, that was the end of the matter. Later that night, however, another meeting was held outside the location and a resolution was passed repeating the demand for eight shillings and six pence a day already put to the private employers.[59] Tuesday 16 December was Dingaan's Day, a public holiday. A meeting held at Ndabeni Location under the auspices of the ICU, the IWA, and the Cape Native Congress was attended by some eight hundred people and presided over by Kraai of the IWA. After condemning the high cost of living and a recent increase in railway fares, it resolved, on the motion of Cetyiwe of the IWA, to approach employers, state and private, on the question of the wages of Black and Coloured workers, and it also protested against the export of foodstuffs.[60]

The strike began at 11.30 in the morning of the day after the holiday, when the stevedores employed by the Union Castle Company on the East Pier, on the instruction of their unions, refused to continue loading foodstuffs on to the *Norman*, as well as on to the *Armadale Castle*, assembling instead outside the dock gates. This meeting, which was addressed by Robert Stuart, resolved to continue the strike, to refuse to handle food exports, and to remain firm on the eight shillings and six pence pay demand.[61] In the afternoon the stoppage spread to the South Arm, where the men failed to report for duty after lunch.[62] The dock authorities were at a loss. In their view the 'raw kaffirs' were scarcely affected

Clements Kadalie – Africana Museum, Johannesburg

A.W.G. Champion and J. Gomas – Forman Collection, University of Cape Town

by the rise in the cost of living and were not badly off, and they attributed the unrest to agitators from the town. In fact, although the labourers of the Docks Location, who received cheap food and lodging, were to some extent insulated from the rise in the cost of living, their dependants in the drought-stricken Eastern Province were not. Those labourers residing outside, especially those living in the city, most certainly were worse off.

At eleven o'clock on the morning of the second day of the strike a thousand strikers assembled at the Parade, an open space in front of the city hall, and were addressed by Dean and Paulse of the ICU, who urged them to persevere, and by E. H. Jones, the local Secretary of the NURHS, who assured them of the support of their fellow workmen,[63] an assurance that turned out to be of little value. This mid-morning meeting on the Parade became a regular event, a means of demonstrating solidarity and keeping up the strikers' spirits; and an evening meeting, too, was held regularly at the bottom of the principal thoroughfare, Adderley Street, the recognized speaking place for radical orators.[64] These gatherings, always addressed by several speakers, opened and closed with hymns. There was very little violence throughout the entire dispute, and though some of the serangs (foremen) complained of threats and assaults, these were isolated incidents.[65]

On the second day the strikers were joined by 150 labourers at the railway goods yard, which meant that only perishable goods could be handled, and on the Friday by Coloured railway workers at the railway workshops. The serangs and sorters and some long-service employees of the Railways and Harbours remained at work, and extra casual labour was taken on. The Administration's cartage men continued to work and White workers stayed at their posts, more being brought in.[66] The NURHS did not bring its men out (perhaps understandably, because strikes by railway workers were illegal under the Railways and Harbours Act of 1912), though it condemned 'scabbing'. Thus a certain amount of work continued to be done throughout the strike and ships got away. In most cases the crews took a hand at bunkering and discharging cargo. Ships avoided Cape Town where possible, and truck loads of coal accumulated.[67]

It was on the second day of the strike that Stuart of the Federation of Trades and Jones of the railway union obtained an interview with H. Burton, the Minister of Railways and Harbours, in order to tell him, in effect, that they would call the strike off if the Government were to impose further limits upon food exports. The hour and a half exchange brought no agreement, but aroused some acrimony, since the labour leaders objected to government attempts to replace Black labour with White 'scab' labour, while Burton accused them of injudiciously exciting the 'natives' and of 'levelling a pistol at the head of the proper constitutional authority of the country'. On the export issue, the Minister insisted that it was a question only of surplus foodstuffs. He rejected the argument that a surplus existed only because the prices were too high for working class pockets and the suggestion that the Government should stabilize the cost of living by fixing prices. The only apparent reference to the dock workers' demand for increased wages was Jones's assertion that it was no concern of his.[68]

On Sunday 21 December a mass meeting was held in a Cape Town cinema. E. H. Jones moved a resolution, which was accepted by a large majority, 'That this meeting of citizens of Cape Town hereby approve of the action taken in stopping the export of foodstuffs from this country until the surplus of such foodstuffs available for export is more clearly and definitely ascertained, and urge that a committee be nominated by workers and exporters to determine whether any permits for export be granted or not'. Jones was totally uninterested in the dockers' wages, in fact advising the strikers to accept the pay offer already made. Robert Stuart followed, moved a resolution condemning the use of White scab labour, and then, striking a discordant note, went on to rebuke the railway union for not taking action itself, but, instead, leaving the dirty work to the Blacks. Finally he threatened to bring out 'every worker in the Peninsula' if food exports did not cease.[69]

By this time the patience of the Government was becoming exhausted. On Monday morning the General Manager of SAR & H, Sir William Hoy, who had come specially to Cape Town, went into conference with the Minister and the local departmental heads. Then, in the late afternoon, an *indaba* was held in the docks, when, with a mixture of threat, blandishment, and cajolery, the authorities sought to induce the men to go back to work. The powerful official delegation, headed by the Assistant General Manager of Railways, Cape Town, was supported by 300 troops and 100 men of the South African Police, dispersed in detachments throughout the docks. The threat, emphasized by the presence of the armed men, was of dismissal and ejection from their huts for the men who lived in the Docks Location.[70] Then, or later, the authorities promised to consider the demand for increased wages provided that the workers returned to duty. Stuart by now was becoming uneasy and apparently advised the strike committee to surrender because of the failure of the NURHS to give genuine support.[71] He subsequently claimed that his advice had been accepted.[72] If so, either the committee changed its mind or it was unable to convince the men.

With the apparent intention of depriving the strikers of trade union sympathy, the Goverment stressed in a statement published on Christmas Eve that there had been a ban on exports of maize and most other foodstuffs ever since the end of October.[73] This satisfied the NURHS.[74] On the same day, the Government, in spite of a last minute appeal by Dean and Kadalie not to use force lest it should evoke a violent reaction,[75] paraded troops in the dock area again and evicted the residents of the Docks Location. It was a rather empty gesture. Clearly the Government would have much preferred the workers to go back to work than itself go to the trouble and expense of getting rid of them and bringing in a fresh batch, even supposing more men could have been readily obtainable. Consequently a last chance was offered to the men to return to work. Few (about thirty) took up the offer, and only some fifty elected to go back to their villages, which was one of the alternatives presented. The rest, the overwhelming majority, were offered accommodation in a tented camp at Milnerton on the outskirts of Cape Town and near Ndabeni location, which few accepted, at least to begin with. Most of the strikers made their way into the city, where they listened to speeches – as many as a dozen on end – and spent the rest of their time waiting outside the offices of the Federation of Trades, walking the streets, or sitting on park benches.[76]

Over the Christmas period most of the strikers from the Docks Location made their way to the temporary location at Milnerton and as many as a hundred went back to work on Boxing Day (Friday).[77] On the Saturday evening the strike committee decided to call the strike off, not because there was much danger of a substantial return to work, but rather because of the difficulty of keeping it up without the support of the White unions. Dean issued a statement blaming '1. The failure of the National Union of Railway and Harbour Servants to keep their promise to the Dockworkers to support them in the event of their deciding to strike. 2. The half-hearted support of the Federation of Trades.' When the decision was communicated to a meeting in Ndabeni Location on Sunday, it encountered considerable incredulity and opposition. It also caused some ill-feeling between the ICU on the one hand and the Cape NC and the IWA on the other, with the Rev. Mahabane claiming that the latter were 'the real leaders of the people' and J. H. Dean suggesting that Congress and the IWA had perhaps gone behind the strike committee's back because 'some of them had white faces'. It appears that on the Saturday morning the leaders of the Cape Congress and the IWA had obtained from the Mayor of Cape Town and the Assistant General Manager of the Railways and Harbours a promise to attend a joint conference of representatives of employers and employees to go into the whole question of Black wages throughout the Cape Peninsula, provided that the men went back to work. Although this promise was passed on to the strike committee at a meeting at the city hall on Saturday evening, the committee had surrendered unconditionally. The result was that there was no general resumption of work on Monday 29 December. As became clear, however, at a further meeting held that day, opposition to ending the strike was weakening. On Tuesday 30 the men streamed back to work and the residents of the Docks Location went back to their huts.[78]

The Cape Federation repudiated any responsibility for the failure of the strike, and to blame it was, indeed, less than just. Most of the strike pay and the expenditure on food distributed among the Blacks of Ndabeni and the Docks Location came from donations made at some sacrifice to the Federation by sympathetic unions and organizations, including the International Socialist League and the South African Industrial Federation, and it assumed responsibility for all liabilities.[79] Understandably relations between the ICU and the Federation were distinctly cool after the strike, and it is evident that in the ensuing months Kadalie did not grow in Stuart's esteem.[80] What the Federation and the ICU did have in common was contempt for the NURHS.[81] Jones, however, answered all charges of betrayal by denying ever having committed himself to support the wage demand, and this was perfectly true. Although one wonders why it did not enter Jones's head that an ally – and a sought-after ally at that – who had fought his union's battle might have some moral claim for aid in waging the rest of the campaign, the fact remains that the railwaymen, unedifying as their behaviour had been, were simply being made a scapegoat. The strike collapsed because no more money was forthcoming. Sympathy was bound to wane once the principal aim of the strike, the ending of food exports, seemed to have been achieved. Besides, the stevedores and dock workers had been offered a pay rise before the strike began. There was something in what Jones said: 'Mr Dean and the strike committee, not being such good generals as to know when they had won the position and having attempted to go further than they were justified, now endeavour to throw the responsibility on this Union.'[82]

One feature of the dock strike that was very ominous for the future of general unions in South Africa was the deployment of soldiers and police and the expulsion of the strikers from the Docks Location, a move which the ICU interpreted as intimidation.[83] It is true that the Government happened to be directly involved as one of the employers and that it acted, for all its display of armed force, with considerable restraint. Nevertheless, it is not to be doubted that, had the strike gone on longer, the contract labourers of the Railways and Harbours Administration would have been shipped back to their homes and replacements recruited.

The strike, then, was a failure. There was little ground for satisfaction even in the matter of food exports, which, as soon as the trouble had blown over, the Government again authorized.[84] Yet, for all that, the 1919 strike was a demonstration of considerable power. It had lasted fourteen days and brought out over two thousand men.[85] The prestige earned by the ICU gained for it an influx of new members, bringing its strength up to two thousand by January 1920.[86] Four hundred members attended the annual meeting held on 16 January 1920, which was presided over by J. H. Dean.[87] Referring, in the course of his annual report, to the dock strike, Kadalie 'thanked the men for the stand they had made for their rights, and also commended their good conduct during the strike, during which they refrained from any hostile or troublesome attitude towards the Government. He was convinced that the authorities now recognised that they were men and not "boys" any longer.' The election of officers followed. Kadalie, out of a job because he had absented himself from his employment during the strike, was elected Organizing Secretary at two pounds a week. Other appointments included James King as President, J. G. Gumbs as Vice-President, and Joe Paulse as Treasurer.[88]

The ending of the dock strike did not put a stop to agitation. Kadalie spoke at a meeting organized at the beginning of February by the Democratic Labour

Party to protest against the high cost of food. Dean, who presided, was cheered for his suggestion of a general strike as a possible remedy.[89] In March, a joint ICU – IWA meeting on Parade called upon the Government to convene a conference of the Railways and Harbours Administration with the unions.[90] Then, in August, 1920, the ICU circulated a letter among all employers of Black unskilled and semi-skilled labour – SAR & H, the Chamber of Commerce, the Manufacturers' Association, and individual employers – requesting the introduction of a minimum wage of eight shillings and four pence a day and ten days' paid holiday a year.[91] Although prices by then had reached their peak and begun to fall, few employees would have admitted it, and the ICU was not alone in its agitation. Other unions of unskilled workers were also seeking pay rises.[92] High prices and widespread dissatisfaction amongst the poorly-paid workers persuaded the Government to call a conference of employers of unskilled labour, which met in early September. There was no question of negotiating with the unions, simply one of concerting policy, for which purpose a committee was set up by the conference. In its discussions, the committee conceded that Coloured workers, who were considered separately from the 'kraal Natives', were entitled to more money, and it was recommended that those employed by SAR & H should receive an additional 'war bonus' of ten per cent upon the existing rate of pay, thus giving married men six and tuppence a day, or thirty-seven shillings a week. Among other recommendations the committee agreed, too, to the eight shillings a day which the stevedoring companies were prepared to pay, because their casual labourers did work 'of a semi-skilled nature, which demands aptitude and experience. The average of earning opportunity may be only three to four days per week.'

Having dealt with Coloured unskilled labour, the committee turned to consider African workers. 'Assuming,' it concluded, 'the correctness of the data showing that the kraal Native at the Docks is to-day enjoying an increased earning capacity of 55% over pre-war conditions, that his cost of housing remains unchanged and that his cost of sustenance has probably increased by 50% to 60% the committee sees no reasonable justification for recommending any increase of pay.' However, it was agreed that Africans unable to obtain accommodation in a location or compound and compelled to live in town, should receive a housing allowance of four pence a working day.[93]

Of all the employers, the shipping and stevedoring firms responded most quickly to the demand for higher wages, receiving an ICU delegation made up of C. Kadalie, J. G. Gumbs, and S. M. Bennett Ncwana, a figure of some importance later, and shortly afterwards making their offer.[94] The administrative machinery of the other employers worked rather more slowly, and an impatient ICU sent off a reminder in the third week of September. At a well-attended meeting on 17 September the Secretary complained of the dilatoriness of the employers, the vagueness of the offer made by some to increase wages or to make 'adjustments', and the failure of all employers, even the shipping and stevedoring companies, to recognize the union. There was some talk of a general strike, but nothing came of it.[95]

'The ICU,' wrote Kadalie in 1928, 'under the writer's leadership, scored a great victory at Cape Town Docks, when the wages of Non-European workers was [*sic*] raised from 4/- to 8/- per day.'[96] This famous victory was a wretched four pence a day extra for rackrented Blacks in Cape Town and nothing at all for those living at Ndabeni or in the Docks Location, and these were the men who had made up the bulk of the strikers. While it is true that Blacks and Coloured casual labourers working for the private stevedoring firms received a substantial increase of two shillings a day (a thirty-three-and-a-third per cent rise), bringing the daily rate from 6s. (not 4s.) to 8s., if they were working only three or four days a week with little prospect of overtime, the extent of the improvement is less striking than the inadequacy of their existing wages. The stevedores' wages fell below the 38 shillings a week that the committee of September evidently considered an acceptable minimum. Altogether it was not such a great victory. The concessions, such as they were, had been bestowed from above, not extorted from below.

By the middle of 1920 Kadalie had attracted the suspicions of the police as a dangerous agitator, possibly under the influence of what was then habitually called bolshevism.[97] In October, the Commissioner of Police suggested to the Chief Immigration Officer in Pretoria that his residence status should be investigated with a view to his deportation, on the ground that he was 'engaged with certain European agitators spreading pernicious doctrines amongst the Coloured persons of the Cape Province',[98] and the outcome was that on 2 November a deeming order was issued by the Minister of the Interior declaring him a prohibited immigrant under Section 4 (1) (a) and (d) of the Immigration Act of 1913. On receipt of the order, which for some obscure reason was not served until 24 November, Kadalie appealed to the Immigration Appeal Board. Help was solicited from the Democratic Labour Party and on 27 November four members of the Party, including Rayner and Dean, at an interview with the Pricipal Immigration Officer in Cape Town 'threatened trouble'.[99] An approach was also made to the Cape Federation of Labour Unions[100] and Dr Abdurahman who later claimed credit for Kadalie's escape from deportation.[101]

Kadalie's case came up before the Board on 2 December and he was represented by Advocate Stuart, MLA, who, having great difficulty in constructing a defence because there was little to go on other than the Minister's deeming order, argued that the order was *ultra vires* on the ground of vagueness and ambiguity. The submission of the Principal Immigration Officer was that the appellant had no right to see the documents in the case and that the Board could not go behind the Minister's deeming order. In a muddled judgment the Board, unsure whether or not the Minister's order was final – and unwilling to believe that it was – and unsure whether or not Kadalie was an alien and therefore not entitled to appeal to the Supreme Court – and unwilling not to let him have the benefit of the doubt – finally agreed to an appeal. Kadalie seems to have been very lucky. As the Chairman of the Board said: 'We have seen the previous cases which have come before the Board for the past two years and in all cases the Board has decided that as far as the Board is concerned the deeming order is final.'[102] Presumably, if the appeal to the Supreme Court had not been allowed, Kadalie would have been deported, since there is no indication that up to that time the Government was going to give way to pressure. The granting of the appeal gave it time to re-consider its decision. Before the appeal came up, the Department of the Interior, on 17 December, instructed the Principal Immigration Officer to stay the proceedings,[103] and on 18 January 1921, the Minister agreed to let Kadalie stay unconditionally.[104]

Grandiloquently Kadalie wrote in his autobiography, 'If the story of the contemplated deportation could be written in full, it would rank as one of the most interesting episodes in the annals of South African history . . . In these pages it is impossible and inappropriate to disclose the secret drama that was responsible for the cancellation of the deportation order.'[105] The explanation for the Government's change of heart does not seem to be so dramatic or mysterious as this suggests. Although it is conceivable that there was a specific understanding made by Kadalie to give support to the government party, the South African Party, in the coming election (and certainly the ICU did so[106]), there is no need to suppose that there was such a formal arrangement, since the volte-face is sufficiently explained by the narrowness of the Government's majority after the 1920 election and its willingness to make a gesture likely to gain it popularity with the Coloured and Black electorate. At this very time the Government was far from popular on account of a disturbance at Port Elizabeth in October, when twenty-three Black rioters had been shot dead by the police and White civilians. Doubtless it had no wish to increase its unpopularity and it is, therefore, surprising that the deportation of Kadalie was even contemplated. It can only be supposed that the proceedings against him, begun some weeks before the Port Elizabeth hullabaloo, had a momentum of their own, and also that the Government was taken aback by the extent of the influential support the ICU Secretary received. What is beyond doubt is that his solicitors, Dichmont and Dichmont, used the impending election to bring pressure to bear on the Government.[107]

The second annual general meeting of the ICU took place in an atmosphere of considerable and justifiable confidence and optimism. Three daughter branches had been founded – at Lüderitzbucht (South-West Africa), Simonstown and Langebaan; members were counted by the thousand; and the financial standing of the union (so it was claimed) had improved. J. H. Dean was not, so far as it is known, present at this meeting, though in the previous November he was still being described as one of the ICU's organizers. It is evident that about the beginning of 1921 a breach appeared between the ICU and the DLP. In February a member of the ICU Executive, William Fife, launched a strong attack upon the former allies of the union, contemptuously dismissing their assistance in saving Kadalie from deportation.[108] Abandoning the ICU, Dean became Chairman (and Rayner Vice-chairman) of the local branch of the Workers' Union, a British general union that had extended its operations to South Africa.[109] The South African organizer of this, Dave Kendall, had in August 1920 persuaded the Simonstown branch of the Industrial Workers' Union to affiliate to his organization,[110] and other poaching activities of his occasioned some indignation in the Cape Federation. It appears that, in 1921, he was even trying to win over the ICU.[111] This, however, seemed to have a bright future all by itself. At the meeting of January 1921, its President, J. G. Gumbs, was looking forward to a membership of tens of thousands by the next annual meeting, a hope that, in the event, did not prove so absurd.

Notes

1. Kadalie, C., 1970, *My Life and the ICU, the Autobiography of a Black Trade Unionist in South Africa*, London, 39–40, and *The Workers' Herald* 17 May, 1927. The two accounts differ slightly in their facts, markedly in their tone. Another, very different, version of the foundation of the ICU, which contains an element of truth, is in Britain, V., 1940, *Testament of Friendship*, London, 199–200. Cf. also *Cape Times* 21 January 1920.
2. *Cape Times* 14 and 16 December 1918.
3. Minutes of the Cape Federation of Labour Unions 10 June and 16 September 1918 (TUCSA Papers), which, however, refers to the 'Industrial Commercial Union'; *Cape Times* 14 August 1920.
4. Secretary, Cape Federation, to Rear-Admiral Hill 12 May 1919 (TUCSA Papers); Minutes of the Cape Federation, Executive Meeting 26 June 1919 (ibid.); *Cape Times* 21 April 1919.
5. Batty's other interests were manifold – Hon. Organizer of the Democratic Labout Party, representative of the Amalgamated Society of Engineers on the Cape Federation (Minutes 31 December 1918), Secretary of the South African Industrial Federation's Co-operative Stores in Cape Town (where he found Kadalie a job for a time in 1919; Kadalie, C. op. cit., 37), and from November 1919, a member of the Government's Cost of Living Commission (*Cape Times* 11 November 1919, and 7 December 1920). He was the representative of the Federation of Trades on various official committees – the Recruiting Committee, the Governor-General's Fund, and the Returned Soldiers Committee (*Cape Times* 11 December 1918; Minutes of the Cape Federation 21 January, 10 April and 31 December 1918, and 19 June and 4 September, 1919; R. Stuart to A. F. Batty 5 September 1919, TUCSA Papers).
6. *Cape Times* 23 December 1919.
7. Minutes 4 December 1919 (TUCSA Papers).
8. Even the foundation of the ICU was not recorded in its minutes.
9. *Cape Times* 11 December 1918; Programme of the DLP, *The Cape Argus* 8 January 1919.
10. *Cape Times* 14 December 1918.
11. *Cape Times* 19 December 1918.
12. *Cape Times* 21 December 1918.
13. 'The exact date of my birth is not known, but it was recorded in the mission register that

I was christened on Easter Day, 1896.' (Kadalie, C. op. cit., 31.) The dates given by him for the beginning of his secondary education and the completion of his teacher training suggest an earlier date, perhaps two or three years before 1896. This is suppoıted by the evidence of the Principal Immigration Officer, Cape Town, who, in November 1920, put his age at twenty-eight (Union of South Africa, *Debates of the House of Assembly*, 20 July 1925, Col. 6291), a piece of information that apparently emanated from Robert Kadalie (Kadalie, C. op. cit., 45–46).

14. For a labour leader and socialist he was oddly proud of his blood relationship with the chief (*The Cape Mercury* 11 January 1928; Kadalie, C. op. cit., 31, 33).
15. *The Cape Mercury* 11 January 1928.
16. Champion, A. W. G., c. 1928, Mr Clements Kadalie's experiences, Forman Collection MSS/26.
17. Kadalie, C. The aims and motives of the ICU in *The Realignment of Native Life on a Christian Basis, Being the Report of the Proceedings of the Seventh General Missionary Conference of South Africa*, Lovedale, 1928, 128.
18. Kadalie, C., *My Life*, 33. He left home before the Chilembwe rising, to which only a single reference has survived: Mwase, G. S., 1967, *Strike a Blow and Die; a Narrative of Race Relations in Colonial Africa*, Cambridge, Mass., 5.
19. Kadalie, C., *My Life*, 44.
20. Ibid., Chapter 1, *passim*.
21. *The Cape Mercury* 11 January 1928.
22. *Rand Daily Mail* 7 May 1928.
23. Kadalie, C., *My Life*, 36.
24. Tyamzashe, H. D., 1941, Summarised history of the Industrial and Commercial Workers' Union of Africa, typescript, 48. E. R. Roux thought him a poet manqué Roux, E. and W., 1970, *Rebel Pity, the Life of Eddie Roux*, London, 40.
25. Tyamzashe, H. D., loc. cit., 46.
26. Burger, John, pseudonym of Leo Marquard, 1943, *The Black Man's Burden*, London, 204.
27. *The Workers' Herald* 17 May 1927.
28. Heaton Nicholls, G., 1923, *Bayete*, '*Hail to the King*', London.
29. Wickins, P. L., 1972, General labour unions in Cape Town, 1918–1920, *The South African Journal of Economics*, XL, 3.
30. *Cape Times* 9 October 1919.
31. The South African Native National Congress, founded in 1912 to prosecute African interests in all spheres, was a loosely organized body made up of provincial congresses that were largely autonomous. The Cape provincial organization was not formally constituted until October 1919 (Mahabane, Z. R., *The Good Fight, Selected Speeches*, Evanston, n.d., 1), when the SANNC adopted its first constitution, but there was a branch of the national organization at Ndabeni before then.
32. Central Archives: Department of Justice 3/127/20, Report of CID, Johannesburg to Secretary, South African Police 28 May 1920.
33. Born 1881 at Thaba Nchu, Orange Free State, ordained 1914, stationed Cape Town 1916, and elected President of the Cape NC in 1919 (Mahabane, Z. R., op. cit., i–ii).
34. *The Cape Argus* 24 March 1919.
35. Letter from C. Kadalie to Editor, *Cape Times* 17 October, 1919 (*Cape Times* 22 October, 1919). This is Kadalie's earliest extant letter and carried the editorial comment, 'We have had to delete portions of this letter which are unintelligible.' Certainly, as printed, it falls far short of his later competence in English. With regard to the composition of the ICU's membership, it can be deduced from the names of the ICU Executive elected in January, 1920, that most of the officials and committee members were Coloured. Of the thirteen only three were indisputably Black, including Kadalie (*Cape Times* 21 January 1920).

Two, J. G. Gumbs and James King, were West Indian, and there may have been others (Kadalie, C., *My Life*, 220).

36. *Cape Times* 9 October 1919.
37. Champion, A. W. G., 1927, *The Truth about the ICU*, Durban, 24.
38. *Cape Times* 9 October 1919.
39. *APO* 12 September 1919.
40. *Cape Times* 14 February 1920.
41. *Cape Times* 21 April 1919.
42. It would be unwise, however, to generalize about ICU policy from isolated speeches. Less than three months earlier the ICU had addressed a letter of sympathy and loyalty to the Acting Prime Minister, F. S. Malan, on the death of General Botha, 'a worthy father and peacemaker' (*Cape Times* 2 September 1919).
43. *Cape Times* 22 November 1919.
44. *Cape Times* 9 and 22 October 1919.
45. *Cape Times* 5 May, 9 October, and 19 and 20 December 1919.
46. *Cape Times* 20, 22 and 23 December 1919.
47. Union of South Africa, *Annual Report of the Factories Division, Department of Mines and Industries, for the Period 1st May, 1919 to 31st December, 1919*, UG 42–1920, 28.
48. *New Africa* 14 September 1929. Batty was occupied with his work on the Cost of Living Commission.
49. *Cape Times* 23 July 1919.
50. *Cape Times* 21 and 23 July 1919. According to D. D. T. Jabavu maize was selling at 30 shillings a bag in the Eastern Province (*Cape Times* 19 December 1919), which was apparently three times the usual price (*Cape Times* 22 December 1919).
51. *Cape Times* 25 November 1919.
52. R. Stuart to unnamed correspondent 6 January 1920 (TUCSA Papers).
53. *Cape Times* 28 November, 22 and 24 December 1919; Minutes of the Cape Federation 27 November 1919 (TUCSA Papers); *The Cape Argus* 19 December 1919.
54. *Cape Times* 18 December 1919.
55. C. Kadalie to R. Stuart 6 December 1919 (TUCSA Papers).
56. *Ilanga lase Natal* 27 January 1922.
57. *Cape Times* 19, 23 and 30 December 1919; R. Stuart to Mayor of Benoni 30 December 1919 (TUCSA Papers).
58. *The Cape Argus* 20 December 1919; *Cape Times* 20 December 1919. 'It is incorrect that the men were offered 6s. per day by the Stevedoring Companies without demand. As long ago as September a request was put through for an increase of pay by the ICU. The companies only found out they were still considering it when it was thought a strike against handling foodstuffs was in the air.' (J. H. Dean, *Cape Times* 23 December 1919.)
59. *Cape Times* 18 December 1919. This must have been the meeting which Stuart attended, or even summoned (*Cape Times* 20 December 1919).
60. *Cape Times* 18 December 1919.
61. *Cape Times* 19 December 1919. Kadalie's account in his autobiography (41–2) is somewhat egotistical. 'I boarded the *Norman Castle* [*sic*] and got in touch with Joe Paulsen [*sic*] . . . I ordered him to "down tools" as a signal to the others . . . I managed to borrow a bicycle and cycled throughout the docks calling on workers to down tools and to follow me outside the dock gates . . . Outside the dock gates I addressed the huge crowd, officially inaugurating what I believe to be the first organised strike of non-European labour in South Africa.' Stuart, however, in a private letter wrote, 'As Secretary I went to the docks and called all those employed in the loading of foodstuffs for exportation to leave off work.' (R. Stuart to G. Spantan 8 April 1920, TUCSA Papers.)
62. *Cape Times* 18 December 1919.

63. *Cape Times* 19 December 1919. There is no mention of Kadalie at this meeting.
64. Kadalie, C., *My Life*, 42.
65. *Cape Times* 20, 23, 24, and 25 December 1919.
66. *Cape Times* 19, 20, 23, and 31 December 1919.
67. *Cape Times* 20, 24, 25, and 27 December 1919; *The Cape Argus* 20 December 1919. According to 'one of the leading officials' of the NURHS, the 'embargo on the export of foodstuffs, as far as the Railway and Harbour Servants' Union is concerned, has been in existence a fortnight', but there is not a shred of evidence to show any action by that union.
68. *Cape Times* 20 December 1919; Minutes of the Cape Federation 18 December 1919.
69. *Cape Times* 22 and 30 December 1919.
70. *Cape Times* 23 December 1919.
71. R. Stuart to P. B. Smith 30 December 1919 (TUCSA Papers).
72. *Cape Times* 30 December 1919.
73. *Cape Times* 24 December 1919.
74. *South African Railway Review* January 1920.
75. *Cape Times* 24 December 1919. They exaggerated somewhat in saying that, if the Docks Location were cleared, 'the wandering about of thousands of men with nowhere to go would be a danger to the people of Cape Town in many ways'. There were fewer than a thousand residents.
76. *Cape Times* 25 and 27 December 1919; Kadalie, C., *My Life*, 44.
77. *Cape Times* 27 December 1919; *The Cape Argus* 27 December 1919.
78. *Cape Times* 30 and 31 December 1919, 5 and 10 January 1920.
79. *The Cape Argus* 20 December 1919; *Cape Times* 24 December 1919; R. Stuart to W. H. Andrews 30 December 1919, to R. Waterston 30 December 1919, and to J. Richmond 20 May 1920 (TUCSA Papers).
80. R. Stuart to C. Kadalie 19 February 1920 (TUCSA Papers); R. Stuart to J. Richmond 20 May 1920 (TUCSA PAPERS).
81. R. Stuart to the Mayor of Benoni 30 December 1919 (TUCSA Papers).
82. *The Cape Argus* 29 December 1919; *Cape Times* 30 December 1919.
83. *Cape Times* 24 December 1919 and 30 August 1920.
84. *The Eastern Province Herald* 21 February 1920.
85. Union of South Africa, *Annual Report of the Factories Division, 1919*, 45.
86. Kadalie, C., 1927, *The Relation between White and Black Workers in South Africa; a Brief Account of the Labour Movement*, Johannesburg and London, 4.
87. *Cape Times* 21 January 1920.
88. Ibid.; Kadalie, C., *My Life*, 44.
89. *Cape Times* 2 February 1920.
90. The meeting (in the evening) was thinly attended (only three hundred present) and presided over by T. Le Fleur, not a well-known figure (*Cape Times* 25 March 1920).
91. *Cape Times* 8 and 30 August and 20 September 1920. Evidently this demand did not cover dock workers, for whom a separate claim had been lodged, viz 12s.6d. for foremen, 9s. for winchmen and gangwaymen, 8s. for labourers (*Cape Times* 12 August 1920).
92. *Cape Times* 22 September 1920.
93. Cape Archives: Agendas, Reports and Résumés Book, City of Cape Town, Conclusions of Committee (set up by employers of unskilled labourers), Volume II, Parcel 88, Item 163, 1920.
94. *Cape Times* 30 August 1920; Kadalie, C., *My Life*, 45. According to Kadalie, Ncwana was a student at Zonnebloem College and, chancing to be visiting the ICU office, was taken along. He must have been wrong, because Ncwana had served with the army in Flanders and apparently had a criminal past, having served a five year gaol term for

theft (Central Archives: Department of Justice 3/1064/18, Commissioner, South African Police, to Secretary for Justice 30 November 1920).

95. *Cape Times* 20 and 22 September and 4 October 1920.
96. Manifesto of 9 July 1928 (B/UCT).
97. A police report of June 1920 connected the ICU with the International Socialist League (Central Archives: Department of Justice 3/1064/18, Commissioner, South African Police, to the Secretary for Justice 14 June 1920).
98. Central Archives: Department of the Interior 1/A/1787 Commissioner, South African Police, to Chief Immigration Officer 1 October 1920; Principal Immigration Officer, Cape Town to Secretary for the Interior 25 October 1920; Union of South Africa, *Debates of the House of Assembly* 20 July 1925, Col. 6290.
99. Central Archives: Department of the Interior 2/A/1787 Telegram Principal Immigration Officer, Cape Town to Secretary for the Interior 27 November 1920.
100. Minutes of the Cape Federation 10 December 1920 (TUCSA Papers). Kadalie also mentions (*My Life*, 47) the Church of Scotland, implying that this had some influence with Patrick Duncan, the Minister of the Interior. The flaw of the story is that the Minister at the time was not Duncan, but Sir Thomas Watt.
101. *Cape Times* 13 June 1924.
102. Central Archives: Department of the Interior A/1787, Proceedings of Appeal Board 2 December 1920.
103. Central Archives: Department of the Interior 3/A/1787.
104. Central Archives: Department of the Interior 5/A/1787, Under-Secretary for the Interior to the Principal Immigration Officer, Cape Town 19 January 1921. It is of some interest that the Governor of Nyasaland inquired about Kadalie's proposed deportation, which he had heard of through newspaper reports. He did not, however, make any comment upon it (Central Archives: Department of the Interior 8/A/1787, Governor of Nyasaland to Governor-General of South Africa 30 December 1920).
105. Op. cit., 47.
106. *Cape Times* 17 February 1921.
107. Union of South Africa, *Debates of the House of Assembly* 20 July 1925, Col. 6292. Cf. also 1926, Col. 296–297.
108. *Cape Times* 15 January and 17 February 1921; *The Eastern Province Herald* 29 November 1921; Union of South Africa, *Debates of the House of Assembly* 20 July 1925, Col. 6291; Union of South Africa, *Social Statistics No. 3 – 1921*, 53.
109. Minutes of the Cape Federation 25 September 1920 (TUCSA Papers).
110. *Cape Times* 14 August 1920 (which gives Kendall's initials as G.H.); Minutes of the Cape Federation 17 August 1920 (TUCSA Papers).
111. R. Stuart to D. Kendall 2 June 1921 (Cape Federation Letter Book, TUCSA Papers).

CHAPTER 3

Urban Discontents in Post-War South Africa – The Wider Perspective

'When there is no smoke in Johannesburg, then it's right to assume that there is no fire throughout the country.'

Naboth Mokgatlo, 1971

While it is true that Cape Town, because of its more liberal atmosphere and the greater sophistication of its Coloured labour force, was especially favourable to the growth of a Black labour movement, labour unrest and the striving to give organizational expression to inchoate protest were to be found in towns big and small the length and breadth of the country. One of the striking features of the incipient Black labour movement was the awareness in every locality of events elsewhere, and the sense of solidarity that followed upon this awareness. Leaders were ever on the move, making contacts and spreading propaganda. Early in its history, the ICU became caught up in a movement to bring together the various Black and Coloured workers' organizations that had sprung up in different centres as a result of post-war restlessness and the soaring cost of living. The origin of this movement can be traced to an exchange of letters in March, 1919 between Clements Kadalie and a labour leader in Bloemfontein, H. Selby Msimang. The latter, who in these early days eclipsed Kadalie in prestige and influence, was born at Edenvale, just outside Pietermaritzburg, Natal, in 1886 and educated at Healdtown. His background was significantly different from that of Kadalie. He was the son of a minister of religion, the Rev. Joel Msimang, and the brother of the solicitor R. W. Msimang, who framed the constitution of the South African Native National Congress, of which Selby himself was a member of long standing. In short he belonged to that able and moderate Black élite, committed to Christianity and imbued with the ideals of western social democracy, that emerged before the First World War. His English was excellent and he was able to meet Whites on equal intellectual terms, endowed as he was with the *savoir-faire* that enabled him to avoid the extremes of bluster and servility with a skill which failed so many ICU leaders, including even Kadalie. Having worked successively as a court interpreter and a clerk in the Volksrust office of the African lawyer, Dr P. Ka I. Seme, he was, at the time of his alliance with Kadalie, the editor of a vernacular newspaper in Bloemfontein, *Morumioa-Inxusa* (*The Messenger*).[1] Although his background was far from industrial, he was drawn into the labour movement because, as a leader of Black opinion, he grasped the fact that the essential Black grievance in the post-war years was economic, a lesson which eluded the Native Congress of the Orange Free State, a body without vigour and influence.[2] While living conditions at the location, Waaihoek, where the residents had the rare privilege of being permitted to build their own houses (though not to own land), were not a source of discontent, wages had failed to respond to changes in the cost of living, and the labour force had a temporary bargaining power in a fortuitous shortage of labour, largely the result of the influenza epidemic.[3]

As early as February 1919, Msimang was voicing the demand for a daily wage for unskilled workers of four shillings and six pence, a modest enough sum, scarcely more than what was paid to Cape Town workers before the war, but even so, far in excess of current wage rates. On 15 February local employers of unskilled labour, including South African Railways, the Public Works Department, and Bloemfontein Corporation, agreed at a meeting to recommend a minimum local wage of two shillings and three pence a day, a recommendation which suggests that existing wage rates were even lower.[4] This offer was quite unacceptable and, since Msimang continued his campaign, the employers thought it expedient to reconsider it. At the end of the month, representatives of the Council, the Master Builders' Association, and the local commercial firms met again and, in spite of some grumbling, they agreed (with the exception of the Railways) to raise their offer to two shillings and six pence a day. Even with Saturday counted as a full day, this still gave only 15 shillings a week, although even the most grudging estimate of the cost of living for a family of five was a pound.[5] The discrepancy between the acknowledged cost of living and the purchasing power of existing wages did not shake the conviction of the authorities that the clamour from the location originated in the agitation of Selby Msimang; and so they had him arrested on 28th February for incitement to public violence, which had the not surprising effect of bringing on this very violence. A mob of several hundreds smashed the windows of the houses belonging to the most unpopular 'blockmen', residents appointed by the municipality to minor posts of responsibility in the location; gathered outside the police station to demand the prisoner's release; and stoned the police, who, displaying commendable self-control, responded by firing over the heads of the crowd.[6]

Msimang was remanded on bail of £500, an enormous sum by the standard of the time.[7] While awaiting trial he continued to hold public meetings and to press for a further improvement in wages, though studiously maintaining a moderate tone and evading demands for a strike.[8] He came up for trial in May 1919, accused of inciting the 'native labourers and residents of Bloemfontein . . . by force and violence to demand and obtain an increase in their wages from their European employers'. He was acquitted.[9]

Msimang's arrest in February 1919 attracted much attention. The Cape Congress, meeting at Ndabeni, protested against it as 'an attempt on the part of the European community of Bloemfontein to intimidate and terrorise the native community against agitation for increased wages'.[10] Kadalie was prompted to send a telegram of support. From Bloemfontein came the reply, 'I thank you for your kind message of sympathy which gives me encouragement. I have begun to organise but I am working single-handed and would be glad if you could send me your constitution and again to send an Organiser from Cape Town to help me'.[11] A copy of the constitution was sent and Msimang, proceeding with the establishment of a general union known as the Native and Coloured Workers' Association, not only adopted this, but also intimated his wish to amalgamate with the ICU. In August he visited Cape Town at Kadalie's invitation and on 9 August, when he gave a talk in the city hall on the organization of labour, he was introduced, so Kadalie later said, as 'an organiser of the ICU in the Free State'.[12] The speech Msimang delivered on that occasion was permeated with the moderation that was characteristic of him: Whites had nothing to fear from the other racial groups unless they persisted in driving them to desperation through the discriminatory legislation that, in the Orange Free State, had reduced Blacks to a state of semi-slavery and compelled them to organize.[13] But more important than this public meeting for the history of the ICU were the negotiations that went on during Msimang's stay in Cape Town to confirm the alliance with Kadalie and to effect an amalgamation with other Black industrial organizations, notably the Industrial Workers of Africa. There seems little doubt that Bloemfontein and Cape Town joined forces under the name of the Industrial and Commercial Workers' Union of South Africa.[14] In the case of the IWA, amalgamation was not easy because of its marked differences from the ICU. Though it appears that Msimang was able to allay the racial suspicions of the IWA leaders and that 'a basis for the amalgamation of the two Unions was arrived at',[15] the IWA in fact maintained a separate existence. Returning to Bloemfontein, Msimang threw himself into the task of organizing the Orange Free State, and at the annual meeting of the ICU in January 1920 (which Msimang did not attend), Kadalie reported a membership of over a thousand in Bloemfontein alone and the opening of other branches in the Free State.[16]

The decisive event in the unification movement was a conference held in Bloemfontein in July 1920, which had a much more ambitious aim than just a consolidation of the alliance between Kadalie and Msimang. The intention was to unite all Black labour organizations and therefore the meeting had an historical importance as the first Black labour conference in South Africa. It is necessary to look at the development of the labour movement in those towns – other than Cape Town and Bloemfontein – that sent delegates to Bloemfontein and to seek an explanation for the absence of representatives from those towns that might have been expected to send them. Styled 'the first annual general meeting of the Industrial and Commercial Workers' Union of South Africa',[17] the conference seems to have originated in a suggestion made by Selby Msimang.[18] In May 1920 the South African Native National Congress, at its annual meeting in Queenstown, Cape, gave its blessing to the project and resolved to send representatives.[19]

None of the provincial Natives Congresses, however, was reported to have sent an official delegation, despite the Queenstown resolution.[20] Although many – probably most – of the delegates were members of Congress, they appear, with possible rare exceptions, to have been at the Conference as representatives of labour organizations rather than of any provincial Congress or of the National Congress. The bodies that did send delegates were the Cape Town ICU; Msimang's organization; the Native and Coloured Workers' Union of East London, Port Elizabeth and Aliwal North; and the Industrial Workers of Africa.[21] Surprising was the total absence of delegates from Natal and the almost total absence of delegates from the Transvaal.

Johannesburg had seen a great deal of industrial and political unrest in the last year or so of the war and during the post-war period, an unrest born, as elsewhere, of the rising cost of living and lagging wages. There was discontent among the mine workers, insulated though they were from the rise in the cost of living by the provision of food and lodging, and this discontent found expression as early as February 1918, in a brief boycott of mine stores on the East Rand. Outside the compounds of the mines the hardships of the urban Blacks were exacerbated by the appalling living conditions – 'a disgrace to civilization and a menace to public health'.[22] As in Cape Town, it had been the outbreak of the plague that had compelled the authorities to make proper provision for the accommodation of Blacks. Between 1905 and 1907 the municipality built huts and barracks for 1 400 people at Klipspruit, some eight kilometres from the centre of the town and next to a sewage disposal works. This location was wholly inadequate, but the only one until the City Council, under the stimulus of the mortality rate during the influenza epidemic, started building the Western Native Township in 1918. Blacks were legally bound to live in locations except those who resided on the premises of their White employers, but since the municipal location was always full, a large number of them found accommodation in White-owned slums.[23] Hundreds crammed into the so-called Malay Location at Vrededorp amongst Coloured people and Indians and – a source of eternal friction – in the neighbourhood of White families. A few property owners there were taking in up to £500 a month in rents, with as many as ten men sleeping in a room, and there was little the authorities could do, short of building more houses for Blacks. Crime and drunkenness were rife.[24] As one observer, who cannot be suspected of excessive sensibility, put it, 'The lot of the native who has lost his place in his kraal and in the tribal lands, or who has been foolish enough to move with his family into Johannesburg, is certainly very hard.'[25] This commentator was that 'latter-day Jefferies',[26] T. G. Macfie.

Macfie was the Johannesburg magistrate who gained much notoriety from the severity of his sentences and the offensiveness of his *obiter dicta* at a trial of strikers in June 1918. This was the so-called bucket strike of Black sanitary workers, who demanded an increase in pay of a shilling a day. Since their strike virtually crippled the sanitary service in most of Johannesburg, they were in a

A.W.G. Champion and C. Kadalie, *The Truth about the I.C.U.* (Durban, 1927) – University of Cape Town, Ballinger Collection

(1. to r.) Harry Snell, George Lansbury, Clements Kadalie, and Arthur Henderson at the House of Commons, *The Workers' Herald* 15 August 1927 – South African Library, Cape Town

A.W.G. Champion and colleagues, Durban – Documentation Centre, Sanlam Library, University of South Africa

strong position, in fact too strong a position, because the gravity of the situation aroused the authorities to swift reprisal. Arrested and charged – with the exception of fifteen who were not under contract – under Section 12 of the Riotous Assemblies Act of 1914, the strikers (or at least the first batch tried, on 10 June) were sentenced to two months' hard labour, and they were told from the bench that 'they would be put back to do their work as convicts under armed guards and if they attempted to escape they would be shot if necessary to prevent their escape, and that if they refused to do the work they would be given lashes.' At the end of the month the sentences were suspended by the Supreme Court.[27]

There was a general feeling among Black workers that a shilling increase in daily pay was a fair demand. Meetings in support of this were held by the International Socialist League, the Industrial Workers of Africa, and the Transvaal Native Congress, and there was much talk about a strike. When, on 1 July 1918, fifteen thousand Black workers on three gold mines stopped work and had to be forced by police and soldiers to go back, it was assumed by the police and the magistrate that this was part of a general strike plotted by agitators. The brief mine strike, however, appears to have been spontaneous except to the extent that the strikers were worked up by the charged atmosphere in Johannesburg following the arrest of the sanitary workers. There does not seem to be any evidence that a general strike was seriously planned for 1 July, or that the organizations active among Black workers had sufficient influence to bring out 15 000 miners.[28] Nevertheless, although the vague talk about striking, especially as it was accompanied by an insistence upon moderation and restraint, can hardly be said to have constituted incitement to public violence, the authorities remained convinced that the International Socialists, the Native National Congress, and the IWA were subversive and a public danger. On 6 July three White members of the ISL were arrested and at subsequent intervals five Blacks, members of Congress and the IWA (including H. Kraai and R. Cetyiwe, later active in Cape Town), all being refused bail. The case against them collapsed when the chief prosecution witness under cross-examination retracted the information he had given and repudiated his own sworn statement.[29]

There was a recrudescence of agitation at the end of March 1919, when the Transvaal Congress began a passive resistance campaign against the pass laws, combined with a renewed demand for increased wages. A request was sent to the Native Recruiting Corporation to open negotiations for higher wages for mine workers, whereupon its General Manager, with the sanction of the Government's Native Affairs Department, invited chiefs to visit the mines; and these duly denied the right of the Transvaal Congress to speak on behalf of the men in the mines, though at the same time making it clear that the demand for more pay was not unjustified. On Sunday 30 March there was a noisy meeting of Blacks at Vrededorp and people were called upon to destroy their passes. The following day a great crowd assembled at the Johannesburg pass office and there was a renewed call for the destruction of passes and also for a strike. The proceedings were then all very good-humoured, but inevitably in the succeeding days violence erupted, especially at Vrededorp and Fordsburg, where hundreds of arrests were made and there was enthusiastic intervention by White civilians anxious to be good citizens.[30] The trouble did not spread to the mines.[31]

Apart from one of those wild rumours that spread from time to time of a country-wide Black conspiracy (in June 1919),[32] there was little hint of trouble on the Rand again until the end of the year, when, perhaps influenced by the Cape Town dock strike and certainly stimulated by the rising cost of living, the Transvaal N.C. resumed agitation for higher wages both amongst the mine workers and amongst the general labourers.[33] Many of the contract labourers on the mines came from areas severely affected by the great drought and all were resentful at the growing gap between wages and prices. The old grievances remained as well: the trading methods used by the concession stores and the exclusion of Blacks from the skilled tasks.[34] Congress, which was pressing for a minimum wage of forty-five shillings a week for single men and ninety shillings for married men (in the case of those not fed and housed by their employers), succeeded in January 1920, in getting a deputation received by representatives of the employers, some of whom responded favourably, offering in a number of cases a 25 per cent advance.[35] For the mine workers the Chamber of Mines recommended a slight increase of wages, and it was because some mines procrastinated in implementing this that the second, and much more serious, postwar strike took place.[36] Beginning on Tuesday 17 February, four days later it was affecting 42 000 men at eleven mines. Altogether it lasted eleven days, with no fewer than 71 000 men involved (37 per cent of the total Black labour force on the Rand gold mines), though the largest number away from work at any one time never exceeded 42 000.[37] Police and troops were used to force a return to work.[38]

The 1920 mine strike owed little to the direct intervention of Congress. The assessment of the International Socialists carries conviction: 'The strike is undoubtedly an instinctive mass revolt against their whole status and pig level of existence. The Native Congress has had very little to do with the movement, other than to hold a watching brief.'[39] In spite of its spontaneity, however, the strike, with its display of solidarity and its picketing, was remarkably well disciplined. Naturally the authorities suspected the machinations of the Transvaal Congress and the ISL, but the suspicion had little foundation. The fact that, while the strike was in process, the compounds were cut off from the outside world and collaboration between mines broke down, with some men going back to work as others went on strike, seems to postulate organization only at compound level, the different compounds being united by a common feeling of expectancy and mutual sympathy. Undoubtedly the Transvaal Native Congress contributed to this climate by demands for higher wages made upon employers and voiced at meetings that mine workers attended,[40] yet its contribution was small enough, if one judges from the mildness of its propaganda. At its meetings of late February its leaders did nothing to incite a strike on the mines and displayed little enthusiasm for extending it, once it had started, from the mines to the town. The outbreak of violence that occurred on the last Sunday of the month, escalating into a racial clash and the loss of eight Black lives, was not the work of Congress but the result of the crowd's anger with its leaders, forever asking for money and forever without any.[41]

Remarkable as these industrial disturbances on the Rand were, they reveal characteristics which explain why Johannesburg did not feature prominently in the Black labour movement of the early 1920s. Although the discipline and cohesion of the 1920 strikers cannot be denied, the fact remains that the nature and composition of the labour force in the gold mines militated against the establishment of a continuing organization. The compounds, with their restricted access, easily isolated at the first sign of trouble, were not conducive to industrial organization. One cannot but notice, too, the ruthlessness with which the authorities on the Rand acted. The display of force during the Cape Town dock strike was very mild compared with the killings and woundings that took place in the Village Deep mine (three killed and forty wounded) in February 1920. But then, the atmosphere was much more violent on the Rand, where sudden death underground or in faction fighting or drunken brawls was not infrequent. Racial animosities as well were much sharper there. White labour in Cape Town, disappointing as its support for the dock strikers proved to be, was far more sympathetic than were the workers on the Rand, where appeals by individual White labour leaders at least to refrain from subverting the efforts of Black labour to achieve better conditions, were scorned.[42] Such encouragement as the Black labour movement in the Transvaal received came from White socialists who were radical and unpopular with White opinion and very different from those respectable and moderate men who helped the ICU in Cape Town.

The organizations that were active on the Witwatersrand, whilst they stirred up and tried to exploit the discontents there, were ill-equipped for the task of organizing and leading a labour movement. The IWA, because of its revolutionary proclivities, invited official suspicion and, in any case, lost whatever influence it had after the strikes of June and July, 1918.[43] The other organization, Congress, had a small membership[44] and was discredited. In December of 1918 it had decided to try once more a tactic that had already proved futile, that of dispatching a delegation to Britain and Versailles to plead the Black cause to the Imperial Government, and also to the Allied plenipotentiaries at the Peace Conference, and once more this had ended in humiliating and wretched failure.[45] 'This, the third Appeal of the Black Sons of Africa,' said the Rev. Z. R. Mahabane at the Queenstown Conference of the Cape Congress in May 1920, 'has again been dismissed with heavy costs. England has finally washed her hands of the innocent blood of the Bantu races.'[46] There followed its indecisive leadership in the wage disputes of 1918–1920. After that the Transvaal Congress turned away from industrial organization to participation in the Johannesburg

Joint Council of Europeans and Natives, an unofficial body founded in 1921 by sympathetic Whites anxious to bridge the racial gap, and also in the consultative machinery (such as it was) set up by the Native Affairs Act of 1920.[47] It is possibly because the Transvaal leadership was reverting to a less militant policy, or because it was disheartened by the disappointing results of industrial action, that it remained aloof from the Bloemfontein Conference.[48]

Durban presents a striking contrast to Johannesburg. It was the only major seaport that did not produce a Black labour union in the post-war period. It experienced sporadic trouble, but nothing of moment. Several possible explanations spring to mind, none very convincing. It is possible, for example, that the Zulus had been cowed by the severity of the suppression of the Bambata rebellion of 1906–1908, but it seems unlikely that that essentially tribal protest had much to do with the problems of urban Blacks. Another possibility is that no Zulu leader capable of organizing a trade union had appeared, and it seems likely that only a Zulu could have done this. The later history of the ICU, especially the experience of Kadalie in Durban, lends support to that possibility. It should be borne in mind that not only did the Black population of the city have a marked degree of homogeneity, but the Coloured element was negligible, while the Indian community kept itself to itself. The leader enjoying the greatest prestige at this period was the Rev. John Dube, former President-General of the SANNC, but his interests lay principally in the field of education and were remote from labour problems.[49] Perhaps there was no labour movement because the Blacks in Durban were less committed to urban life than those in Ndabeni or the locations of Port Elizabeth and Johannesburg. The impermanence of the Black labour force is shown by the very small number of women, children, and elderly people living in the city.[50] Another possible explanation lies in the restrictive policy pursued by the municipal authorities, who forbade public meetings for Blacks, both indoors and outdoors.[51] The imposition of this restriction, which hampered trade union activity, was facilitated by the character of the accommodation provided by the City Council. There were married quarters for only a couple of hundred men, women, and children, and the rest of the accommodation, housing some three thousand men and a hundred women, was of the barrack or hostel type,[52] which helped exclude undesirable outside influences. It is true that thousands of men and women, very many of them domestic servants, lived in single quarters on their employers' premises in town, but they were widely dispersed and subject to strict control. They often lived in deplorable conditions.

In the other Natal towns there was unrest that took the form of complaints about low wages during the post-war inflation and occasional brief strikes.[53] As in the case of Durban, however, no trade union was thrown up. The fact that none was established among the coal miners must be explained to some extent by the same factors that inhibited labour organization in the gold and diamond mines. Grievances do not seem to have been so acute as on the Rand, partly because wages were comparatively good and accommodation reasonable.[54] The labour force was partly Indian and partly Black, and no doubt this racial division tended to discourage common action.

Kimberley, East London, and Port Elizabeth were represented at Bloemfontein and had their labour organizations, though Kimberley, where there were some stirrings, but not much industrial unrest, produced no spontaneous union of any consequence. De Beers Diamond Mines, the biggest employer in Kimberley, with a reputation of being a good one,[55] took steps to safeguard its workers against the effects of the rising cost of living by selling food and clothing at a loss in the compound stores and also by increasing wages.[56] The very fact that their men were in compounds, even (or, perhaps, especially) well-run ones, would tend to discourage trade union ideas spreading from outside. Delegates from the town attended the Bloemfontein Conference simply because Msimang's organization had established a branch there.

East London had no big employer like De Beers with its compounds. The city had very little industry and was economically dependent upon its port. Most Black labourers, apart from domestic servants, worked for the municipality, various commercial enterprises, and South African Railways and Harbours, and they lived in two somewhat unruly locations, the East Bank (the bigger of the two) and the West Bank.[57] Early signs of an incipient labour organization appeared among the dock workers, who were not contract workers, but casual labourers whose precarious livelihood made them particularly vulnerable to unemployment in times of depression and to hardship in times of rising prices. They tended to be restless and easily roused. Demands for a wage increase were made in July 1918, as a result of the rising cost of living, but, in spite of the precocity of its Black labour movement, going back to before the war, East London experienced no violence and wage demands were made in a spirit of compromise and without bitterness. One reason for this was that employers tended to be tolerant and to display understanding. Another was the moderating influence exerted by Dr Walter Rubusana, the minister of the Congregational Church in the East Bank Location and a Vice-President of the South African NNC until the establishment of the Bantu Union, to which he transferred his allegiance. At the end of August a committee of the local Chamber of Commerce, receiving a delegation led by him, offered, after preliminary comments upon the law-abiding character of 'the Natives as a whole' and upon the respect enjoyed by Dr Rubusana, to recommend that employers should increase wages by six pence a day, an offer which the delegates' leader agreed to commend to the workers. This bargain lasted until the beginning of 1920, when as a result of the continued rise in prices there were renewed demands for higher pay.[58]

In February 1920, a letter was circulated among employers from an organization calling itself the East London Native Employees' Association and claiming a membership of two thousand. The Chamber of Commerce described the Association's demand of an extra two shillings a day 'most unreasonable', but it was not outrageous as a negotiating gambit, and the employers were prepared to talk. A conference of employers appointed a sub-committee to inquire into the cost of living, and this recommended a further six pence a day, which came to be the offer made to the men.[59] This offer, following as it did so soon after the previous increase, must have allayed popular discontent. At least, the Association was not sufficiently active again to attract the notice of the White press. It seems that, when the Chamber of Commerce tried to get into touch with it to request it to send a delegation, there was no response and the six penny offer, in March, 1920, had to be announced by the Superintendent of Locations.[60] However, it is apparent that Dr Rubusana was associated in some way with it and that it received a measure of support from local White radicals.[61]

The report of the delegations to the Bloemfontein Conference suggests that the East London Native Employees' Association linked up with similar organizations in Port Elizabeth and Aliwal North, to form the Native and Coloured Workers' Union of East London, Port Elizabeth and Aliwal North. Aliwal North, with its Black population of fewer than 3 000, could have been of little importance, and its unlikely appearance during this phase of Black labour history can have been due only to the influence of events in East London. It was at Port Elizabeth that the most exciting developments occurred in 1920.

At this period Port Elizabeth had a larger Black population than greater Cape Town had (11 472 compared with 3 707 – 1921 census), slightly smaller than that of East London (11 601); and also a very substantial Coloured population (13 203 Coloured and Asian, compared with only 2 006 in East London). The Blacks were accommodated in a government location, New Brighton, built in 1903, eight or so kilometres outside the city, but many had settled and bought land at Korsten, a village which lay outside the municipal boundaries and had, besides Black residents, a very mixed population of Cape Coloured, Indians, Chinese, and Whites.[62] Living conditions in New Brighton (which was overcrowded) and Korsten, though not uniformly bad, were undoubtedly a cause of dissatisfaction, especially in the latter.[63] New Brighton, intelligently administered and provided with facilities, such as water and lighting, that Korsten lacked, had an Advisory Board of six members, four of whom were elected, and an elected Chairman of Public Meetings responsible for their conduct. There was strict control over the consumption of liquor, only limited quantities of 'Kaffir beer' being allowed. Nevertheless, if the rent was low, the housing was rudimentary. Korsten, where in contrast liquor was freely obtainable and some of the houses were 'undescribably filthy and insanitary',[64] was much more turbulent, though the location too did not lack an unruly group.[65] In short, there was an environment likely to foster a radicalism that was prepared to exploit the grievances of unemployment and of a decline in wartime and post-war real wages.

According to an appraisal of December 1920, the cost in Port Elizabeth of foodstuffs and other necessities 'ordinarily consumed and used by natives' rose

105 per cent between 1914 and 1920. As in East London, discontent among the unskilled Black workers was voiced as early as 1918, when employers agreed to a six penny daily rise, bringing 1914 wages up to three shilling a day for men and two for women. Dissatisfaction was expressed much more forcibly from the beginning of 1920, no doubt influenced by events in Cape Town. At a meeting held on the morning of Sunday 11 January and attended by 4 000 people from a wide area, there were clear signs of the emergence of a new radical group, which attempted to seize control of the proceedings. This was the first occasion that the claim which was to be constantly reiterated in the coming months, for ten shillings a day for male workers, was heard. There was also talk of a general strike. A few days later, the Railways and Harbours Administration granted a rise of six pence a day, plus seven pence a day war bonus, an increase that evoked little gratitude among its employees, who complained that their wages would still be below Cape Town's. Other employers were also stirred into action and a meeting, presided over by the Mayor, agreed to invite a delegation from the locations to hold a discussion on the wages issue. A deputation was got together, clearly representing the old moderate leadership, and was received by the employers on Saturday 17 January and offered a rise of six pence a day for all those earning less than 27 shillings a week, with the exception of those in the building trade.[66]

On Sunday 18 January the deputation, accompanied by the Superintendent of the location, passed the offer on to a mass meeting at New Brighton, but it appears that it had a mixed reception from the crowd, because, after the Superintendent's departure, the official meeting broke up in disorder and another, unauthorized, one was immediately held by the radicals, the most important of whom was Samuel M. M. Masabalala.[67] Masabalala, born in 1877 at Uniondale in the Cape, was some years older than Msimang and considerably older than Kadalie, and had had a somewhat chequered career. After accompanying, as a young man, the first White settlers in Southern Rhodesia and serving in the Boer War, he had worked for some time as a teacher, but in 1920 was employed as a clerk by an insurance company. As a labour leader, he seems to have been something of a demagogue and an indifferent organizer, while his command of English was inferior to Kadalie's and, most certainly, to Msimang's. Kadalie's later strictures upon his competence cannot be considered unprejudiced, but they are supported by the evidence. As the treasurer of the Cape Congress, Masabalala enjoyed the backing of the Rev. Mahabane.[68]

An 'unofficial' delegation led by Masabalala which interviewed the Mayor on Monday 19 received short shrift,[69] but in the struggle that ensued between the moderates and the radicals Masabalala came out on top as the most widely supported leader. The moderates, in order to escape from the emotional atmosphere of mass meetings, secured, on 27 January, the election by the residents of Port Elizabeth, Korsten, and New Brighton of a committee of twelve (the members of the official deputation of 17 January all being elected to it), known as the Native Employees' Committee, that would negotiate with employers in an effort to get better terms than the unacceptable six pence a day increase. Masabalala responded by forming a general union, which very soon had 4 000 members.[70] It was the new union that made the running. The employers were unmoved and refused to budge from the existing offer, and the Black workers continued to seethe with indignation. The crisis came in October 1920, when the Bloemfontein Conference was already in the past.

Masabalala probably attended the Conference of the National Congress at Queenstown, and he almost certainly went to the Bloemfontein Conference as well.[71] On his return from the latter he plunged into a further bout of agitation for higher wages. In August his organization held its annual meeting, at which he, after being re-elected President, delivered a speech, larded with scriptural allusions and expressions of loyalty to the Empire, repeating the demand for a higher wage.[72] The following month, his tone becoming more threatening, the Mayor granted him an interview, which resulted in the offer by the employers of an additional six pence a day, bringing the minimum daily rate from three shillings and six pence to four shillings and six pence, still far short of the ten shillings demanded.[73] Mass meetings continued to be held and there was a great deal of talk about striking. Such excitement was aroused that on Sunday 17 October, at a Korsten meeting, Dr Rubusana who, being in Port Elizabeth for a church function, had been asked by the conservatives to throw his influence on to the side of moderation, was assaulted.[74]

The violence done to Dr Rubusana seemed most opportune to the public authorities, who regarded Masabalala as a dangerous extremist, especially after Monday 18 October, when his union (despite the opposition of some of its committee, who thought that there were insufficient funds at its disposal) announced the beginning of a strike on 3 November. Early on Saturday 23 October Masabalala was arrested (without warrant and at the initiative of the District Commandant of the South African Police) on affidavits made by Rubusana and another man (Kala or Kale), alleging that it was his inflammatory speech that had brought on the assault of the previous Sunday.[75] In the course of that morning a crowd of two or three hundred gathered outside the police station where Masabalala was in cells and, when the request by a deputation for the prisoner's release on bail was refused by the District Commandant and the Acting Magistrate, threatened to release him by force if he were not set free by five o'clock. The deputation, which included the Secretary of Masabalala's union, Alfred Sidzumo, endeavoured to pacify the crowd, but with no success. In the meantime some of the police had been armed and stationed on the steps leading to the main entrance.

As the afternoon wore on hundreds of people, as many as three thousand, of all races, men, women, and children, were attracted to the scene, as much by idle curiosity as by a desire to take part in the demonstration. To disperse the crowd a charge was made by four mounted policemen, but this had only a temporary effect, as did 'the jet of a moderate-sized water hose', which was soon out of action because the nozzle fell off. However, the comedy of the situation was soon blighted by the intervention of a number (about thirty) of civilians, mostly ex-servicemen, who made their way into the police station, armed themselves with rifles and posted themselves, some on the steps, others, the majority, on the balcony. Although Captain Halse, the District Commandant, accepted these voluntary additions to his garrison, he omitted to place an officer or NCO in charge of the men on the balcony and, it seems fairly certain, neither he nor the Acting Magistrate gave them definite instructions not to fire without orders. After the fiasco of the moderate-sized water hose the crowd began throwing stones at the men on the balcony. Then firing broke out and the crowd attempted to scramble to safety. Sixty seconds later two dozen people – one of them White – lay dead or dying.

What was established subsequently beyond all doubt was that neither of the two police officers in charge gave an order to fire. What is also certain is that, whether or not the first shot came from a revolver in the crowd (and not only does the evidence cast doubt on this, but also it is clear from the tone of its report that the commission of inquiry into the events of the day was highly sceptical about it), the firing was wild and prolonged beyond even the most generous estimate of the danger to the men in the police station. Again, it is apparent that the temper of the crowd was not so menacing as to frighten off a number of Whites who mingled with the demonstrators right up close to the police station steps. The White girl who died from a blow on the head was struck down by a Black already mortally wounded. Much indignation was expressed about the fate of this victim of 'senseless savagery'; but there was more reticence about her companion, shot in the head by rifle fire; and about the White spectator, struck by a bullet that passed through his body with such velocity that it killed a Black standing at his side.[76]

The events of the afternoon shocked and frightened the White residents, and the belief that a cunning conspiracy was afoot possessed them. Although the local newspaper, which had reported only in a cursory way the attack upon Dr Rubusana, had given no hint that violence was anticipated, people remembered now that their servants had told them stories of impending disturbances. Police reinforcements were hurriedly summoned from Grahamstown and places further afield, and patrols of police and armed civilians sent out. There were two clashes during the night, one with a group of men that was thought to be aiming to sabotage the power station, the other with a small party trying to set fire to a petrol store. The former group broke under fire, leaving behind one man killed and seven too badly hurt to move. Fear was not confined to the Whites. For, after the shooting, hundreds of location residents left for the country.[77]

Events in Port Elizabeth stirred up indignation throughout Black South Africa, not least in Cape Town, where large, though orderly, protest meetings were held to demand a commission of inquiry on which 'the non-European shall be directly represented'.[78] In appointing a commission the Government was actuated no doubt by the same consideration that swayed it in the case of Kadalie's threatened deportation, viz. its need for maximum electoral support in the pending general election. This is borne out by the composition of the commission, which was made up of Dr Abdurahman and Dr A. W. Roberts of Lovedale Mission (tacitly watching over Coloured and Black interests respectively) and C. A. Schweizer (a former South African Party member of the Legislative Assembly), the chairman. The commission reported on 11 January, 1921. While condemning 'in the strongest terms' the behaviour of the crowd 'in assembling in force . . . with the avowed determination of forcibly effecting the release of Masabalala', it was, at the same time, highly critical of the action of the police. The District Commandant was censured for refusing bail and for his failure to impose a proper discipline upon the civilians who had volunteered their services. Its final words were a stern indictment: 'That all the firing which took place after the mob broke away was directed against fugitives; that it was unnecessary, indiscriminate, and it was moreover brutal in its callousness, resulting in a terrible toll of killed and wounded without any sufficient reason or justification.[79]

It need hardly be said that the commission's report aroused intense anger in some quarters. The Secretary of Police at Pretoria invited comments from the Deputy Commissioner of the Eastern Cape and the District Commandant, Port Elizabeth, and these were published with the report (with consecutive pagination). Inspector Halse in particular considered that at least one commissioner, Dr Abdurahman, came to Port Elizabeth with his mind already made up; and he also claimed that, in spite of everything, he had been right to arrest Masabalala and that he had been legally unable to grant bail. The rest of the police witnesses, displaying a united front, whether commended or censured by the report, insisted that the whole crowd and not just a few hundred demonstrators in front had been bent upon violence from the beginning and armed with a variety of weapons; that the first shots had come from the crowd; and that an order to fire would have been given before long in any case. Such police afterthoughts incensed in turn the commissioners, who protested vigorously to the Acting Prime Minister at their attachment to the report, 'as a reflection upon the impartiality of the members of the Commission' and pointed out that there were discrepancies between the police comments and the police evidence of the previous year.[80]

After the riot, in the absence of Masabalala, who was taken to Grahamstown and detained until late in November, when he was committed for trial and charged with incitement under the Riotous Assemblies Act, the local Black leaders summoned Selby Msimang by telegram from Bloemfontein to represent their interests. The first thing he did after his arrival on 27 October was to persuade the men to withdraw their threat of a strike, which, contrary to the advice of the local union officials, who wanted the whole idea to be abandoned, had been brought forward from 3 to 1 November, and when this had been done, he led the employees' delegation at a joint conference with the employers, presided over by the Mayor, on Tuesday 9 November.[81] Msimang was clearly uncomfortable about the demand for ten shillings to which the local leaders were committed, and would have preferred a demand for a more realistic six shillings, which itself had no chance of acceptance. The employers resisted a further rise in wages, but agreed to the appointment of a committee of employers and employees to examine jointly the real cost of living of working families.[82] The committee met the following week and arrived at a settlement of four shillings and six pence a day for all Black workers except those in the building trade.[83]

Later in November Masabalala, released on bail, came back to Port Elizabeth, where he was enthusiastically welcomed by 2 000 supporters. Carried away by the excitement of the occasion, the crowd spurned the four-and-six minimum and decided to persist in the demand for ten shillings.[84] Such a demand was more unrealistic than ever, as prices were tending downwards once again, and as the cost of living declined anger and resentment subsided. By the end of the year the police were able to report that the 'native position' was back to normal, though trials of Blacks arrested in connection with the riot were going on into December, with severe sentences being passed. Masabalala was released when Dr Rubusana withdrew charges. The 'Native problem' slipped once again from the immediate attention of the White public.[85]

Notes

1. Interview with Mr Msimang, 29 June 1971; Mweli Skota, T. D., *The African Yearly Register, Being an Illustrated National Biographical Dictionary (Who's Who) of Black Folks in Africa*, Johannesburg, n.d., 218.
2. *The Friend* 22 July 1920.
3. Union of South Africa, *Annual Report of the Department of Justice for the Calendar Year 1919* (UG 35–1920), 120; *The Friend* 28 February 1919.
4. *Cape Times* 18 February 1919.
5. *The Friend* 28 February 1919.
6. *The Friend* 3 March 1919.
7. *The Friend* 4 March 1919.
8. *Cape Times* 7 April 1919; Interview with Mr Msimang, 29 June 1971.
9. *The South African Law Reports (1919), Orange Free State Provincial Division (1919 OPD)*, Rex *v.* Msimang, 38–44.
10. *The Friend* 12 March 1919.
11. *Ilanga lase Natal* 20 January 1922.
12. Ibid. Interview with Mr Msimang, 29 June 1971.
13. *Cape Times* 8 and 9 August 1919.
14. In March 1920 Msimang submitted to a committee inquiring into the pass laws evidence on behalf of 'the Free State Division of the Industrial and Commercial Workers' Union of South Africa', claiming a Free State membership of 7 000 (*Cape Times* 8 March 1920).

15. *Cape Times* 9 October 1919.
16. *Cape Times* 21 January 1920. He also reported branches in Natal, but there is no confirmation elsewhere of their existence.
17. *The Friend* 7 January 1920.
18. *Ilanga lase Natal* 20 January 1922.
19. *The Queenstown Daily Representative and Free Press* 27 and 29 May 1920; Central Archives: Department of Justice 3/127/20 Inspector P. J. Whitaker, South African Police, Queenstown to Deputy Commissioner, Grahamstown 2 June 1920.
20. It has been suggested that S. M. Makgatho, who was President of both the Transvaal Congress and the National Congress, was opposed to the formation of a separate industrial organization Johns, S. W. III, The birth of non-white trade unionism in South Africa, *Race*, October 1967. He had not attended the Queenstown Conference (*The Queenstown Daily Representative and Free Press* 29 May 1920).
21. *The Friend* 7 July 1920; *The Eastern Province Herald* 7 July 1920; *Cape Times* 7 July 1920.
22. According to S. M. Pritchard, the Native Affairs Department Director of Native Labour (*The Eastern Province Herald* 16 July 1920). Cf. Union of South Africa, *Report of the Native Affairs Commission for the Year 1921* (UG 15–1922), 8, which speaks of 'decent men and women in decent homes' and conditions 'so disgraceful and immoral that the thought of them murdered sleep'.
23. Maud, J. P. R., 1935, *City Government, the Johannesburg Experiment*, Oxford, 137.
24. Central Archives: Department of Justice 3/127/20 Sub-Inspector F. V. Lloyd, South African Police, Western Area, Johannesburg to Deputy Commissioner of Police, Johannesburg 3 September 1919.
25. Union of South Africa, *Report of the Department of Justice for the Calendar Year 1918* (UG 36–1919), 111.
26. Cope, R. C., *Comrade Bill, the Life and Times of W. H. Andrews, Workers' Leader*, Cape Town, n.d., 197.
27. Union of South Africa, *Report of the Department of Justice for 1918*, 110.
28. The absence of precise plans emerges from speeches made at meetings of the IWA at Johannesburg on 27 June 1918, attended by 150 Blacks and 5 Whites, and of the Transvaal Congress the following day (Central Archives: Department of Justice 3/527/17 Report of District Commandant, South African Police, Krugersdorp, evidently drawn up by a Black detective or informer).
29. Central Archives: Department of Justice 3/882/18 S. P. Bunting to Minister of Justice 10 October, 1918; Deputy Commissioner, CID, Transvaal to Deputy Commissioner, SAP Transvaal 21 October 1918; *Cape Times* 8, 9, 16, 17 and 18 July 1918.
30. *Cape Times* 4 April 1919. According to Kadalie in 1922 the infant ICU 'exerted its influence with the Government and protested at the deplorable action of the police' (*Ilanga lase Natal* 20 January 1922).
31. Central Archives: Department of Justice 3/1064/18 Provost Marshal of the Union of South Africa to the Minister of Justice March, 1919.
32. *Cape Times* 16 and 27 June 1919.
33. Central Archives: Department of Justice 3/527/17 Deputy Commissioner, CID Transvaal to Secretary, SA Police 7 January 1920.
34. Central Archives: Department of Justice 3/127/20 Deputy Commissioner, CID Transvaal to Secretary, SA Police 19 February 1920.
35. *Cape Times* 16 January 1920; *The Eastern Province Herald* 25 February 1920.
36. Central Archives: Department of Justice 3/127/20 Deputy Commissioner, CID Transvaal to Secretary, SA Police 19 February 1920.
37. Diamond C. R., 1969, African labour problems on the South African gold mines, M.A. thesis, University of Cape Town, 47.

38. Central Archives: Department of Justice 3/127/20 Commissioner, South African Police to Secretary for Justice 26 February 1920.
39. *The International* 27 February 1920.
40. Central Archives: Department of Justice 3/527/17 Deputy Commissioner, CID Johannesburg to Secretary, SA Police 27 November 1919 and 3 February 1920.
41. Central Archives: Department of Justice 3/127/20 Deputy Commissioner, CID Johannesburg to Secretary, SA Police 17, 23, and 26 February, and 1, 2, and 5 March 1920; South African Police, Fordsburg to Deputy Commissioner, Johannesburg District 1 March 1920.
42. R. C. Cope, op. cit., 15.
43. A reasonable inference from Central Archives: Department of Justice 3/527/17 Report of District Commandant, SA Police, Krugersdorp, n.d. and from the removal of H. Kraai and R. Cetyiwe to Cape Town.
44. Central Archives: Department of Justice 3/527/17 Deputy Commissioner, CID Johannesburg to Secretary, SAP 27 November and 18 December 1919.
45. Walshe, P., 1970, *The Rise of African Nationalism in South Africa, the African National Congress 1912–1952*, London, 62–5; *Contact* 30 July 1960.
46. *Abantu-Batho* 28 October 1920.
47. Walshe, P. op. cit., 96–9.
48. Such an hypothesis finds no support from the police report of the SANNC Queenstown Conference previously cited (P. J. Whitaker to Deputy Commissioner, Grahamstown 2 June 1920), which speaks of the 'fire-brand types . . . from the North'.
49. Walshe, P., op. cit., 228; *Ilanga lase Natal* 24 October 1924.
50. Union of South Africa, *Census of Population 1921, Part VIII – Statistics Regarding Non-Europeans* (UG 40–1924).
51. *The Workers' Herald* 15 May 1925.
52. Saunders, F. A., 1920, *Municipal Control of Locations, a Paper Read at the 13th Session of the Association of Municipal Corporations of the Cape Province*, Grahamstown, 11.
53. For example, on the coal mines in April 1919 (*Cape Times* 29 and 30 April 1919) and among municipal workers in Pietermaritzburg in January 1920 (*The East London Daily Dispatch* 31 January 1920).
54. The South African Native Races Committee, *The South African Natives; their Progress and Present Conditions*, London, 1908, 36–7; S. T. van der Horst, op. cit., 187.
55. H. M. Robertson, loc. cit., 11–12.
56. *Cape Times* 8 July 1919.
57. Cape Archives: Minutes of Meetings of Cape Town Native Affairs Committee Vol. II, Parcel 107, Item 339, Senior Inspector, South African Police to Deputy Commissioner, Cape Town 25 May 1927.
58. Smith, H. H., 1949, The development of labour organization in East London, 1900–1948, M. Econ. thesis, Rhodes University, Grahamstown, 152–8.
59. *The East London Daily Dispatch* 20, 21, and 25 February and 20 March 1920.
60. H. H. Smith, loc. cit., 160–1.
61. *The International* 20 February 1920.
62. Union of South Africa, *Report of the Native Economic Commission, 1930–1932* (UG 22 – 1932), 70.
63. *Cape Times* 24 December 1919.
64. Union of South Africa, *Report of the Native Economic Commission*, 70.
65. Ibid., 70; F. A. Saunders, op. cit., 14; *Cape Times* 24 December 1919.
66. *The Eastern Province Herald* 14, 15, 16, and 22 January and 3 February 1920.
67. *The Eastern Province Herald* 19, 20, and 21 January 1920.

68. T. D. Mweli Skota, op. cit. 187; *The Eastern Province Herald* 27 January, 28 October and 2 November 1920; C. Kadalie, *My Life*, 52–3; *Abantu-Batho* 28 October 1920.
69. *The Eastern Province Herald* 21 January 1920.
70. Union of South Africa, *Report of the Commissioners Appointed to Enquire into . . . the Native Disturbances at Port Elizabeth*, 3; *The Eastern Province Herald* 21 January, 3 February and 22 November 1920.
71. He does not figure in the list of delegates in *The Friend* 14 July 1920, but, since he was certainly in Bloemfontein at that time (*The Friend* 22 July 1920), he must have attended.
72. *The Eastern Province Herald* 26 August 1920.
73. Builders' labourers, who had caught up to 3s.6d., remained at that (Union of South Africa, *Report of the Commissioners*, 1).
74. *The Eastern Province Herald* 18 and 19 October 1920.
75. For an account of the events of 23 October and the preceding month, see Union of South Africa, *Report of the Commissioners*, 1, 12; *The Eastern Province Herald* 24 and 28 September, 12, 15, 25, and 28 October and 22 November 1920.
76. Union of South Africa, *Report of the Commissioners*, 8.
77. Ibid., 15, 21, 22; *The Eastern Province Herald* 25 and 29 October 1920.
78. C. Kadalie to Editor, *Cape Times*, published 26 October 1920. Cf. Kadalie, C. *My Life* 197. There was little reaction in Durban. 'So far, the recent native trouble at Port Elizabeth has had no perceptible effect on the local natives; in fact few of them appear to be aware of the recent happening at that place.' (Central Archives: Department of Justice 3/1064/18 Commissioner, SA Police to Secretary for Justice 30 November, 1920) Cf. also 3/127/20 Deputy Commissioner, CID, Transvaal to Deputy Commissioner, CID for the Union 9 November 1920.
79. Union of South Africa, *Report of the Commissioners*, 8–9.
80. Union of South Africa, *Letter Addressed to the Acting Prime Minister by the Members of the Commission Appointed to Enquire into the Native Riots at Port Elizabeth on the 23 October, 1920* (Ann. 656 – 1921).
81. *The Eastern Province Herald* 25, 26, and 28 October, 3, 10, 20, and 22 November 1920.
82. Ibid., 10 November 1920.
83. Ibid., 20 November 1920.
84. Ibid., 24 and 26 November 1920.
85. Central Archives: Department of Justice 3/1064/18, Acting Commissioner, South African Police to Secretary for Justice 31 December 1920; *Cape Times* 7 December 1920; *Contact* 30 July 1960.

CHAPTER 4

ICU and ICWU, 1920-1925

'*At our first labour Conference held at Bloemfontein in July 1920 we had the "One Big Union Movement" in view, but, owing to our being young at the game, blinded with that spirit of sectionalism and tribalism we were unable to launch out the gigantic task before us. It was no less discouragement to the determined ones, however, it was only a temporal* [sic] *setback.*'

(Clements Kadalie, September 1923)

Although the Bloemfontein Conference of July 1920 was summoned with the intention of establishing a national Black labour organization, the only major towns that had vigorous and spontaneous labour unions represented at the Conference were Cape Town, Bloemfontein, and Port Elizabeth. Kimberley, though sending no fewer than four delegates, had no union of its own, and there is no evidence of the presence of a delegate from East London, which does not, however, necessarily mean that none attended. The delegation from Cape Town was a strong one – Clements Kadalie, Joe Paulse, J. G. Gumbs, and Bennett Ncwana from the ICU, Reuben Cetyiwe and Hamilton Kraai of the IWA, and Impey Ben Nyombolo, of importance in due course, of the Cape Congress (and possibly of the ICU or the IWA too),[1] but the rest of the Cape Province (apart from the area contiguous to the Orange Free State) sent only five men, one of them, it is to be reasonably presumed, Samuel Masabalala.[2] Of the thirty or so representatives who attended the Conference, two-thirds came from branches established by Selby Msimang or under his influence in the Orange Free State, the northern Cape, and Basutoland. It was Msimang who acted as chairman. In his opening address he spoke of the enemies of the Black workers. 'The white worker,' he said, 'has only the capitalist as his foe, while we have the capitalist and the Trade Unions to fight against.[3]

The first act of the Conference was to establish what was bravely called 'one great union of skilled and unskilled workers of South Africa, south of the Zambezi', which was to seek 'equitable rates of wages and reasonable conditions of labour' for Black workers, including farm labourers and women workers in industry and domestic service, through negotiation, and to provide welfare benefits for its members. The new organization was given the cumbersome title of the Industrial and Commercial Coloured and Native Workers' (Amalgamated) Union of Africa, the Industrial and Commercial Workers' Union of Africa (ICWU) for short.[4] The Conference then proceeded to discuss the recruiting system ('detrimental to the progress of all native races in the sub-continent'), the pass laws ('unjust and degrading and a direct encouragement to the increase of criminal practices amongst the natives'), South African representation at the International Labour Conference to be held at Geneva in 1921, the cost of living, the establishment of a minimum wage for Black workers, equal pay for women, working hours, and education.[5]

'From the beginning to the end,' wrote Clements Kadalie in 1922, 'the Conference was a failure.'[6] Put out no doubt by the dominant role played by Selby Msimang, who was elected President of the new union,[7] he chiefly resented the election of Ben Nyombolo as Secretary instead of himself, disqualified by his alleged ignorance of 'any of the South African Native languages'.[8] Later he complained that the Conference was nothing but a plot hatched by Msimang, 'the idea being that the local people at Bloemfontein would place him in power ... We tried our best to make the Conference a success but achieved nothing for the race which is so desired, seeing that everyone who attended that conference aimed at being on top of the ladder ... What is it then when a man of intellect such as Mr Selby Msimang does not realise courtesy? What vindicates the idea of ignoring your own recognised mother? Without any hesitation Mr Msimang during the Bloemfontein Conference deliberately showed that he was not a member of the ICU and he even ignored what this Organisation had achieved for them and for the race in general ... We are now confronted as to what made the Bloemfontein Conference a failure. I could only sum it [*sic*] with this fact that self-aggrandisement was the main reason.'[9]

However, if Kadalie was disappointed with the outcome of the Bloemfontein Conference, this did not become immediately apparent. Indeed, it appears to have induced a certain euphoria in Cape Town. Mass meetings were held to report on it, and that of 25 July resolved, in conformity with the Conference's decision, to set up 'a non-European Workers' Federation, to include Indians, Malays, Coloured and natives . . . to work and manage its own affairs independently of the whites' Federation of Trades'.[10] In September, however, a quarrel developed between Kadalie and the Branch Secretary of the Cape Congress at Ndabeni, Simon Jordan, over the way in which the ICU was handling the current Cape Town wage demand. Jordan complained that Kadalie had failed to consult the other unions and the General Secretary of the ICWU.[11] As a result of this dispute the Executive of the ICU, adopting a motion of Bennett Ncwana, repudiated the proceedings of the Bloemfontein Conference and decided to preserve its separate identity.[12]

When this breach between the ICU and the ICWU appeared, Masabalala remained loyal to the latter, and it was his flamboyant behaviour that attracted most attention. In the general election of 1921 he became absorbed in politics, with comic and curious results. His support was enlisted by the opposition National Party in Uitenhage, which subsequently came to regret its decision because of the embarrassment he caused it. In a speech delivered on its behalf at Enon, a Coloured mission station near Uitenhage, in January, Masabalala was reported by Reuter to have said that, 'God could not help the native and coloured people, nor could his angels; but only the Nationalists could do so . . . if the Nationalists got into power the coloured people would be given rifles and the Kaffirs and Boers would unite . . .'[13] Although Alfred Sidzumo, in a letter to *The Eastern Province Herald*, claimed that Masabalala was misreported,[14] the mere fact that he lent his support to the Nationalists, scandalized many Blacks, not least Kadalie, who expressed righteous horror at the 'idiotic and obnoxious action adopted by Mr Masabalala in advising the natives and coloured electors to vote for a Nationalist Government'.[15] Yet within the year Kadalie and Masabalala were close comrades. This surprising development followed the first anniversary conference of the ICWU.

The ICWU Conference of 1921 was opened at Ndabeni by the Location Superintendent on 20 July. There were several odd features about this meeting. For one thing, unlike the Bloemfontein Conference where delegates from the Orange Free State predominated, the Cape Town Conference apparently had no representatives at all from that province, even Selby Msimang, who presided, representing several Cape 'constituencies'. Although this can be explained partly by the change of meeting place, the total absence of Free State representatives does not point to the survival there of a very vigorous organization. The published (though probably incomplete) list of delegates included only fifteen names, one being Msimang himself, and, apart from one from Johannesburg, J. W. Dunjwa of the SA Native National Congress, who may have chanced to be in Cape Town when the Conference convened, all the representatives were from the Eastern and Western Cape.[16] Another perplexing thing was the listing of Clements Kadalie of the ICU, who had in fact broken with the ICWU. There is no evidence at all that he attended, though S. M. Bennett Ncwana, who was in the Kadalie camp, certainly did, and he spoke in favour of co-operation and unity.[17]

On the proceedings of the conference the King William's Town newspaper, *Imvo Zabantsundu*, reported sourly, 'All the stock grievances were ransacked, and a long boohoo pronounced on them . . . Fancy demonstrations were indulged in about Bulhoek and the Port Elizabeth riots.'[18] Bulhoek, just outside Queenstown, had witnessed, just two months before the Conference, the massacre of the Israelites, a bizarre sect that resisted eviction from crown land. In commemoration the ICWU and the Cape Congress organized a Sunday demonstration during the period the labour congress was in session.[19] The Conference also resolved to send a deputation to the Government to request relief for the relatives of the victims, to keep the anniversary of the massacre, 24 May (as well as that of the Port Elizabeth tragedy, 23 October), 'as national days for all workers of non-European descent', and to establish a relief fund.[20]

The 'stock grievances' that were 'ransacked' were low wages, the high cost of living, the pass laws, the maldistribution of land, farm labour conditions (including 'the blatant shooting of workers on the farms'), the recruiting system for the mines ('nothing other than forced labour and tantamout to slavery'), and, a problem of growing concern as the economy slid into depression, unemployment.[21] Selby Msimang was anxious to persuade rural emigrants 'to turn their hands to something useful and to make them realise the wealth lying dormant in the lands they occupy'.[22]

In his speeches President Msimang stressed the need for conciliation and moderation and for organization 'to strike heavy blows – not rebellious or violent – for a larger freedom',[23] and these sentiments were echoed by other speakers.[24] His presidential report, on the evening of the second day of the Conference, had some harsh references to the industrial colour bar imposed by the Government ('a club of incorrigible magnates') and White trade unions and to the great gap between the wages of White workers and those of Black workers, the 'actual workers and producers of the country's wealth'. While his remarks on the Israelites show that he had no sympathy with their religious beliefs, it is apparent that he regarded them as victims of the country's land laws and the insatiable desire of European employers for cheap Black labour. The burden of his speech was an indictment of White rule in South Africa, 'too much greed, too much Europeanisation, too much prejudice'. Yet, 'How much are we worth?' he asked, 'Perhaps we suffer for our own sluggishness, foolishness, selfishness, and want of co-operation, selfhelp, and all the other virtues which go to the full sum of national progress.' There was criticism for the behaviour of the hot-heads in the Black labour movement, who embarked upon premature and ill-organized strikes and indulged in 'wild talk which serves merely to rouse the passions of the people'.[25]

For whom were these strictures intended? They were probably directed at Masabalala, who had uttered many wild words during the Port Elizabeth wage dispute and the 1921 election campaign, and whom Msimang must have had in mind in criticizing the advocates of the ten shilling a day minimum wage.[26] At, or just before, the end of the Conference Msimang and Masabalala quarrelled, for reasons that can only be surmised. Perhaps the latter resented the tone of the presidential speeches; perhaps he was offended at not being chosen, in the new elections, for an official position in the union, other than membership of the Supreme Executive Council; or perhaps his loyalty had been undermined by Kadalie. On the day before the Conference ended, on Monday 25 July, he had been received with enthusiasm by the assembled members of the ICU and, in the course of a typically extravagant speech, had expressed his thanks to the ICU for sending £150 after the Port Elizabeth riots to pay his bail and 'to feed the hungry'. At Port Elizabeth, he said, the people had 'thought it time to go to their Father, the Government, for food . . . The only reply they got from the Government was through machine guns, which killed 150 (*sic*) persons.' At the same meeting Kadalie explained why he had taken no part in the ICWU Conference, 'giving as the principal reason that the ICU stood for constitutionalism'.[27] This latter claim was no doubt an innuendo aimed at Msimang, whose assumption of the presidency of the ICWU at Bloemfontein was represented as a breach of constitutional propriety.

In his farewell speech on the last day of the Conference Msimang, doubtlessly realizing that the rift in the ICWU was beyond healing, was more explicit in his references to 'some of the leaders of the people whose system and manner of speech at public meetings seemed to take up a tone that made things difficult even for the most sympathetic of our enemies to think kindly of them,' a denunciation that may have been aimed equally at Kadalie and Masabalala. He again emphasized the necessity to abandon a sterile conflict with constituted authority, to seek remedies for grievances in organization and self-help, and to avoid 'wild phrases and flowery words'.[28]

Masabalala then defected; nor was he alone in his defection. He took with him five other delegates from his own part of the Cape, four of them, like himself, members of the newly-elected Supreme Executive Council of the ICWU. The deserters waited upon Kadalie at the ICU office to inform him of their decision to dissociate themselves from the ICWU Conference and to request the ICU to convene a conference at Port Elizabeth instead.[29] This competing conference was opened on Saturday 22 October 1921, by a Member of the Legislative Assembly, D. M. Brown of the South African Party. Apart from South-West Africa, which was unlikely to have been represented by anyone other than delegates from the ICU branch at Luderitzbucht, the Cape Province alone was represented, and in fact, the 1921 Port Elizabeth Conference led simply to the establishment of an ICU Cape Town-Port Elizabeth axis.[30]

Almost the first task of the Conference was to recall in a fitting manner the events of twelve months before. On the first anniversary of the riot a procession of several thousand people, led by a band, made its way to the cemetery for a religious service.[31] In its deliberations during the ensuing days the Conference passed resolutions calling for an end to the contract labour system, which the delegates regarded as a device used by South African Railways and Harbours and other employers for undercutting Black urban labour.[32] Other resolutions demanded an investigation into the working conditions of Black miners in the Transvaal and into conditions in South-West Africa; called for the repeal of the pass laws and for Black representation at the International Labour Conference; and condemned the practice of wine farmers in the Cape of issuing wine in lieu of wages and not giving their labourers decent accommodation. Delegates also protested at the Government's decision to confine the payment of compensation for injuries in the Port Elizabeth disturbances to those who had been permanently injured and who had not been willing spectators.[33] Such resolutions were much the same as those that had come out of the Bloemfontein Conference and the ICWU Conference earlier in the year.

The main business of the Conference was to bring the Eastern Province organization into an enlarged ICU, a project which was nearly frustrated by differences of political policy. While the Eastern Province delegates were in favour of rendering support to the Labour Party, the Cape Town people, who had supported the South African Party in the previous election, were hostile to any commitment to the Labour Party as long as the White trade unionists, especially in the Transvaal, did not accept their common interest with the Black workers. It is true that the ICU was no longer attached to the SAP and, indeed, Kadalie himself, with or without the consent of his colleagues, had already made overtures to the National Party, just before the ICWU Conference of July, when he had written to General Hertzog a letter apparently endorsing his policies and appealing for a contribution to an ICU fund for the Bulhoek victims. Hertzog's response was a donation of a guinea, accompanied by his celebrated letter, in which he spoke, in stiff and laboured terms, of 'our common endeavours' and the necessity for 'faith in and sympathy with one another' on the part of 'the white and black Africander'.[34] Whatever Kadalie's private views were, however, and in spite of Masabalala's enthusiasm for the Nationalists in the general election earlier in the year, majority Black opinion could not yet stomach support for Hertzog, however disenchanted it was with the SAP Prime Minister, General Smuts. After protracted debate it was decided to postpone any decision upon political affiliation, though even this compromise secured only a narrow majority.[35] The final result was a resolution by the enlarged union 'to dissociate itself from any political body whatever, but . . . solely to propagate the industrial, economic and social advancement of all African workers through industrial action on constitutional lines'. It went on to say 'that this Organization does not foster or encourage antagonism towards other established bodies, political or otherwise, of African peoples'.[36]

In the election of officers at the end of the Conference, Masabalala was given the position of Organizer-in-Chief, Kadalie becoming General Secretary, while William Fife of Cape Town was elected President. James La Guma of the Luderitzbucht branch was transferred to Port Elizabeth as Branch Secretary,[37] becoming in 1923 Assistant General Secretary. Authority was vested (between conferences) in a General Executive Council and its sub-committee, the Board of Arbitration.[38] In practice it seems that the Port Elizabeth and Cape Town branches, understandably given the great distance between them, remained virtually autonomous, and it also appears that East London did not go in with the enlarged ICU.[39]

At the end of the 1921 Conference Bennett Ncwana, who had defected from the ICWU, deserted in turn the ICU, upon which he launched a bitter attack on 26 November 1921 in the newspaper he had started the previous year just after the Bloemfontein Conference, *The Black Man*.[40] He threw in his lot with the ICWU again, being appointed its General Organizer, and in 1922 started with its General Secretary, Nyombolo, and a self-styled professor, James S. Thaele, an African Land Settlement Scheme, the object of which was 'to assist the Government by inducing Natives living in towns to settle on the land'.[41] Nyombolo, the dominant figure in the union in its later years, ran a newspaper called the *African Voice*.[42]

Early in 1923 there was talk of a move to bring together the ICU and the ICWU, and it was even reported that a reunion had been effected.[43] In September 1923, however, the *African Voice* resumed the offensive, accusing Kadalie of being in the pay of Moscow, a charge that was indignantly repudiated.[44] It is rather curious that this attack coincided with a recrudescence of police suspicions. Scarcely a month before, the Commissioner of Police was pressing the Secretary for the Interior to reconsider the decision of 1921 not to deport Kadalie. 'Secret information,' he wrote, 'has now been received from New Scotland Yard that Clements Kadalie is in touch with John Campbell, who is Secretary of the International Transport Workers' Propaganda Committee in Hamburg. I may add that Campbell has been specially commissioned from Moscow to win over the transport workers to the Red International of Labour Unions . . . This Coloured emissary of the Soviet Government at Moscow is at the present time addressing a series of meetings in Bloemfontein with a view to organising the coloured workers there, ostensibly for industrial purposes, but in reality with the object of spreading communistic propaganda.'[45]

Despite the contempt with which he habitually referred to the ICWU Kadalie took the rival union sufficiently seriously to propose at the Fourth Annual Conference of the ICU, held in January 1924, that the ICU change its name to the African Workers' Federation because 'certain individuals have adopted and styled their union [*sic*] as the ICWU, a name associated and derived from [*sic*] that of the Industrial and Commercial Workers' Union of Africa – the ICU. This union, ICWU, which is at present non-existent, is now used for purposes of exploitation of the African workers.'[46] The proposal met with a hostile reception and he was compelled to withdraw it.

The 'non-existent' union held its annual conference at Grahamstown in July of that year. Typically the Conference passed resolutions expressing loyalty to the King and 'great alarm and consternation' at the spread of Bolshevism.[47] Anti-Communism and a servile support of the South African Party seem to have been cardinal features of ICWU policy,[48] and in later years Kadalie was to allege that the rival union had been financed by 'the exploiters of our people',[49] by which he presumably meant the Chamber of Mines or the South African Party.

In 1924 the ICWU followed the ICU into Natal when the latter began its propaganda there;[50] and there is evidence of its existence as late as 1925.[51] By then it was in a state of confusion, with the annual conference of 1925 suspending both President[52] and General Organizer, Ncwana, who responded by setting himself up as a rival General Secretary. Thus it displayed the usual characteristics of a disintegrating organization. When the newspapers associated with Nyombolo and Ncwana disappeared is not clear, but they evidently had gone bankrupt by 1927.[53] Even though these two men themselves do not yet drop out of the story, their union can safely be presumed dead.

Notes

1. Kraai, Ncwana, and Nyombolo were reported present by the South African Police, who noted that Nyombolo, a former interpreter in a magistrate's court, had served a prison term for an unnamed offence (Central Archives: Department of Justice 3/1064/18, Commissioner, SAP to Secretary for Justice 30 November 1920), the others by *The Friend* 14 July 1920.
2. Two delegates from Aliwal North are recorded (presumably representing the Native and Coloured Workers' Union of East London, Port Elizabeth and Aliwal North), one from Queenstown, and another from Touws Rivier in the Western Cape (ibid.).
3. Ibid.
4. Ibid.; *Cape Times* 23 July 1921.
5. *The Friend* 14 July 1920; *The Eastern Province Herald* 7 and 16 July 1920; *Cape Times* 30 August 1920.
6. *Ilanga lase Natal* 20 January 1922.
7. *The Friend* 14 July 1920.
8. Manifesto of 9 July 1928 (B/UCT).
9. *Ilanga lase Natal* 20 and 27 January 1922.
10. *Cape Times* 9 and 30 August 1920.
11. *Cape Times* 24 September, 1920; Central Archives: Department of Justice 3/1064/18 Commissioner, South African Police to Secretary for Justice 27 August and 30 November 1920.
12. *Ilanga lase Natal* 27 January 1922; *Cape Times* 4 and 6 October 1920, and 17 February 1921. Kadalie makes no mention of the Bloemfontein Conference in his autobiography, though it counted in the ICU canon as the first of the national conferences. It seems that the IWA coalesced with the ICU.
13. *The Eastern Province Herald* 27 January 1921.
14. *The Eastern Province Herald* 29 January 1921.
15. *Cape Times* 31 January 1921.
16. *Cape Times* 21 July 1921.
17. Ibid.
18. 2 August 1921.
19. *Ilanga lase Natal* 29 July 1921.
20. *Cape Times* 22 and 27 July 1921.
21. *Cape Times* 22 and 23 July 1921.
22. *Cape Times* 23 July 1921.
23. *Cape Times* 21 July 1921.
24. Cf. especially *Cape Times* 26 July 1921.
25. *Cape Times* 23 July 1921.
26. Ibid.
27. *Cape Times* 26 July 1921.
28. *Cape Times* 27 July 1921.
29. *Ilanga lase Natal* 27 January 1922.
30. *Cape Times* 26 October 1921.

31. Ibid., Kadalie, C. *My Life*, 51–2, which, however, does not refer to the Conference.
32. *Cape Times* 26 October 1921.
33. *Cape Times* 29 October 1921.
34. The letter is printed in full in Kadalie, C. *My Life*, 58–9. The original is in the Ballinger Collection, University of Cape Town.
35. *Cape Times* 26 and 29 October 1921.
36. *Cape Times* 23 January 1923.
37. Kadalie, C., *My Life*, 53.
38. At least this was so by 1923, as may be surmised from *Imvo Zabantsundu* 9 October 1923, It is not clear when Kadalie assumed the grander title of General Secretary.
39. *Imvo Zabantsundu* 9 May 1922.
40. *Ilanga lase Natal* 20 January 1922. No copies of *The Black Man* survive. For its beginnings see *Cape Times* 30 August 1920.
41. *A.P.O.* 8 April 1922, which expresses contempt for both the scheme and its initiators.
42. For further information about the ICWU cf. *Cape Times* 27 July 1921; *Ilanga lase Natal* 13 June 1924.
43. *Umteteli wa Bantu* 14 and 21 April and 9 May 1923.
44. *Imvo Zabantsundu* 9 October 1923; *The Workers' Herald* 22 October 1923.
45. 2 August 1923 (Central Archives: Department of the Interior 10/A/1787).
46. *The East London Daily Dispatch* 25 January 1924.
47. *Umteteli wa Bantu* 26 July and 9 August 1924.
48. *APO* 8 April 1922; *Umteteli wa Bantu* 22 September 1924.
49. Manifesto of 9 July 1928 (B/UCT).
50. *Ilanga lase Natal* 24 October 1924.
51. Cape Archives: City of Cape Town, Minutes of the Native Affairs Committee, Volume I, Parcel 107, Item 338.
52. Presumably Msimang. Cf. Manifesto of 9 July 1928 (B/UCT).
53. H. D. Tyamzashe to Editor, *The Star*, undated (F1927/142); Silburn P. A., 1927, *South Africa; White and Black – or Brown?*, (London, which speaks of the ICWU as still active at that date – 'The ICWU is a rival of the ICU, also in the hands of communist agents [*sic*].' 93.

CHAPTER 5

The General Election of 1924

'We shall render General Hertzog
All the help that we can give;
To save our country from all sweating,
Make it so that all may live.

'In the words of General Hertzog,
"Sweated labour is a curse";
And, South Africa must be rescued,
Ere she sinks from bad to worse.

'We natives therefore are determined,
Forthwith, to ask for better pay,
Surely this can't be denied us,
Now that Hertzog's paved the way?'
(ICU poem c. 1925)

The early 1920s were not a favourable period for trade unions. After the wartime 'price boom' broke in the middle of 1920, South Africa entered a brief depression that reached its deepest point in March 1922, when there was a general strike on the Witwatersrand. Depression saw a reduction of employment and wages and a lengthening of working hours and a much tougher attitude among employers.[1] There can be little doubt that the ICU lost ground in 1921. Support among the contract labourers of the Docks Location in Cape Town was certainly lost,[2] and in East London enthusiasm for the cause of unionism had so diminished by 1922 that Kadalie was forced to make a fresh start there.[3] Even at Port Elizabeth, where the shared experience of 23 October 1920 must have helped keep the organization together, there had been a schism in the ranks, generally a sign of sickliness, though in this case it can plausibly be put down to distaste among some supporters either for Masabalala's style of oratory or for his espousal of the Nationalist cause in the election of 1921. At all events adherents and critics engaged in an exchange of anathema and excommunication.[4]

Economic recovery, beginning in the second half of 1922, lasted until 1929, when the country fell victim to the international depression. However, if during the prosperity of 1922–1929 new job opportunities were created, more people – landless Whites as well as Blacks – were making their way into the towns to take advantage of them, and the obstacles to Black trade unionism remained – the vast reserves of unused labour; the illiteracy, indifference, and instability of the labour force; and the hostility of employers and Government. There were, indeed, instances of labour shortage – in the Durban docks in 1923, in the gold mining industry almost all the time – but they did not stimulate so much the workers to organize as the recruiters to cast around for additional supplies – on their own terms.[5] Above all there was no longer the pressure exerted during the wartime boom of the continuous rise of prices that urged men to desperate remedies, to jeopardize employment for the sake of securing a tolerable wage.

Until 1923 the ICU was essentially a Cape organization. At its Conference of January 1923, all thirty delegates came from the Cape Province, with the exception of one from South-West Africa. At that Conference, however, influenced perhaps by the improving economic situation, meagre as were the advantages that it offered to Black labour, the ICU decided upon a nation-wide publicity campaign for extending the union beyond the boundaries of the Cape.[6] Perhaps it was a sign of its expanded ambition that the ICU now started calling itself the Industrial and Commercial Workers' Union of Africa, no longer just of South Africa. An important feature of the campaign was the foundation of its newspaper, *The Workers' Herald*, which began publication in May 1923.

Kadalie had in mind, to use his expression, an invasion of the mines, and he publicly said so at an open-air meeting at the time of the 1923 Conference.[7] However, it was not the Transvaal and the mines, but the Orange Free State that was invaded first. At Bloemfontein, in response to a local invitation, Kadalie, paying his first visit since the Conference of July 1920, set up, in August 1923, a branch with J. B. Mancoe as Branch Secretary. In 1924 Keable 'Mote, a teacher from the Orange Free State, but hailing from Basutoland, was recruited, subsequently one of the best-known and most colourful leaders of the ICU.[8]

A more vigorous campaign of extension was inaugurated by the Fourth, East London, Conference of January 1924.[9] This was also named the First African Labour Congress and invitations to attend it were sent (though it is doubtful whether any accepted) to 'kindred labour, social and economic organisations.'[10] The intention was to set up an African Labour Federation based upon the ICU. In his unsuccessful attempt to change the name of his union Kadalie made the point that its existing one did not sufficiently indicate the ICU's comprehensive nature as the organization for all Black workers, skilled and unskilled.[11]

The outcome of the East London resolution was a tour made by Kadalie from June to November 1924. In his annual report presented to the Conference of April 1925, he claimed the establishment of 12 new branches since the preceding Conference. Two of these were situated in the important Cape towns of Kimberley and King William's Town, but Kadalie's tour also took him outside the province, first, at the end of July, to Durban, where, in the face of the prevalant apathy, he succeeded in founding a branch, entrusting it to Alex Peddie Kajno Maduna. The General Secretary had to contend not merely with Zulu indifference, but also with White opposition. The municipal authorities refused to give him permission to hold public meetings, and it was only through the assistance of a European sympathizer, Mrs Mabel Palmer, who was able to arrange for Kadalie to see the British Colonial Secretary, J. H. Thomas, then in South Africa at the head of the visiting Empire Parliamentary Delegation, that the ban was removed, though only temporarily. In September he moved to Johannesburg where, assisted no doubt by the publicity he had acquired in Durban, he met with more rapid success than he had done in Natal. As in Bloemfontein, local enthusiasts had already started a branch, and soon afterwards others were started at Roodepoort and Benoni.[12]

In all probability the growth of the ICU owed much to the fact that it came to be the focus of Black and Coloured discontent, eclipsing other pressure groups in popular favour. Although it always disclaimed any intention of usurping the functions of other bodies and insisted that it was an industrial, not a political, organization, the ICU was inevitably drawn into politics because, once the cost of living had markedly declined, the grievances of its members and sympathizers were largely political: the pass laws, the industrial colour bar, the inequitable incidence of taxation and distribution of government expenditure, and so forth. Perhaps more important was the nature of its membership. While it had its staunch following among the Cape Town stevedores and enjoyed fairly substantial support among railway workers, for the most part members were of all sorts, unskilled workers in every type of employment – laundry workers, farm labourers, employees of the oil companies, municipal labourers, domestic servants, and miscellaneous factory workers. Subsequently on the Rand, although the ICU made some converts among mine workers – chiefly, it would seem, among those living outside the compounds – and although the iniquities of the recruiting system became a staple of conference denunciations, there seems to be no evidence for assuming significant penetration of that semi-enclosed and largely impermanent labour force. The fact that the ICU Conference of April 1925, after eighteen months activity by the union on the Rand, resolved upon 'special efforts . . . to organise mine workers' would indicate that it had made little progress in winning them over.[13] To stick its growing heterogeneous membership together, politics was only cement.

The increasingly political character of the ICU posed for it two problems, its relationship with the South African Native National Congress (from 1923, the African National Congress) and its attitude towards the White political parties. After their deterioration in 1920 when Simon Jordan was the Branch Secretary in Ndabeni, the ICU's relations with Congress in the Western Province improved when, sometime in 1923, J. S. Thaele, Mahabane's successor as the President of the latter, joined the ICU. [14] In some respects, however, he was a dubious gain, because he was also associated with that militant Black organization, the Universal Negro Improvement Society of Marcus Garvey, a body whose aims were incompatible with the basic ICU striving (for all the rebuffs suffered) for a single multi-racial South African society and for the solidarity of the working class.

In the Transvaal, when it commenced operations there in September 1924, the ICU had a mixed reception from Congress officials. Although Makgatho, still President of the national organization, was entirely hostile and R. V. Selope Thema, the General Secretary, unhelpful, some of the other officials were friendly. In Natal also Congress attitudes varied, though in no instance downright hostile. It was J. T. Gumede who issued Kadalie with an invitation to start work in that province and gave him every assistance when he arrived at Durban, while *Ilanga lase Natal*, John Dube's paper, gave the ICU a more cautious, but not an unfriendly, welcome.[15]

In White politics the debate among Black voters in the early 1920s was whether it was better to cling to the devil they knew or risk their future with the devil they did not. Smuts, as Boer general and architect of the hated Act of Union, was an object of a suspicion that was in no way lessened by his Savoy Hotel speech of 1917, when he 'painted the Bantu as a menace to European civilisation'.[16] Then, while he was remembered by White labour as the ruthless suppressor of the 1922 Rand strike, to the Black workers his reputation was stained by the bloodshed of Port Elizabeth and Bulhoek and of the Bondelzwarts affair in South-West Africa.[17] Although he could hardly be held responsible for the Port Elizabeth shooting, any more than for the Bondelzwarts slaughter, he would have gained some esteem with the Black communities if he had made some substantial reparation for the loss of life that had been due to police mismanagement and miscalculation in Port Elizabeth. But no: a special commissioner appointed to investigate claims for compensation for death and injury of persons who 'were not willing spectators' eventually recommended *ex gratia* payments of such grossly inequitable division between Black and White victims as could not have been better calculated to arouse resentment.[18]

The Smuts Government was responsible for a number of legislative measures which introduced some solid reforms, but incorporated features repugnant to Blacks. Among them was the Native Affairs Act of 1920, which set up the Native Affairs Commission, a continuing body to inquire into and make recommendations upon Black interests and grievances and also 'to recommend that conferences of Natives be convened by the Governor-General to ascertain the sentiments of the Native population in regard to any measure in so far as it may affect such population'.[19] In addition the Act provided for the extension elsewhere of the local councils already found in the Transkei. Its provisions evoked a variety of feelings among Blacks, with such enthusiasm as there was, however, evaporating rapidly. The Native Affairs Commission had no Black members and in any case seemed to have little influence with the Government, while the proposed local councils were not mandatory. The Cape Native Congress was suspicious of the Act's implications of political segregation.[20]

The 1920 Act was followed by the Natives (Urban Areas) Act of 1923, which provided for the accommodation of urban Blacks in locations. While it had its beneficial side, since it insisted that municipalities establish locations of reasonable standard, and thus rescued Blacks from the rack-renting of slum landlords, and since it provided for advisory boards chosen from amongst the residents, nonetheless the Act entailed racial segregation and meant more compulsion, a limitation upon freedom of choice of residence.

A third piece of legislation was the Industrial Conciliation Act of 1924, which began its passage through Parliament at the beginning of 1923. It established conciliation machinery for industrial disputes, but excluded from its operation 'pass-bearing Natives'. Another numerous body of workers placed outside the scope of the Act was composed of farm labourers, though not because they carried passes, but simply because it did not apply to the agricultural industry. Such an exclusion was no less founded in racial discrimination, seeing that almost all farm workers were Black. In 1924 relatively few members of the ICU worked in agriculture or were 'pass-bearing Natives', either because they were Coloured or because, if Black, they were largely free of the pass system. The union, however, was affected, although it was not realized at the time, by a provision of the Act that had nothing to do with racial discrimination. The conciliation procedures laid down by the Act did not allow for general labour unions such as the ICU, indeed intentionally excluded them, thus making possible the registration only of unions organized on industrial or craft lines.[21]

The political sympathies of the ICU tended to waver. Despite the declaration of October 1921, at the beginning of the following year Masabalala and other ICU leaders were appearing on the same platforms as Cape Town Labour politicians.[22] This burgeoning relationship, however, did not survive the shock of White racial intransigence in the Transvaal during the 1922 strike, which saw sporadic attacks upon Black workers. Blacks found their sympathies all on the side of General Smuts in his endeavour to crush the ensuing rebellion.[23] The Third ICU Conference of January 1923 reaffirmed its political neutrality. Although it was opened by the visiting British Communist, Tom Mann, who had been invited to South Africa by the White labour movement, the ICU took care to point out that his presence did not imply acceptance of his political views; and, in fact, he was asked to perform the ceremony only because the Mayor of Cape Town declined to do so.[24] Mann called upon his audience to maintain close ties with the Cape Federation, whose Secretary was also present. The assembled delegates remained unmoved by this plea and were more ready to castigate the White labour movement than the South African Party as the author of their troubles. It was the White workers rather than the Government that bore the odium for the increasing practice of substituting White for Black labour on the railways and in other fields of employment. The memory of Port Elizabeth was still fresh, but the Conference's resolution on the subject was moderately phrased. It urged – unsuccessfully – the authorities to compensate the dependants of those killed. Curiously the Conference did not discuss, or so it seems, the legislation, then impending, that was later to be a fruitful source of complaint. It was concerned rather with the questions of unemployment and wages and conditions of work, especially of railway and farm workers. Other matters discussed included the question of Black representation at the International Labour Conference; the establishment of labour bureaux 'in every centre controlled by the ICU'; education, which led to a resolution calling upon the public authorities to improve facilities; the need for a sanatorium for Black victims of phthisis, the miners' disease; and the acquisition of a building for the ICU and a printing press.

The Conference, which was disappointed in its hope that a deputation would be received by the Prime Minister to hear the resolutions that had been passed, did gain the ear of J. W. Jagger, the Minister of Railways, who was called on by five ICU representatives, including the President, the General Secretary, and the Organizer-in-Chief. The interview was cordial, the Minister sympathetic, the deputation deferential. While holding out no hope for improved wages for railway and dock workers, who, he thought, were already adequately paid in relation to the cost of living, Jagger promised to look into certain grievances regarding housing and rations that the ICU had raised.[25]

By the time the next Conference of the ICU assembled, the Fourth, at East London in January 1924, the political situation in South Africa had been transformed by the conclusion of an electoral pact between Hertzog's Nationalists and the Labour Party, led by Colonel Creswell. Nonetheless, the Conference found the union still politically neutral. The thirty-odd delegates (all apparently from the Cape Province apart from one or two from South-West Africa and John Mancoe from Bloemfontein) were, it is true, welcomed to East London by a Labour Member of the Legislative Assembly, James Stewart, but he had been asked only because the Mayor of East London had refused to do so. The principal speaker was Professor D. D. T. Jabavu, of Fort Hare Native College, who urged the members of the ICU to be loyal to their leaders, to work for the co-operation of 'those two sections of the African people, coloured and native, with a view to building up a new, strong, united race', and expressed his admiration and staunch support for the union.[26] The presence of the son of Tengo Jabavu, a figure of prestige and influence, undoubtedly gave a cachet to the Conference. Tengo's other son, A. M. Jabavu, also came out in support of the ICU and, since he was editor of *Imvo Zabantsundu*, the union now had a respectable mouthpiece in the Eastern Province. Further support from the Black 'establishment' came from Dr Rubusana, who, after declaring that he was there 'as a listener', spoke at what must have been some length, echoing the sentiments expressed by Professor Jabavu. The breach between him and Masabalala was evidently closed.

The Conference got down to business. There was still no sharp criticism of the Smuts administration. The Industrial Conciliation Bill escaped comment, and there was only an expression of disappointment with one of the provisions of the Urban Areas Act and with the refusal of the Government to lease crown land to Blacks in the Eastern Province. It was not the segregation feature of the 1923

Act that disturbed the Conference, which paid tribute to the Government for 'its endeavour to ameliorate the lot of the African race', but Clause 12, which empowered municipal authorities to register Black residents. Registration was associated with the pass laws and labour contracts, 'barbaric systems responsible for the continual degradation of the African races'. The Conference concluded by repeating its policy of non-alignment with any political party and remaining outside politics, but paradoxically accepted the principle of putting up ICU candidates in provincial and municipal elections in the Cape Province.

In spite of its continued political neutrality it is clear that the ICU felt that its future lay with a national, colour-blind labour movement and even looked beyond South Africa to the British labour movement. The Conference, congratulating the Labour Party upon its 'steady ascendancy . . . in the Imperial Parliament', expressed the hope that its growing strength would ultimately be of benefit to 'those worst paid toilers, the African workers of the Union of South Africa'. Although the South African Native National Congress had appealed in vain to the Imperial Parliament, the hope of external assistance – and there seemed no better source of such help than the United Kingdom – died hard. Even better would have been an alliance with the White labour movement in South Africa, and the ICU regretted its failure to respond. The time would come, it was hoped, when the White trade unions would open their doors to Black workers and adopt 'an enlightened policy, on the basis of which may be expected friendly co-operation and ultimate fusion of all labour forces into one big union.'[27]

The East London Conference left the ICU still in a political limbo, as uneasy about the policy of the party in office as it was out of sympathy with the opposition parties. When in April of that year, 1924, the Governor-General, on the advice of General Smuts, dissolved Parliament, Kadalie's union took the initiative in summoning a meeting of Black leaders, to be known as the All African Convention, to decide what advice to give to Black voters in the coming general election. An invitation to 'all leaders of the present existing organisations of non-Europeans of South Africa' was issued at Port Elizabeth by Clements Kadalie, S. M. Masabalala, and S. M. Bennett Ncwana. Ncwana was in this case not representing the rival ICWU, but acting in his capacity as General Organizer of the Cape Native Voters' Association, a body dedicated to mobilizing Black voters in support of the South African Party.[28]

The Port Elizabeth invitation speaks of 'a race co-operative movement of African peoples . . . already under consideration by various organisations in Cape Town',[29] and a few days after it was issued, when Kadalie and Masabalala must still have been in Port Elizabeth, a 'United non-European Congress' was inaugurated in Cape Town 'to protect and further the educational, commercial, political and industrial interests of the non-European peoples of South Africa',[30] with La Guma of the ICU as Secretary and S. Reagon of the African People's Organization as President. Within the next fortnight, however, the ICU took up a position of hostility to both SAP and Pact, and this put an end to any chance of working with the pro-SAP Cape Native Voters' Association and APO. At the end of April James Thaele, President of the Cape section of the African National Congress, as it was now, and a member of the Board of Arbitration of the ICU, presided at a meeting in Cape Town at which the General Secretary of the Cape Congress, Johnson Dlwati, expressed in strong terms Black disappointment with the Government, though at the same time repudiating the segregation favoured by the National Party. He ended by saying that 'a black man should never cast a vote in favour of a white man'. The meeting adopted the slogan 'No policy, no vote'.[31]

This militant neutrality was not maintained for long. Soon the ICU leaders were advocating, not a boycott of the election, but a vote gainst the Government, which in practice meant a vote for the Pact. In May, Thaele, Dlwati, Kadalie, and Masabalala travelled north to Bloemfontein to take part in the Conference of the ANC and to try and persuade the national body to endorse the policy already formulated by the Cape Congress and the ICU.[32] Kadalie's autobiography would have us believe that his intervention was decisive.[33] In fact, that the ANC's policy would have been different had the ICU delegation not attended the Conference is dubious. A substantial body of Congress opinion, it is clear, had moved, before the Conference took place, in the direction of political neutrality. Such was the prevailing disappointment with the record of the SAP that the Conference delegates were pushed without much difficulty into displaying their resentment against it by urging the Black electorate 'to vote solidly for a change of Government.'[34]

At the conclusion of the ANC Conference Kadalie, Masabalala, Thaele, and Dlwati had a meeting with General Hertzog in Bloemfontein.[35] Although the initiative appears to have come from the ICU and the Cape Congress,[36] the overtures of Kadalie and his companions could not have been unwelcome. Hertzog was under the impression, if not at that time, then later, that the Black vote was decisive in twelve of the fifty-one Cape constituencies.[37] At that meeting a bargain was struck, the details of which are, at least in part, recorded in Kadalie's autobiography. The Nationalists printed and distributed the anti-Government resolution adopted by the ANC Conference[38] and also printed, on their Cape Town presses, ten thousand copies of an election edition of *The Workers' Herald*, which was given out free.[39] There is no hint of any more solid benefits for the Black workers, and it can only be supposed that Hertzog's temporary allies were duped, getting nothing other than a short-lived sense of being at the hub of affairs. One may also suspect that Kadalie, who was not immune to White flattery, fell victim to General Hertzog's charm and courtesy.

From Bloemfontein Kadalie and Masabalala, fortified by their 'great victory',[40] proceeded at the expense of Hertzog and Arthur Barlow, the Bloemfontein Labour MLA, to King William's Town, where the All African Convention, attended by the representatives of some dozen organizations, opened on

15 May. As in the case of the ANC Conference, Kadalie's account of this meeting arouses some scepticism. 'We urged,' he says, 'the conference to follow the lead given by the African National Congress in Bloemfontein, and to be guided by the European electors who desired a change of government. In the early hours of the morning we challenged a division on the two motions [*sic*]. Our motion for a change of government, as adopted at Bloemfontein, won the day.'[41] For one thing the question of deciding what party the Black voters were to support, though the most contentious issue before the Convention, was not the only one. The subjects of discussion were outlined, in an opening speech, by Prof. D. D. T. Jabavu, and they included the extension of the vote to White women, which threatened to devalue the Black vote; a minimum wage for Black employees; 'the new pass law which had come in behind their backs, under the Native Urban Areas Act, and which was put through without any consultation with black people and was operating in Cape Town and other places'; and the colour bar.[42] After this opening address there was a procedural dispute: should the Convention first decide between Smuts and Hertzog and then draw up for a presentation to candidates a manifesto that would list the major Black demands, or should the manifesto be drawn up and the Black voters then decide between the parties in the light of the reception accorded to the manifesto? Kadalie and Masabalala argued, not for a vote against Smuts, but for supporting that party prepared to implement the manifesto,[43] and it was this point that they won.

During the course of an all-night sitting the Convention drew up its manifesto and agreed to support whichever party or candidate would subscribe to its terms. The more important requests that were enumerated were Black access to the facilities of the Land Bank, amendment to the Urban Areas Act to permit Black freehold rights in towns, the repeal or amendment of the Natives Land Act of 1913, the appointment of Black court interpreters, the extension of the Cape franchise to the other provinces of the Union, repeal of the pass laws, a ban on the importation of foreign Black labour, minimum wage regulations, and a national system of Black education. Almost the only request likely to commend itself to the Pact was that for 'minimum wage regulations, which would protect the workers in all kinds of occupation by compelling employers to pay not less than a fixed minimum wage for all skilled and unskilled labourers, irrespective of race and colour'.[44] This the Pact implemented as part of its 'civilised labour policy', fixing wages so high in fields of employment where Whites found jobs that employers saw taken away the only reason (in most cases) for employing Black labour – its cheapness.

When the Convention closed (16 May) Kadalie returned to Cape Town. Although during the ensuing years he had occasion to say many harsh things about the Pact, looking back twenty years later upon the events of 1924, he appeared to have no regrets about his real or imagined successes at Bloemfontein and King William's Town. 'Jubilant and strengthened by these two political

eral Hertzog's proposed solution to the Native Problem as embodied in his recent Bills laid before Parliament has given the Non-European people food for thought.

The Workers' Herald 15 June 1926 – South African Library, Cape Town

COMING EVENTS.—
Socialism can only be brought about by unity of all Workers, irrespective of colour or creed.

The Workers' Herald 14 October 1926 – South African Library, Cape Town

victories,' he wrote in his autobiography, 'I returned to Cape Town, where an enthusiastic reception awaited me from all sections of the population.'[45] His triumphant progress passed largely unrecorded in the newspapers.[46]

The ICU position in the 1924 election is by no means explained by revulsion against the sins of the Smuts Government enumerated by Kadalie in his autobiography – 'the shootings at Port Elizabeth in 1920, the Bulhoek massacre, the calling of troops to the Cape Town dock strike in 1919',[47] since these grievances were not new and the Government's handling of the Cape Town dock strike and the Port Elizabeth riots had not prevented the ICU from supporting the South African Party in the 1921 election. Neither can hostility to the Government be attributed to any violent reaction against the Urban Areas Act or the Industrial Conciliation Act. It was the sins of omission, not those of commission, that offended the Black voters, who felt that the SAP took an interest in them only when there was an election in the offing. The influence of Advocate Morris Alexander must have swayed many people in Cape Town. A member of the old Unionist Party, Alexander had been unable to overcome his repugnance for the South African Party when his own merged with it, and he preferred to remain in the House of Assembly as an independent. In 1924 he stood for election in a predominantly Coloured constituency of Cape Town and gained support both from ICU leaders – Gumbs and Fife, as well as Kadalie and Thaele – and from deserters from the APO. He appeared on the platform at National Party meetings, condemning what he called the autocracy of Smuts' government and complaining that the SAP had dishonoured all its 1921 election pledges.[48]

In the absence of any sense of loyalty to the existing Government it is hardly surprising that some voters succumbed to the blandishments, during the election campaign, of those Pact candidates who offered the Coloured community economic (though not social) integration into White society and sometimes denied the intention, or at least the feasibility, of disfranchising Blacks in the Cape.[49] Even segregation, if equitable, possessed a certain attraction. General Hertzog seemed to be offering a fair division of the country, Smuts to be implementing segregation in an underhand and unfair way, exemplified by the residential segregation of Blacks in towns under the Urban Areas Act and of Indians in the Class Areas Bill of 1924. 'I would welcome segregation,' said the Rev. Z. R. Mahabane at the 13th Annual Conference of the African National Congress at Bloemfontein in May 1924, 'if the land was divided so that 50 per cent was allocated for occupation by the white people and 50 per cent for the black, but not as at present where only 13 per cent is allocated to five million natives and the rest to one and a half millions of whites.'[50] Kadalie himself, in a speech that did him little credit because it contradicted his fundamental belief in a racially integrated society, declared that 'segregation was natural'.[51]

Only an analysis of South African constituencies in 1924 could give any indication of how much the ICU influenced the course of the election. Given the anti-Government swing in the White electorate and the widespread disillusionment with the Smuts Government among the Black voters, the ICU's weight in the scales was probably slight. It is likely that, while some Coloured voters deserted the South African Party in spite of (or because of) Dr Abdurahman, Blacks preferred to stick to Smuts whatever his faults.[52] Even the Congress leaders seem to have had second thoughts. A prominent Nationalist, Tielman Roos, in an unguarded moment exclaimed at an election meeting early in June, 'The Native is not an asset to the White man in this country – he is a curse.'[53] This was a timely reminder to the Black voter of what value was put upon his people by a party that was intermittently trying to gain his support.

Kadalie was convinced that he had made a major contribution to the Hertzog-Creswell victory.[54] Three months later, in September, he had his reward. When the member for Pinetown, one of the Durban constituencies, J. S. Marwick, complained in the House of Assembly about Kadalie's activities in Durban, he was rebuffed by the new Minister of Justice, Tielman Roos, who stated that there was nothing to stop Black workers from forming trade unions.[55] It was indeed a meagre reward; yet it is difficult to see what more was to be anticipated of a coalition pledged to safeguard the White worker and the White farmer.

Notes

1. Cf. Union of South Africa, *Social Statistics No. 4 – 1922*, 94; H. H. Smith, loc. cit., 161.
2. So much may be gathered from a remark made by a Cape Town official (John Gomas) in 1926 (*The Workers' Herald* 28 April 1926).
3. Kadalie, C. *My Life*, 53–5.
4. *The Eastern Province Herald* 17 and 31 March 1921.
5. *Cape Times* 16 July 1923.
6. *Cape Times* 22 and 23 January 1923.
7. *Cape Times* 18 January 1923.
8. *The Workers' Herald* 25 September 1923.
9. *The East London Daily Dispatch* 25 January 1924; *Cape Times* 26 February 1924; *The Workers' Herald* 15 May 1925.
10. *The Workers' Herald* 22 October 1923.
11. *The East London Daily Dispatch* 25 January 1924; *Cape Times* 10 January 1924.
12. Kadalie, C. *My Life*, 61–5; E. & W. Roux, op.cit., 35; *The Workers' Herald* 9 January, 2 April, 15 May, and 15 June 1925, and 14 September 1926.
13. *The Workers' Herald* 2 April and 15 May 1925, and 20 February, 28 April and 27 May 1926; *Cape Times* 30 August 1920; Minutes of National Council, ICU November 1927 (F 1927/124); Kadalie, C., *My Life*, 72; interview with Mr Gomas 18 May 1970.
14. *The Workers' Herald* 21 September 1923.
15. Kadalie, C., *My Life*, 62, 64, 65, 67; *The Workers' Herald* 15 May 1925; *Ilanga lase Natal* 4 July, 15 August and 24 October 1924.
16. *Imvo Zabantsundu* 27 May 1924.
17. In 1922 the Bondelzwarts tribe lost 115 men killed in action against government troops and, when its flocks and herds were bombed, suffered casualties among its women and children.

The issues involved were complicated, but the basic tribal grievance was loss of land and freedom (W. K. Hancock, *Smuts: the Fields of Force 1919–1950*, 100–10).

18. *Umteteli wa Bantu* 3 February 1923.
19. Union of South Africa, *Act No. 23 of 1920*, Section 16(1)
20. P. Walshe, op. cit., 100–2.
21. There was a fourth discriminatory Act, the Apprenticeship Act (1922), but less obviously inimical to Black interests.
22. *APO*, 11 February 1922.
23. Kadalie, C., *My Life*, 50; E. Roux, *Time Longer than Rope. A History of the Black Man's Struggle for Freedom* (2nd ed. Madison, 1964) 151. In May, 1922, the Minister of Mines and Industries, F. S. Malan, who was well-disposed to Black aspirations, received an ICU delegation reporting the resolutions of the Port Elizabeth Conference of October 1921. Kadalie urged the Minister to consider the claim of his union to be the most representative of the majority of workers in the country, and he, without definite promises, agreed to take notice of the request, as well as other pleas (Johns, S. W., loc. cit., 187).
24. *Cape Times* 20 January 1923.
25. *Cape Times* 20, 22, and 23 January 1923; *The Workers' Herald* 21 July 1923.
26. *Imvo Zabantsundu* 22 January 1924; *The East London Daily Dispatch* 23 January 1924.
27. *Cape Times* 10 January and 26 February 1924.
28. *Imvo Zabantsundu* 15 April 1924; *Cape Times* 9 April 1924; *Umteteli wa Bantu* 14 and 21 April, 4 August and 1 September 1923; *Ilanga lase Natal* 1 June 1923.
29. *Imvo Zabantsundu* 15 April 1924.
30. *Cape Times* 14 April 1924.
31. *Cape Times* 28 April 1924.
32. *Cape Times* 10 June 1924.
33. Op.cit., 58.
34. *The Cape Mercury* 3 June 1924.
35. *Cape Times* 10 June 1924.
36. Kadalie, C., *My Life*, 58.
37. Tatz, C. M., 1962, *Shadow and Substance in South Africa, a Study in Land and Franchise Policies Affecting Africans 1910–1960*, Pietermaritzburg, 39, 42–3.
38. *Cape Times* 10 June 1924.
39. Kadalie, C., *My Life*, 58–9.
40. Ibid., 59.
41. Ibid., 59–60; *Cape Times* 17 May 1924.
42. *The Cape Mercury* 16 May 1924.
43. The 'proceedings were by no means amicable'. (Ibid.)
44. Ibid., *Cape Times* 17 May 1924.
45. Kadalie, C., *My Life*, 60.
46. Cf., however, *Cape Times* 11 June 1924.
47. Kadalie, C., *My Life*, 58.
48. *Cape Times* 13 June 1924.
49. *Cape Times* 29 May 1924.
50. *Cape Times* 26 May 1924.
51. *Cape Times* 11 June 1924.
52. *The Cape Mercury* 17 June 1924.
53. *Cape Times* 11 June 1924.
54. *The Workers' Herald* 12 May 1928.
55. Kadalie, C., *My Life*, 62–3; Union of South Africa, *Debates of the Assembly* 2 September 1924, Col. 1186.

CHAPTER 6

Civilization Preserved, 1925-1926

'Depending upon the slogan of the Pact Government for a "Civilised South Africa", all workers, both black and white, had pinned their faith on their new bride, who was to "deliver the goods" which were kept in store for the exclusive use by big finance. The goods were "delivered", but to our disappointment, instead of supplying the child with bread, our Pact bride gave the child stones in the form of the Colour Bar Bill, enforcement of Pass Laws upon our women in the Transvaal, the retrenchment of Natives from state undertakings such as the Railway, etc. Thus, instead of coming to attend the wedding feast of the King's son, we met in Johannesburg last April sorely disappointed, and we vociferously protested against such unjust measures introduced by our new Government.'

Clements Kadalie, April 1926

The Pact Government did not delay in introducing measures designed to alleviate the 'poor White' problem and to set at rest the fears of White workers that their privileged position would be destroyed. As soon as it was elected, it began to prosecute with greater vigour a policy that had already been applied by General Smuts' Government, the replacement of Black workers (despite extra expense) in government employment (especially on the railways) by unemployed Whites and, in some cases, in the Cape Town docks, for example, by unemployed Coloured workers.[1] Private employers were also encouraged to take on Whites in preference to Blacks. All this activity was euphemistically termed 'the civilized labour policy'.

In February 1925, the first legislative proposals of the coalition were made to the House of Assembly. 16 February saw the first reading of two major Bills, the Mines and Works Act (1911) Amendment Bill, popularly known as the Colour Bar Bill, and the Wage Bill. The former was likely to make little practical difference. For, although the colour bar of the original Mines and Works Act had been judged *ultra vires* by the Transvaal Provincial Division of the Supreme Court in 1923, the mine companies, bearing in mind the 1922 general strike, had not dared to antagonize White labour by taking advantage of the legal decision. The Wage Bill, on the other hand, was an ambiguous measure. The intentions of its framers were clear enough – to reserve for Whites any fields of employment where they were likely to come into competition with Blacks and where the possession of a particular skill and the proposed Colour Bar Bill did not provide a safeguard. By preventing employers from sweating their labour, the Government hoped to ensure that the unsweated labour would be White. A Wage

Board would make enquiries into different types of employment and recommend to the Minister of Labour a wage sufficient for a worker to live 'according to the European standards'. Since the wage for each occupation where a determination was made was to prevail throughout the entire labour force engaged in that occupation, Black labour would no longer, it was hoped, hold any attraction for employers. This was where the ambiguity arose. If the intention of the Bill was clear, it was not explicit. In theory race was not the criterion, but 'civilization'. However, the discriminatory intention was demonstrated all too clearly by the exclusion of two classes of workers from its scope, farm labourers and domestic servants, who were overwhelmingly Black. Yet the apparent racial impartiality of the machinery proposed under the Bill[2] and the need to deal with the very real problem of sweating in South Africa, commended it to men for whom the industrial colour bar was indefensible, for example Advocate Alexander.[3] There was, besides, a possibility for action beneficial to the Black unskilled, because, in the event of the Wage Board's inability to recommend wages upon which the 'employees may be able to support themselves in accordance with civilised habits of life', the Minister might still direct it to recommend such wages as it considered suitable.

The ambiguity of the Wage Bill perhaps helped Kadalie to persist in his belief that General Hertzog was a 'fine fellow', and Colonel Creswell too, while Smuts was a 'soldier who always wanted trouble' and 'the English were hypocrites'. As late as May 1925, J. S. Marwick was complaining in the House of Assembly that Kadalie was flourishing at his meetings the letter that Hertzog had written to him in 1921 and claiming that he enjoyed 'to some extent the moral and financial support of the Prime Minister'. Kadalie, in his reluctance to revise his trust in the good intentions of the Pact, looked around for excuses. When it proposed to extend the pass laws to Black women, he blamed the civil servants, suggesting that they were 'trying to bring the Pact Government into disrepute with the natives'. Other scapegoats found by the ICU leaders were unnamed 'extremists' of the National Party, who, it was still being alleged well into 1926, were holding captive not only the Prime Minister, but even Tielman Roos as well.[4]

It was difficult, however, to maintain the fiction that the Pact's beneficent purposes were being frustrated by sinister forces, and there was growing disillusionment with the Government. This coincided with a change in the forces of the radical left. In 1921 the International Socialist League and other Marxist groups united to form the Communist Party of South Africa, and from 1924 the Cape Town branch of the party actively engaged in winning adherents among Black and Coloured people; and it must have been then that James La Guma, the Assistant General Secretary of the ICU, joined it. At the Communist Party conference in Johannesburg at the end of 1924 a policy of proselytising the Blacks was adopted by a narrow majority.[5] Making little headway among Blacks, the party saw in the ICU a means of making its influence felt. For its part the union had hitherto always been at pains to dismiss the suggestion that it had anything to do with Communism, but by 1925 the situation changed. The circumstances of South African political life meant that Black political objectives could be achieved only through influencing the White political system, and, in spite of their complaints that they had lost confidence in the White man, it was into that system that the ICU leaders wanted to penetrate. Although the CP was small and uninfluential, it appeared to be the only possible ally after an election in which one of the three major parties had been derided and abused and the other two had, it was thought, accepted comradeship only to betray it almost at once. Therefore, not only did the ICU not object to its officials joining the Communists (though few did so), but it also admitted into its ranks men who were already members of the party.

By the time the 1925 Conference of the ICU was held, Communist influence was apparent. Members of the ICU began to call one another 'comrade', and 'capitalism' and 'imperialism' featured more frequently in the speeches of the leaders. It may be suspected, however, that for many of them the charm of Communism did not extend beyond their delight in what one critic called its 'curious lingo'.[6] There was a certain ambivalence, moreover, in the attitude displayed towards the British Empire, the villainous oppressor of colonial peoples, yet the fount of justice and fair-play. In the issue of *The Workers' Herald* dated 27 March 1926, by which time the front page regularly carried the legend, 'The Herald exposes the "good boys" ' – Blacks associated with White liberals – 'as tools of imperialistic hypocricy [*sic*]', one finds 'British Imperialism in Africa must be exposed and attacked vigorously'. In the very same issue, however, South Africa is described as 'this great Dominion of the British Empire'. Sometimes the Crown, to which loyalty was pledged, was distinguished from its representatives in South Africa, who were accused of abusing that loyalty;[7] sometimes the monarchy itself was assailed.[8]

In a superficial way the Communists influenced the new constitution adopted by the union in 1925. For this contained the famous preamble based on that of the Industrial Workers of the World, but modified in a Marxian direction.[9] It was singularly ill-suited to the ICU, speaking as it did of the class struggle and the proletarian confiscation of the means of production, which were meaningless in the South African racial situation.[10] If the class struggle meant anything at all, it was a private war for Whites only. The preamble came to be a source of acute embarrassment, particularly in 1927, when the union was anxious to prove its moderation and respectability. Grappling with the problem, one of its leaders, A. W. G. Champion, came up with the surprising gloss that 'the Preamble (which we frankly admit could be better worded) is an attempt to put into modern language the teachings of Christ, namely "Love thy neighbour as thyself", and prove and test it by conduct by "Doing unto others as ye would they should do unto you".'[11]

The new constitution set up a National Council, composed of the chief officers of the union. The Board of Arbitration was retained from the earlier organization to act as an executive committee. A new arrangement was the appointment of Provincial Secretaries for the Western Cape, the Eastern Cape, Transkei and Border, Transvaal, Orange Free State, and Natal. Among the officers appointed under the new constitution familiar names appeared – Kadalie as National Secretary, largely responsible for propaganda, James La Guma as General Secretary, largely responsible for administration, J. G. Gumbs, who, having earlier succeeded Fife, remained as President, an honorary post, A. M. Jabavu, who filled the second most lustrous honorary position, Senior Vice-President, and A. P. Maduna, J. B. Mancoe, and Theo B. Lujiza, who had helped Kadalie to establish the ICU in East London,[12] Provincial Secretaries of Natal, Orange Free State, and Transkei and Border respectively. Some old names disappeared. In December 1924 Masabalala had been dismissed, following complaints from the East London and King William's Town branches, for 'negligence and carelessness', for falling 'into his old bad habit in spoiling the work done by others', whatever that meant.[13] Another casualty was Thaele, fully occupied with Congress in the Cape.[14] There were also new names, then or shortly afterwards: M. E. A. Johnson, Junior Vice-President, James Dippa, Provincial Secretary of the Eastern Cape, Eddie Khaile, Financial Secretary, H. D. Tyamzashe, who started off as Assistant Provincial Secretary of the Transvaal,[15] John Gomas, Provincial Secretary of the Western Cape,[16] and, above all, the Provincial Secretary of the Transvaal, A. W. G. Champion, whose background is best told in his own words.

'Mr Allison Wessels George Champion . . . was born of Zulu parents in 1893, near the mouth of River Tugela [*sic*], in the small Mission Station, Sans Souci. His father, George Champion, was adopted by an American missionary[17] about 1835. Mr Champion's mother could not read or write, not even in Zulu, but she was determined, like all good mothers, that her only son should go to school and she was always interested in his education. Mr Champion attended the Amanzimtoti Boys' School and passed standard VI.[18] But, being of a studious nature, he followed his studies while earning his living and, as he prefers to put it, the rest of his education and practical experience of the problems of life were picked up around the mine dumps of Johannesburg.

'After serving two years in the South African Police, Champion severed his connection with them to begin a new life on the mines. He was first employed by the Simmer and Jack Proprietary Mines as a time-keeper.

'After an attack of malaria fever which necessitated his returning home to Natal, he returned to Johannesburg and . . . again went to the mines as time-keeper for the Roodepoort United Main Reef Gold Mines Co. Ltd, but left to try his luck as diamond digger at the Riversdale Diggings, Taungs. When he came back, a wiser but poorer man, he found employment at the Crown Mines as time-keeper and remained in their employ from 1919 to 1925. It was during these years and since that he has shown that he has, in a marked degree, the high qualities of leadership . . .

'When he resigned his appointment at the Crown Mines to join the ICU nearly all of his colleagues tried to prevent him from doing so and warned him of the risks he was taking, but he was always known as "the lion-hearted young Zulu", and when the call came for leadership in the greater field of the ICU he could not be kept back by any fears or threats of consequences. The Divine urge within him forced him to go forward to greater service for his people'.[19]

When his 'Divine urge' began to trouble him, Champion by his own account was attending ICU meetings in order to make reports on them to his employers.[20] His was a complex character, formidable, even devious. Capable at times of apparent subservience and sycophancy, he had a sharp tongue and a keen sense of his own worth and dignity.[21] As an indefatigable founder of organizations and businesses, he was perhaps less interested in their objectives than in finding, as he says, 'an outlet for his abilities'. When the ICU presented him with an enlarged opportunity to exploit his talents, he forsook without much regret the respectable bodies, such as the Joint Council of Europeans and Natives, with which he had hitherto been associated and for which the ICU leadership expressed contempt.

In July 1925, Champion was sent to unravel a financial scandal in Bloemfontein, where he was responsible for securing the prosecution of two ICU officials, John Mancoe and Simon Elias, who were accused of embezzling funds, and, in the face of local opposition, for reorganizing the Bloemfontein branch.[22] In September he was back in Johannesburg, only to be sent at the end of the month to Durban, as part of a general reshuffle of appointments. Becoming Natal Provincial Secretary, he relinquished the Transvaal post to Tyamzashe, who had himself spent a brief and, according to Champion, inglorious spell in Bloemfontein.[23] Maduna, though with great reluctance, took over as Provincial Secretary at Bloemfontein. No great success had attended his efforts in Durban, and, indeed, he was implicated in a financial scandal to do with a proposed business venture and the purchase of uniform badges.[24] On his arrival in Durban, Champion, by his own account, was hampered by hostility from the old membership and the authorities, as well as the organizational chaos left by his predecessor.[25] However, it was not long before ICU fortunes picked up, and soon he was bombarding Head Office with demands for membership cards and copies of the constitution.[26]

Champion had joined the union after attending its 1925 Conference as a 'distinguished visitor'. [27] This, the Fifth Annual Conference, the Third African Labour Congress, met in Johannesburg on Monday 13 April 1925, an assembly of fifty-four delegates from fifteen branches, presided over by J. G. Gumbs. For the first – and only – time in its history the ICU secured the services of a mayor to open its conference. After the preliminary ceremonies the Wage Bill, wages and conditions of service in the docks, and the 'civilized labour policy' were the subjects of the opening debates. While the delegates welcomed the Wage Bill in principle, they were highly critical of the proposed exclusion from its operation of agricultural labourers and domestic servants, amongst whom the ICU had a following. They went on to demand the extension of the rate of pay (eight shillings a day) current since 1920 in the Cape Town docks to the other ports and the termination of the practice at Cape Town of hiring dock labour by the hour or by the quarter day. The Conference decided to make representations to the Select Committee of the House of Assembly on the Wage Bill and to the Minister of Labour.[28]

The debate upon the 'civilized labour policy' gave a superb opening for Kadalie's style of oratory. 'Here,' he said, 'we have white people who have come out here with the professed idea of civilising the blackman. But by what means? Has civilisation ever been introduced into any country through the instrumentality of oppression, tyranny and the iron heel method to crush and grind down democracy? These people have come here to batten on us, and live on the fat of the land. We did not go to Europe to invite the whites to come here, nor did we want them. No, but the whites, influenced by their own selfish ends, came along and we received them as good fellows. But to what purpose? To acquire what is known to them as civilisation, but to us and the freedom-loving world slavery . . . Our people are being replaced by what we are told are poor whites, but let me tell you that they are not poor whites, but lazy – . . . The fact is that this civilised labour policy is nothing less than an attempt to oust you from every sphere of labour, and to place you in such a state as to imperil your very existence and exterminate you.' He warned that 'in the absence of a definite scheme of land settlement as a compensating measure the enormity of injustice inflicted upon victims of this one-sided policy is incalculable and will positively provoke a deep-seated sense of resentment which the country will ill-afford to ignore'.

The sessions of Thursday and Friday, 16 and 17 April, dealt with the grievances of the mine workers, the iniquities of the contract labour system, the inadequacy of accident payments, the Colour Bar Bill, and the exclusion of Black mine workers from the operation of the Industrial Conciliation Act. A resolution was adopted comparing the work conditions of contract labourers with that of convicts and calling for an amendment of the Native Labour Regulation Act and for a conference with the Minister of Labour to work out an alternative system. The delegates also took time to consider the pass laws, especially their proposed application to African women in the Transvaal. Clearly it was not only the humiliating restrictions of 'this unchristianlike system' that were resented, but also the sheer cost of acquiring passes. A resolution condemned them as 'an institution of the present capitalistic system of Government to reduce the African workers to a state of abject servility so as to facilitate their utmost exploitation'. Attempts by White liberals to devise a compromise formula that would lessen the burdens of the system but retain what were thought to be its advantages, were attacked. The ICU resolution demanded 'total abolition' and threatened 'a passive resistance movement . . . with the co-operation of other organised bodies of the African peoples, particularly the African National Congress'.

On Saturday 18 April the new National Council met for the first time at the ICU's Johannesburg offices in Fox Street. *The Workers' Herald* was under discussion. It was agreed that the union would subsidise the paper for six months and that, in an effort to make it more widely read, more of it would appear in the vernacular languages. The idea of sending a man to England – 'with a view of studying the World Labour Movement' – was mooted and found favour with the Council's members, who decided to call upon the branches to provide the necessary money. The Fifth Annual Conference was brought to a conclusion on Sunday morning.

After the Conference Kadalie returned to Cape Town to lead a deputation to present the views of his union to the parliamentary Select Committee on the Wage Bill. Since they were not received, they had to make do with the submission of a memorandum on Black wages, based upon the resolutions of the late Conference. Representatives of the union, however, were seen by the Minister of Mines and Industries, W. F. Beyers, who was presented with a protest on the Colour Bar Bill and a request for increased death benefits for Blacks under the Miners' Phthisis Consolidation Acts Bill.[29] Attention, however, after the 1925 Conference was fixed not on Cape Town, but on Bloemfontein.

On the very day the Fifth Conference broke up there began a brief but bloody riot there that was the second of the two blood-lettings associated with the ICU. It had in reality little to do with the union, although 'hotheads like Kadalie' were blamed for stirring up 'mainly imaginary grievances'. The trouble originated in the attempted arrest of women who were brewing 'Kaffir beer' and became serious as the result of the death of one of the crowd that threw stones at a police detachment which was sent into the location to assert authority. On the next day, Monday 20 April, Black pickets prevented those who wanted to from leaving the location, and a thousand-strong crowd gathered. The authorities received a deputation – 'not the leaders of the mob, but the responsible leaders of the native community' – which complained of police provocation, but promised to try and get the crowd to disperse. When it refused to break up, it was charged by a force of four hundred regular police and special constables. Four Blacks died of bullet wounds and eighteen were injured, and two Whites were severely hurt by stones. Seventy or so people were arrested. The whole affair provoked intense anger among Blacks, who were particularly incensed by the part played in the affray by White civilians. 'Every white man was walking around Bloemfontein with a rifle,' complained one member of the deputation received by the authorities, and he went on to suggest that 'some of the white people were always ready to kill the natives'.[30] Apart from the special constables, who had been largely responsible for the deaths and wounds during the attack on the location and had been rebuked by the magistrate for firing indiscriminately, other civilians had apparently joined in and, according to Colonel Beer, the Deputy-Commissioner of the South African Police, 'hampered and embarrassed the police'. It seems likely, moreover, that a White bystander had fired the shot which mortally wounded the man whose death had caused the marked deterioration in the situation.[31]

The Bloemfontein disturbances proved to be an occasion of scandal for the ICU. Keable 'Mote turned king's evidence against an arrested fellow member of the union.[32] Yet the riots were not wholly disastrous for the Blacks of the town. White people seem to have had an attack of conscience. The City Council granted the local branch of the ICU a lease on a site in the location for the erection of a hall and office, and it set up a Native Wages Commission, composed of an equal number of representatives of employers and employees, the latter represented by four members of the Native Advisory Board and four from the ICU. Its task was to inquire into and make recommendations on what constituted a 'fair basic wage' for Blacks doing unskilled work. It recommended a 3s. daily wage, and in March 1926, the Council requested a Wage Board inquiry in order to compel all employers to pay the accepted rate. The ICU, after a little hesitation, insisted on its original demand for 3s.6d. and withdrew from the Commission. Since the Wage Act did not recognize racial distinctions, the Board declined to investigate the wages of Black unskilled labour and the arrival at a suitable formula to permit its intervention meant that it was April 1927 before it began to take evidence.[33]

The ICU also put forward wage demands in East London in 1925, asking for a 2s. addition to the daily wage. The Town Council received a deputation and expressed a willingness to raise wages if other employers would do the same. The Chamber of Commerce 'made some frivolous excuses', while the local offices of the South African Railways and Harbours Administration suggested an approach to the General Manager. After the ICU had submitted evidence about living costs in the city, an offer of an extra six pence a day was made.[34]

In Johannesburg, too, the union was active. It became involved in a minor industrial dispute in September 1925, when the management of Maytham's Limited, a firm of tinsmiths, locked out its employees. The sixty workmen concerned called upon the ICU for support and through the good offices of the Inspector of White Labour, who intervened after an appeal to the Native Affairs Department had achieved nothing, the dispute was settled in favour of the workers.[35] A careful scrutiny of the columns of *The Workers' Herald* and of the ICU's evidence to the Economic and Wage Commission in September 1925 shows that, as in Cape Town in its early years, the ICU on the Rand investigated individual grievances and made representations to employers and the Native Affairs Department, taking legal action if necessary.

The ICU did not regard itself as a political body, but as the industrial wing of the Black labour movement, of which the African National Congress was the political wing. However, the ICU leaders found it impossible to stay out of politics because industrial issues were inextricably intertwined with politics. There was also the fact that making speeches was Kadalie's chief interest and almost the only function enjoined upon him by the union's constitution. Thus in January 1925, he made the widely reported and discussed speech at Bloemfontein in which he threatened to make 'such an agitation everywhere that Parliament House will tremble'.[36] For its part, the ANC was reluctant to go so far in defiance as the ICU claimed it was itself. In the agitation against the extension of the pass system to women the ANC preferred a challenge in the courts – which was successful – to a campaign of passive resistance.[37] The situation, however, changed when General Hertzog, in November 1925, made his celebrated Smithfield speech. After a protracted gestation his 'Native Policy' reached parturition. The principle was to be segregation of Blacks from Whites, the means four 'Native Bills', first published in July 1926, which, among other things, sought the removal of Black voters in the Cape from the common electoral roll and the 'substitution of a mock representation in the Union Parliament'[38] by White members of the Assembly elected on a limited franchise and with restricted legislative rights. There was to be in addition a General Native Council, also elected on a limited franchise and with derisory powers. As some sort of compensation more land was to be set aside for Blacks. Alarmed by the Smithfield speech, the ANC summoned a special congress to Bloemfontein and issued an invitation to the ICU to attend.

Although the ICU welcomed the ANC initiative with enthusiasm,[39] its delegates – Kadalie, Lujiza, and Maduna – found much to criticize at the conference, held on New Year's Day, 1926. Not least they thought there were too many Whites – and too many churchmen – on the platform and altogether too much praying. 'The proletarian delegates "gingered up" the old political thoughts at Bloemfontein into action,' said Clements Kadalie. The action referred to was a number of resolutions and the threat of passive resistance if the franchise were taken away.[40]

Kadalie spent most of 1925 on the Rand, though the Head Office remained in Cape Town. Early in June he was invited to attend the American Negro Labour Congress and, hastening back to Cape Town to consult the Board of Arbitration, was authorized to accept, but, as soon as he returned to Johannesburg, the Board changed its mind.[41] It seems likely that it was becoming impatient with its National Secretary; if not then, certainly in the ensuing months. The vast majority of the National Council lived in the Cape, and there was Kadalie playing an independent role on the Rand, where he was ruling (with the assistance of his henchman, Tyamzashe, the Transvaal Provincial Secretary) the Johannesburg branches like a personal fief. There was not much that the National Council or the Board of Arbitration could do to keep Kadalie under control, since they met only intermittently, and it became even more difficult to keep him on a tight rein after the Head Office moved from Cape Town to Johannesburg (in April 1926), while most of the National Council remained behind. In the course of time the Board of Arbitration fell into disuse and was replaced, sometime in 1926, by a so-called National Council Executive Bureau, which appears to have lent a spurious collective authority to Kadalie's personal decisions. At a National Council meeting in January 1928, the Senior Vice-President, A. M. Jabavu, had to ask who the members of the Bureau were, and Tyamzashe, who was one, could recall only one meeting of the Bureau ever having been held.[42] Yet Kadalie in 1926 was sending off letters in its name. What particularly angered the Board of Arbitration in 1925 was Kadalie's acquiring without its consent a hall – the Workers' Hall – on lease and running up a considerable debt in connection with it, a debt that had to be settled by the Board 'to save the situation and the prestige of the Organisation'.[43]

The Workers' Hall was opened in September 1925. Three ill-matched sponsors were present at its opening, the Rev. B. R. Hattingh, the Nationalist M.L.A. for Krugersdorp, who sang the praises of segregation as the best guarantee to the Black that he would 'develop on the right lines and according to his own interests and capabilities'; W. H. Andrews, the Secretary of the Association of Employees' Organisations (the successor to the South African Industrial Federation, discredited after the 1922 Rand strike), who emphasized the need for working class organization; and C. F. Glass, the Secretary of the Witwatersrand Tailors' Association, who, much to the agitation of the Rev. Hattingh, dwelt on the class struggle and the common interests of White and Black workers. The speeches of all three were impartially applauded by the audience.[44]

In the same month that the Workers' Hall was opened Kadalie, assisted by Tyamzashe and Champion (a day or so after his return from Bloemfontein and before his transfer to Durban), submitted a memorandum to the Economic and Wage Commission and gave oral evidence. The ICU put forward the argument that Black workers were as dependent upon wages as White, even the migrants from the congested 'native territories' and that their wages had not kept pace with their advancing civilization and standard of living.[45] Typical budgets were handed in for the principal cities, all of them showing that current wages were far from sufficient to meet the needs of Black families, and the resolutions of the Fifth Conference. Although some slight attention was paid to the plight of farm labourers,[46] most of the written evidence supplied by the union was an onslaught upon conditions in the mining industry, an indictment that was almost certainly drawn up by Champion. The grievances aired were much the same as those discussed at the April Conference, viz. inadequate accident compensation, low wages, brutal and callous discipline, poor and insufficient food, the lack of married quarters, the sale of 'soft jobs' (police and clerical) by compound managers, the iniquities of labour recruiters and the inadequacies of the Native Affairs Department.[47] The ICU called upon the Government to assume responsibility for bringing the workers to the mines and to prohibit imported labour.[48] The written evidence concluded with a moderate plea for the removal of obstacles to Black unionism, the humane treatment of Black workers, and a recognized role for their representatives in the determination of wages. The very last sentence was an important comment upon the objectives of the ICU – 'Non-European workers do not ask for equality in any way with the whites in all things social, but will insist at all times on the proper distribution of equal opportunities in all spheres of labour.'[49]

The union's representatives were questioned by the Commission on 16 September. The questions touched upon the membership of the ICU, then estimated at thirty thousand, about half of them regular subscribers, a claim which the Commission treated with some scepticism,[50] and the condition of farm workers,[51] but most of the oral, as of the written evidence, concerned alleged abuses on the gold mines and the ineffectiveness of the Native Affairs Department as the guardian of Black interests, its indifference to complaints by employees, its alacrity in investigating complaints by employers. Although it is clear that the ICU speakers were forthright and unintimidated by the Commission, one is forced to admit that their evidence was not impressive. One cannot doubt the authenticity of the instances of harshness and corruption and official indifference that clearly fell within the experience of, in particular, A. W. G. Champion, nor can one deny the brutality of the system against which they were protesting. It was their vagueness and lack of preparation that vitiated their testimony.

The ICU's evidence, half-baked as it was, did present the true feelings of Black mine workers, and the leaders of the union always looked back upon their performance as one of their major achievements and considered that they had made a deep impression.[52] In the event, however, half the Commissioners rejected their charges and suggestions. 'We are unable,' they reported, '. . . to recommend the abolition of the compound system, the prohibition of organised recruiting, or the making of contracts of six months or more illegal . . . Charges were made against compound managers and the larger recruiting organisations that were completely refuted by representatives of the persons charged. Similar charges were made against the Department of the Director of Native Labour,[53] which were shown to be equally without justification; on the contrary, our investigation of them led us to form a high opinion of the sympathetic care and efficiency with which that Department performed its function.' (S. Mills, H. Clay, and J. Martin.) The other three Commissioners, however, were more favourably disposed to the ICU evidence. They were on the whole opposed to recruiting and thought that there had been abuses, especially in the recruitment of labour for agriculture in Natal. After suggesting the setting up of state employment bureaux for Blacks looking for work, they turned to the ICU's allegations. 'Complaints of unjust, harsh and illegal treatment of natives in various industries and compounds were made to us by the native trade union – the Industrial and Commercial Workers' Union. Into a number of these cases the Director of Native Labour, or his Department, had made inquiries and several were found to have been correctly stated. This union claimed that natives do not receive sympathetic consideration of their grievances from many officials with whom they have to come in contact. It was not within our sphere to make a detailed examination of these complaints. Even if there is no ground for them, the fact remains that a belief in their reality does exist in the minds of a number of natives' (W. H. Andrews, F. A. W. Lucas, and W. H. Rood).[54]

The Commission issued two reports. Both contained something of comfort for Black workers, though it cannot be thought that the ICU's views carried much weight among those of the many witnesses giving evidence. The whole Commission, Mills, Clay, and Martin emphatically, the others cautiously, admitted the impossibility of achieving economic segregation. 'We assume,' said Mills, Clay, and Martin, 'that the ultimate destiny of, at any rate, a majority of the native population of South Africa is to be absorbed in and assimilated to the economic system which Europeans have introduced'. 'As far as the detribalised natives are concerned,' reported Andrews, Lucas, and Rood, 'it would appear to be too late for any other policy than that of adoption into the European economic system.'[55] Both groups of Commissioners accepted the view that unskilled wages were too low and work opportunities for Blacks too restricted.[56] While Mills, Clay, and Martin were clearly in favour of bringing Black wage earners under the protection of statutory wage-fixing procedures,[57] the other three Commissioners, including Lucas, the first chairman of the Wage Board, were in favour of a repeal of Section 3, sub-section 3, of the Wage Act, which laid down the 'civilized habits of life' criterion for wage recommendations by the Board, because they thought that, in cases where it was inappropriate, it needlessly delayed the determination of a minimum wage.[58] Furthermore, Mills, Clay, and Martin considered that 'a complete survey of the economic position of the native people' should be undertaken,[59] and the delay of the Government in taking up this suggestion became the subject of complaint by Blacks.[60]

Altogether 1925 was a very full year for the ICU, a year when it attracted much publicity. 'It is not out of place here,' says Kadalie modestly in his autobiography, 'to characterise the 1925 session of Parliament as the "Kadalie Session" or, in other words, "the ICU Session".'[61] Undoubtedly Kadalie was a thorn in the flesh of the Government, which was subjected to alarmist reports from Natal, and clearly Hertzog was losing patience. In the new session of Parliament, in March 1926, he introduced a Prevention of Disorders Bill, popularly known as the Sedition Bill, aimed at curbing inflammatory speeches and publications.[62] This, however, increased the Prime Minister's difficulties rather than providing a solution to his problem. It caused much uneasiness among the Labour supporters of the Pact, who feared that it would hamper legitimate trade union activity.[63] Consequently it was dropped, to reappear the following year under the guise of the Native Administration Bill.

Even before the dropping of the Sedition Bill, having apparently already made up its mind that it furnished no immediate escape from its embarrassment, the

Government decided as a temporary expedient to place limitations upon Kadalie's freedom of movement. The National Secretary was told of this decision verbally just before the 1926 ICU Conference was due to meet.[64]

Notes

1. *Ilanga lase Natal* 29 August 1924.
2. Lucas, F. A. W., The determination of wages in South Africa, *The South African Journal of Economics*, I, 1 March 1933, 49–57.
3. Union of South Africa, *Debates of the House of Assembly*, 1925, Col. 1664–1665.
4. Ibid., Col. 1764, 2891-2892; *The Workers' Herald* 20 February 1925, 28 April, 15 May and 14 September 1926.
5. Roux, E., 1944, *S. P. Bunting, a Political Biography*, Cape Town, 66–8; E. and W. Roux, op.cit., 38.
6. Rev. R. Phillips to the Editor, *The Workers' Herald*, 2 June 1925 (F/Joint Council File/30).
7. *The Workers' Herald* 15 June 1925.
8. Cf. *The Workers' Herald* 20 July 1925 on the visit to South Africa of the Prince of Wales.
9. The preamble must have been supplied by a member of the Communist Party (cf. Roux, E. R., *Time Longer than Rope*, 400), perhaps S. Buirski.
10. There are those who would not agree. Cf., for example, Martin Legassick, 'South Africa: forced labor, industrialization, and racial differentiation' in Harris, R. 1975, ed., *The Political Economy of Africa*, New York, etc., 1975, 229–70 and Wolpe, Harold, Capitalism and cheap labour-power in South Africa: from segregation to apartheid, *Economy and Society* I, 4, 1972, 425-56.
11. Champion, A. W. G., 1927, *The Truth about the ICU*, Durban, 6.
12. Kadalie, C., *My Life*, 53–5.
13. *The Workers' Herald* 9 January and 15 May 1925.
14. There is no evidence of a quarrel. Thaele attended the 1925 ICU Conference and appeared at an ICU meeting at Pretoria as late as February 1926 (*The Workers' Herald* 27 March 1926). Cf. also *The Workers' Herald* 14 September 1926.
15. Tyamzashe (Oupa), of mixed Black and White blood, was a Lovedale-trained printer working for an Indian firm in Johannesburg (Tyamzashe, H. D., loc. cit, 7, 51 Kadalie, C., *My Life*, 78). He was also sub-editor of *The Workers' Herald*.
16. Gomas, of mixed blood, came from the Malmesbury district of the Cape, where his father was a farm labourer. He himself was a tailor. In his autobiography Kadalie speaks rather slightingly of him: 'Although not an outstanding organiser, Gomas was however an able speaker on the platform. During his period at the Cape, the ICU slowly declined'. (99) In 1926, however, he spoke differently of him, as one who had 'fully repaid the confidence entrusted in him and considerably aided in increasing the membership of the branches of the Western Province.' (*The Workers' Herald* 28 April 1926).
17. Daniel Lindley. Champion's father, who had fought on the British side at Isandhlwana, died in 1921 (F/MSS/55).
18. Champion told me that he was expelled for attacking another boy (Interview 28 June 1971).
19. *The Truth about the ICU*, 20–3.
20. Kadalie, C., *My Life*, Editor's note 1, 87–8.
21. 'A dangerous morose and powerful native dreamer' with 'a vision of himself with his

THIN A FEW DAYS THE UNION PARLIAMENT OPENS. IT WILL BE A "NATIV E" SESSION. THIS CARTOON DEPICTS THE ACTUAL POSITION.

The Workers' Herald 12 January 1927 – South African Library, Cape Town

THE AFRICAN WORKERS RECEIVE INTERNATIONAL RECOGNITION THROUGH THE AFFILIATION OF THE I.C.U. TO THE INTERNATIONAL FEDERATION OF TRADE UNIONS THE SOUTH AFRICAN WHITE WORKER IS ANNOYED AT THE VICTORY OF THE BLACKS

The Workers' Herald 18 March 1927 – South African Library, Cape Town

arms round the pillars of the house of Africa, like a destructive Samson, ready to destroy the white man.' (Mrs E. Lewis to Lord Olivier 2 April 1928 B/UCT).

22. Autograph fragment of Champion's in the Forman Collection.
23. *The Workers' Herald* 28 April 1926; A. W. G. Champion to J. A. La Guma 12 November 1925 (Wits CP).
24. A. W. G. Champion to C. Kadalie 18 January 1926 (F/ICU Copies of Letters/3); A. P. Maduna to A. W. G. Champion 22 January 1926 (F 1926/2).
25. A. W. G. Champion to J. A. La Guma 19th October 1925 and to C. Kadalie 2 November 1925 (Wits CP).
26. A. W. G. Champion to C. Kadalie 2 November 1925 and to J. A. La Guma 12 November 1925 and 6 January 1926 (Wits CP).
27. Kadalie, C., *My Life*, 73. The proceedings of the Conference were reported in *The Workers' Herald* 28 April, 15 May and 15 June 1925.
28. Kadalie, C., *My Life*, 75; ICU to Select Committee May 1925 (F 1925/2).
29. *The Workers' Herald* 28 April 1926; *Evidence of Industrial and Commercial Workers' Union of Africa, Submitted at Johannesburg on September 19 1925* Johannesburg, 1925 (i.e. to the Economic and Wage Commission), 30.
30. *Cape Times* 21 April 1925.
31. *Cape Times* 22 April 1925.
32. *The Workers' Herald* 15 October 1925.
33. *The Social and Industrial Review*, Special Edition, I, 17, 29 June 1928/447–51; 15 May 1926.
34. *The Workers' Herald* 17 May 1927.
35. Champion, A. W. G., *The Truth about the ICU*, 14.
36. *The Workers' Herald* 20 February, 15 May and 15 June 1925.
37. *The Workers' Herald* 15 May 1925 and 28 April 1926; C. Kadalie, *My Life*, 79.
38. *The Workers' Herald* 12 May 1928.
39. *The Workers' Herald* 15 November 1925.
40. *The Workers' Herald* 28 April 1926.
41. Ibid.
42. Minutes of the National Council January 1928 (F 1928/1).
43. General Secretary's Report of Inspection of Branches 6 March 1926, 2, 6 (F 1926/6). The Johannesburg branch also ran an unprofitable tea-room.
44. *The Star* 7 September 1925.
45. *Evidence to the Economic and Wage Commission*, 2–4.
46. Ibid., 6–7.
47. Ibid., 7–10.
48. Ibid., 10.
49. Ibid., 13–15.
50. Ibid., 19, 40–2.
51. Ibid., 28–9.
52. *The Workers' Herald* 28 April 1926.
53. An official of the Native Affairs Department.
54. Union of South Africa, *Report of the Economic and Wage Commission, 1925* (U.G. 14–1926), 158, 331–2.
55. Ibid., 155, 323.
56. Ibid., 171, 232.
57. Ibid., 158.
58. Ibid., 296.
59. Ibid., 9.
60. *The Workers' Herald* 17 May 1927.

61. Op.cit., 72. According to *The Workers' Herald* 15 June 1926, 1926 was the 'Kadalie session'.
62. Union of South Africa, *Debates of the House of Assembly, 1926*, Col. 1900, 2056.
63. Ibid., Col. 2054–2055, 2065–2066.
64. According to C. Kadalie, *My Life*, 91, Kadalie was served with a notice on 1 March, but more than a month after this the ICU was complaining that no written statement had been sent by the Native Affairs Department (*The Workers' Herald* 28 April 1926).

CHAPTER 7

Moscow versus Amsterdam, 1926

'There is no government in the world sympathetic to the workers except the Russian government.' – Clements Kadalie, September 1926

'In all countries the Communists have been banned as cut-throats and anarchists who have no intelligent policy – except murder – to place before the workers.' – Clements Kadalie, April 1927

The Sixth Annual Conference of the ICU, the Fourth African Labour Congress, was held at the Workers' Hall in Johannesburg from 5 to 11 April 1926, and was attended by more than ninety delegates. The South African Trades Union Congress, the successor to the Association of Employees' Organisations, declined to send an official to open the Conference, and the only dignitary found to perform the ceremony was the eccentric Colonel P. A. Silburn, a former Natal MLA and an advocate of racial purity, whose speech seems to have left his audience somewhat bewildered.[1]

On the week-end preceding the opening of the Conference the National Council met, its deliberations being prolonged throughout the night. It must have been an invidious meeting, because it involved a dispute about the disposal of the union's money and had some bearing upon the removal of the Head Office to Johannesburg, a move that was unpopular in Cape Town. It appears that a plot had been hatched, in which Gumbs and La Guma were implicated, to prevent the National Secretary from removing the funds to Johannesburg, and about which he learnt from the Secretary of the Cape Town branch, Stanley Silwana. Kadalie was able to use the support of those members of the Council who did not come from Cape Town, including the Financial Secretary, Khaile, to thwart the conspiracy. There was some risk of secession, which did not, however, materialize.[2]

The opening debate of the Conference was on the Colour Bar Bill, which had twice been defeated in the Senate. Though naturally united in their detestation of the Bill, the delegates differed in the extent to which they were prepared to defy the Government. Loose, but well-defined, groups emerged during the Conference, the Moderates, 'whose policy was to face facts and to deliberate soberly and moderately on them'; the Die-hards, 'whose policy was that "Nay was Nay and Yea was Yea" '; and the Ginger Group, 'composed of all the young bloods, their policy was "Direct Action" '. In short, there were the Moderates, the Radicals, and what one might almost call the Lunatic Fringe. The known Gingerists were Keable 'Mote (re-admitted to the union after his betrayal of the previous year), T. W. Thibedi, formerly of the International Socialist League and the Industrial Workers of Africa, Thomas Mbeki, Dixon Mogaecho and John Gomas.[3] Mbeki, Thibedi and Gomas were members of the Communist Party, but two other Communists, La Guma and Khaile, were Die-hards. Champion was a Die-hard, while Kadalie, though unlabelled, tended to support the middle group against the Moderates, who were mostly from the Eastern Province and whose principal spokesmen were Theo Lujiza and James Dippa.

On the afternoon of Tuesday 6 April James Dippa moved a resolution of great importance: 'That in view of the rapid development in the introduction of fundamental changes in the Native policy under consideration . . . this conference instructs the National Council of the ICU to enter into negotiations for the affiliation of this organisation to the British Trades Union Congress, with the further object of bringing the case of the African worker before the League of Nations and public opinion in Europe.' In his contribution to the motion the National Secretary spoke of 'the white workers of Britain, who are not narrow-minded like most of our South African white comrades, and who have great influence universally'. Events in South Africa compelled the Blacks 'to go elsewhere for help'. The Natal Provincial Secretary, speaking in support, said he would like to see a delegate sent overseas if the money could be found. The motion was carried – without opposition from Gingerist or Communist – and the delegates went on to condemn the Sedition Bill as 'a public danger', 'diabolically iniquitous'.

On Wednesday 7 April the Cape Town Communists, La Guma and Gomas, mounted an attack upon the Government's segregation policy, proclaiming the solidarity of working class interests and the danger that segregation brought to White workers as much as to Black. Parliament, they alleged, was the instrument of the capitalists, who exploited race prejudice to the detriment of workers of all races. The 'white workers sell their principle for the little favour they receive from the capitalists' (La Guma). 'Segregation fosters the separation of workers, and the white workers look upon themselves as an aristocratic class in comparison with the blacks' (Gomas). Yet delegates were still disinclined to attack General Hertzog, and it was rather Smuts who was the target of wrath.

After condemning the Industrial Conciliation Act and the pass laws, whose operation excluded many Blacks from the benefits of the Act, the Conference debated the civilized labour policy. The Senior Vice-President, A. M. Jabavu, introducing a motion expressing the delegates' disapproval, said that the Black people contributed abundantly to the revenue of the state, relatively more abundantly than Europeans to railway revenue, and were entitled to employment, including state employment. The Government had no right to solve the poor White problem at the expense of the Blacks. Speakers who followed cited instances of dismissal of Blacks on the railways and the transfer of Black railway clerks to manual labour to make way for Whites. Morever, it was not only a question of subordinating Black interests to White. The Cape Town delegates, M. E. A. Johnson, a West Indian, and John Gomas, a Coloured worker, indignantly denounced the Government for fostering a division between Blacks and the Coloured people. Johnson, who had earlier expressed his distaste for the very terms Native and Coloured as a device for splitting up 'the African race still further', bitterly attacked the pass system, and Gomas, in a forceful and fluent speech, accused the Government of creating 'ill-feeling between the Coloured and Native people, by recruiting Coloured loafers from the country to replace the Natives at the docks. These loafers are misled into thinking that they are white people.'

The discussion moved to the minimum wage question. What was to be done? Speaking in character, Keable 'Mote, the turncoat of Bloemfontein, 'passionately urged for a movement of passive resistance. "Let us all be arrested."' Alex P. Maduna, the Orange Free State Provincial Secretary and a Die-hard, claimed that at Bloemfontein 'he could engineer a strike at any time. Mere resolutions do not always carry weight, direct action was sometimes wanted.' This, however, found little favour. Lujiza, a Moderate, advised the ICU, before calling a strike, to consider whether the time was really ripe; or, at least, if it was set on a strike, to make it a general strike. He claimed that his people in East London were ready for industrial action. James Dippa, on the other hand, said that he had discouraged strikes at Port Elizabeth and that the best course open to the union was to win over the chiefs. Shortly after Kadalie intervened to complain about the spinelessness of the Eastern Province officials. Although he was prudent enough to add that the strike weapon 'should not be played with or grossly encouraged before the workers were properly organised', his intervention earned him a rebuke from the Senior Vice-President, who was acting as chairman. Some disorder ensued. Champion 'demanded that the rules of debate must be followed, no matter whether the heavens fall', but Kadalie was willing to run that risk and was difficult to quieten.[4] 'Mote took advantage of the confusion to demand strong action, with the result that an exasperated delegate requested the chairman, to 'ask that man to sit down, or ask the Sergeant-at-Arms to bundle him out head first'.

The debate was continued on Thursday morning. Even Thibedi of the Ginger Group supported the view that the strike should be used only as a last resort. Jabavu, insisting that the Cape at least was not ready for one and arguing that the only way to proceed was through the Wage Board, called upon the National Secretary or the Bloemfontein representative to report upon the progress that had been made in obtaining a minimum wage determination. Kadalie reviewed the state of negotiations both in Bloemfontein and in East London. There was some discussion of the value of the Wage Board. John Gomas expressed some impatience with the policy of having recourse to it, and in this he received support from President Gumbs, who was also sceptical about its effectiveness in the case of unskilled labour and was in favour of pressing for a national minimum wage. The Board was defended by Maduna, Die-hard, and by Khaile, Gingerist.

There followed a lengthy debate upon the system of recruiting labour for the mines. The main speaker was A. W. G. Champion, who began by saying that he had worked on the mines for ten years and therefore could be considered an expert on working conditions there. He continued: 'Recruited mine labourers are like slaves . . . No questions are to be asked, otherwise the sjambok and boot would be introduced . . . usury and extortion were largely practised in the compounds, and many poor Natives pay as much as 15 per cent on loans offered them by the indunas . . . he had seen men die in mine hospitals without proper care being taken of their cases. The underground white overseers had no human feeling in them . . .' A. M. Jabavu attacked the system from the other end, the abuses in the recruiting grounds. 'Down in the Native territories,' he said, 'where most of the mine labourers came from, conditions were appalling, and through the economic pinch many Natives have to sell themselves to traders . . . The recruiting system was sheer profiteering on the part of the traders in Native territories . . . the recruiting system should be boycotted.' Mbeki took up Jabavu's suggestion of a boycott and said that the ICU should persuade the chiefs to discourage enlistment, and the National Secretary revived the old idea of ICU-run labour bureaux as a substitute for the recruiting agencies. Mzazi, a Die-hard from East London, said it was silly to talk of boycotting the recruiting system unless the workers could be provided in some other way with their fares to the mines. 'The only way to smash the recruiting system,' he said, 'was to open country stores so as to feed the people and lend out money on security at reasonable rates of interest. If this proposal is followed the ICU could be rich in one year, and the traders would have to "get out of it".' At that point the debate broke off when Kadalie intervened to read out a letter from the Native Affairs Department confirming the restriction placed upon his movements.

Because of the ban Clements Kadalie, having, after the Conference rose, participated in a great May Day demonstration in Johannesburg, was unable to make his usual jaunt round the country. He did not comply with a resolution passed by the Conference before it disbanded instructing him to travel to Natal, which he was specifically forbidden to enter, with those delegates going home there. Loyal telegrams, such as one from Cape Town, 'We must prepare face imprisonment of Kadalie for not being allowed to organise', did not spur him on. It is not easy to determine the exact nature of his ban and to discover upon what statutory authority the Native Affairs Department was relying. The Government, it appears, insisted that outside the Cape Province, where he was a registered voter, Kadalie must be subject to the pass laws, which meant that he was supposed to (but did not) carry a pass in the Orange Free State and Transvaal and, under Natal Law 48 of 1884, obtain an 'inward pass' whenever he entered that province. Sidney Bunting, a solicitor and a member of the Communist Party, advised him to test the law in the Transvaal and then test it in Natal by entering without a pass. Accordingly he made an application for a certificate of exemption from the operation of the Transvaal pass laws under Ordinance 28 of 1902. For a long time he heard nothing. At last, in August, his application was rejected on the ground that, in the opinion of the Minister of Native Affairs, he was 'not a Native deserving of the privilege'. He re-applied to the Sub-Native Commissioner and Chief Pass Officer in Pretoria, who claimed that he was unable to issue the certificate for the reason already given by the Minister. Thereupon Kadalie applied for a court order requiring the Pass Officer either to grant the certificate or 'to acquaint the applicant of any evidence prejudicial to his application and to afford him an opportunity of correcting or contradicting such evidence'. But the case did not come on until August of the following year.[5]

In the meantime the National Secretary displayed extreme reluctance to test the Natal ban, and it is unlikely that he would ever have moved if Champion, who had been advised that Law 48 of 1884 was a dead letter, had not prodded him from May onwards.[6] Shortage of money was one difficulty. The response to the National Council's call to branches for funds was disappointing.[7] Towards the end of July Kadalie was thinking of going to the Cape to try and raise money there,[8] but evidently decided against it lest he could not get back again to Johannesburg, and at the end of the month La Guma, Khaile, and he decided that the General Secretary, La Guma, should go to the Eastern Province to endeavour to arouse the branches from their 'extreme lethargy', while Kadalie himself should concentrate on the Reef, where his freedom of movement was not interfered with.[9]

At last, on 12 August, Kadalie, after informing the Government of his intentions, made a move. In an extended military metaphor he explained the situation in his annual report to the 1927 Conference at Durban: 'The only medium between the Headquarters of the Organisation and Branches was fortunately [*sic*] our Official Organ – *The Workers' Herald*. Therein both the Sub-Editor[10] and I sent out each month words of encouragement to our soldiers on the battle front which was on the retreat. With all our inspiring writings, the results were not promising: the soldiery desired to see someone from the War Office who could verbally arouse them. The organisation was on the collapse [*sic*], the Government had a temporary victory. And what brave General could have permitted his army to be disintegrated in this way by his enemy? The moment for decision would soon arrive. The old saying comes into my judgment – "It is a noble thing and heroic thing to die fighting" . . . I resolved to proceed to Natal to test the legality of the ban on my free movements after legal opinion had been obtained. I must pay great tribute in this connection to Comrade A. W. G. Champion . . . I doubt if we would be assembling here to-day as a Trade Union had Comrade Champion not encouraged me to cross the border. Comrade Champion did not only encourage me to cross the border, but actually came to Johannesburg to escort me into Natal. I know of one official of the Organisation[11] who had hinted to me that Comrade Champion's object was to put me into a tight corner and leave me there to suffer the consequences alone. But this ill talk proved in vain.'[12]

In Durban, where he stayed ten days, Kadalie addressed large meetings and applied for an inward pass, which the local official would not issue without instructions from the Native Affairs Department. Returning to Johannesburg, he was given an enthusiastic welcome, when he triumphantly suggested to the crowd that the best way to deal with the pass laws was to defy them. On a second trip to Durban, on 24 September, he was arrested and charged with entering Natal without an inward pass.[13] On 15 October a fine of £3 (with the option of 14 days hard labour) was imposed on him in the magistrate's court. His sentence, however, was set aside on appeal by Justice Tatham in the Supreme Court at Pietermaritzburg on the ground that, as secretary of a trade union, he was entitled to a concession under the law that permitted people on legitimate business (in his case auditing the books of the ICU branch in Durban) to stay inside the province for up to seven days without a pass, and he had in fact been in Natal for less time than that.[14]

Kadalie treated this episode as a victory 'against the despotic and tyrannical Native Affairs Department officials'. It was, however, but a limited victory. While it is true that he had broken the ban, he was still not free to stay as he wished in Natal, since to remain there for longer than a week still necessitated an inward pass. Besides, it would have been easy enough for the Government to make things more difficult for him by framing new regulations under Law 48 of 1884. If it did not do so, it was presumably because more draconian legislation was in the offing in any case. The question does arise, nevertheless, why it was that the Government simply did not deport him. The answer was that it did not have the power to. Unless he committed an offence under Section 22 of the Immigration Act, he was immune, because once the Minister of the Interior had permitted a prohibited immigrant to remain, the decision was binding upon himself and his successors, and in Kadalie's case the discretion had already been exercised in his favour in 1921.[15]

By October 1926, when the National Secretary's appeal in Natal had been upheld, the ICU was coming increasingly under the influence of what the late Prof. E. R. Roux derisively called 'certain "good people" who had never before displayed any interest in African trade unionism . . . Among these were religious people, college professors, humanitarians and the like.'[16] Hitherto the ICU leaders had been hostile to and contemptuous of liberals and missionaries. Christianity as practised by Whites was seen as a gigantic piece of hypocrisy, a trick perpetrated on the Black man to make him submissive. It was not a question of attacking, though it was assailed on occasion, a religion that probably most of them accepted, but a belief that the White man had departed from its true practice and used it as a device for exploitation. Indeed, ICU propagandists chose to regard Christ as the archetypal radical and agitator.[17] White priests and ministers, with some exceptions, responded with indignation or indifference.

'"Down with everything that's up, and up with everything that's down" seems to be your policy,' wrote the American missionary Ray Phillips to *The Workers' Herald* in June 1925.[18] He was Secretary of the Bantu Men's Social Centre (founded in 1924 and given the blessing of moderate Black leaders, including the Rev. J. L. Dube and R. V. Selope Thema[19]), which itself came under attack as a 'dangerous institution', built on 'capitalism and parasitism'.[20] Quotations in that vein could be multiplied, as could assaults on the Johannesburg Joint Council of Europeans and Natives, another butt for ICU scorn.[21] Its Black members were the 'good boys', the dupes of the Chamber of Mines, which was the arch-villain of the capitalist plot.

This deep suspicion felt by the ICU for these two organizations was never wholly allayed. It was lulled, but it broke out again in due course, perhaps even more sharply. In point of fact, however, although the men involved in the Joint Council movement were brought somewhat gingerly into contact with the ICU, the influence that now came to bear on it issued from a rather different quarter. The new influence was exerted by a female triumvirate with a wide circle of friends and acquaintances among liberals and socialists in South Africa and England. The first of these women was Mrs Palmer, who had been of some assistance to Kadalie at the time of his first propaganda efforts in Durban in 1924 and who liked to think that she had some sway over Champion. In 1926 she was fifty years of age and had been in South African since the end of the war, after having been prominent in the Suffragette and Fabian movements. In Durban in the 1920s she was lecturing in economics at the Natal Technical College.[22] It was she who had arranged a meeting between the ICU leaders and Winifred Holtby,[23] a member of the British Independent Labour Party, a pacifist, a contributor to *The New Leader*, *Time and Tide*, and *The Manchester Guardian*, and a novelist of some distinction.[24] She was much the youngest of the three women, being twenty-eight in 1926. From February to June 1926, she made a tour of South Africa that was partly financed by a series of lectures she delivered for the League of Nations Union. Her first impressions of the ICU leaders – Champion: 'extraordinarily dignified, efficient and moderate'; 'reasonable, courteous, patient beyond description'; Maduna: 'highly cultured and intelligent'; Kadalie: 'extremist, suspicious, sensitive, vain, sincere'[25] – came in the course of time to be significantly modified. Displaying a great interest in the work of the union, Miss Holtby promised to see, on her return to England, what help could be given to it.

In Johannesburg Winifred Holtby met Mrs Ethelreda Lewis, the third member of the trio, to whom she had already been introduced in England in 1923.[26] Mrs Lewis, who had lived in South Africa since the beginning of the century and was a year older than Mrs Palmer, was also a writer. Her chief claim to fame is her association with Trader Horn, whose adventures she was committing to paper in 1926, but she also wrote a number of novels that achieved a modest popularity. The 'Native problem' had long interested her, and she had contributed on that subject to English periodicals. To term Mrs Lewis a liberal would be far from accurate, unless the description can be properly applied to any White person in a racially-mixed society who is willing to work with or on behalf of Blacks. In fact she was a firm supporter of the South African Party, to which she had come from the Unionist Party. Terrified of Communism, she was willing to overcome her distaste for socialism of the non-Communist variety and steer the ICU in that direction on the principle that an inoculation of a mild dose of the disease would be a prophylactic against its more virulent form, though it would be unfair to suggest that she was not concerned to promote 'native rights in their own native land'. With considerable misgiving, on the day after the passage, in May 1926, of the Colour Bar Act, which she deplored, she approached Clements Kadalie to try and convince him that 'he would find better, safer, more stable white friends for himself than the white communists – people who will never let him down again to the ultimate necessity of falling back on communist friends or fighting quite alone for the rights of black workers.'[27]

Mrs Lewis coupled with her detestation of Communism a nice sense of what was proper for a woman in her position. The fact that her husband, who was a doctor, was employed by the Government made it difficult enough, she thought, for her to become too openly involved in the ICU, but her uneasiness extended further. 'I felt deeply,' she recorded later, 'the hopelessness of a woman, and a woman of my age, trying to put her shoulder to such an enormous wheel. And far more than that I felt the bitter incongruity (I felt it as a sort of outrage to myself no less than to the natives) of a woman trying to help natives. In the full knowledge . . . that no black man so recently in the kraal as the SA native can respect or look up to a woman my action was a humiliation not only to the natives I sought to help but to myself.'[28] She looked, therefore, for men to assist her, but all the help she got took the form of occasional lectures delivered by Professor Edgar Brookes of the Transvaal University College and F. S. Livie-Noble, the Secretary of the Pretoria Joint Council, at the Workers' Hall.[29]

Of the three women Mrs Lewis was the most patronizing, or rather was actuated by the crudest kind of paternalism. On the day before she went to see Kadalie in May, 1926, she read an address to a Church synod in Johannesburg that reveals her attitude with great clarity. Speaking of 'our dark countrymen clamouring like children at the skirts of the white man as a boy at its father's coat . . . the infant race whose playground the white man burst into three centuries ago', she went on to suggest that what South Africa stood in need of was a John Chinn, the hero of Kipling's *The Tomb of His Ancestors*, or rather an army of John Chinns, each 'devoted to his work, making it his pride – a sort of holy inarticulate pride – to understand each the different race or caste or tribe under his special jurisdiction . . . We need S. Africans of both white races, who have been brought up to look at the Native with a familiar, an unsentimental eye. And we need to train that eye, which has known the Native all its life, to be imaginative, to be just, to be pitiful, to be brotherly, but never to be sentimental . . . These workers to be location masters, to run hostels and hospitals, to teach agricultural methods.'[30] And, presumably, to guide the ICU.

In accepting the offer of help from the three women, Kadalie was not being seduced by White flattery – as acceptable as he found it – to follow a policy that was against his better judgment. Rather did he see open before him an avenue to a prize for which he had long striven, the integration of his union into the main stream of the labour movement. It cannot be emphasized too strongly that he was not adopting a new policy, but pursuing one that had been under discussion ever since the Bloemfontein Conference of 1920, an appeal to international labour. When the 'civilized labour policy' came to be implemented in such a way that the ICU leaders could no longer deceive themselves about the real intentions of the Government which they had helped into power, the idea of appealling to Great Britain recurred with greater urgency. In July 1925, Kadalie was saying that the British labour movement must be woken from its slumber and expressing his confidence in the ability of the British Labour Party to influence events in South Africa.[31] Such was the background to the resolution moved by James Dippa on 5 April 1926, at the Sixth Annual Conference. International pressure would, it was hoped, not merely force the Government to modify its policy, but also shame the White workers in South Africa into displaying a comradely spirit towards Black workers. Bitter disappointment with Colonel Creswell and his narrow-mindedness did not destroy the hope of a colour-blind proletarian solidarity. Such hopes and plans were not the product of new liberal influences, which did no more than foster and encourage them.

It was through Mrs Palmer and Miss Holtby that the ICU made contact with the labour movement in Britain, a direct approach two months after the 1926 Conference to the British Trades Union Congress, after some delay caused by the General Strike, having brought a terse reply referring the ICU to the International Federation of Trade Unions, the headquarters of which were in Amsterdam.[32] During the period when he was confined to the Johannesburg area Kadalie was in correspondence with Winifred Holtby (as was Mrs Lewis) and, when he went to Durban in defiance of his ban, he renewed his acquaintance with Mrs Palmer. Through the efforts of these two women a gift of books came from England in response to an appeal by Miss Holtby in the columns of *The New Leader*.[33] Furthermore, Mrs Palmer, on a visit to England in 1926, discussed the ICU with her socialist friends, Sidney Webb, Bernard Shaw, H. N. Brailsford (editor of *The New Leader*), and Arthur Creech Jones, the National Secretary of the Administrative, Clerical and Supervisory Group of the Transport and General Workers' Union. Winifred Holtby was also in touch with Jones and Brailsford, like herself members of the Independent Labour Party. It was from this party that support came rather than from the main Labour Party, which, like the British TUC, was reluctant to offend the White labour movement in South Africa by what might be construed as intervention in its domestic affairs.[34] Brailsford suggested the setting up of an informal committee –

'a sort of "Friends of Africa" group' – to consult on measures to assist the ICU, and he advised an application for affiliation to the British Labour Party.[35] In October Kadalie wrote to Creech Jones. Although in this, his first letter, Kadalie, not yet appreciating Jones's unemotional, almost bureaucratic, turn of mind, spoke of men and women having been 'shot in cold blood under General Smuts' Government, simply because they asked an increase of wages to enable themselves to have a civilised life',[36] scarcely more than a partial truth, he soon adapted his own style to his correspondent's; not, however, that Creech Jones was ever less than courteous and sympathetic.

Creech Jones pressed the needs of the ICU upon the 'imperialism committee' of the ILP, but saw no chance of its affiliation to either the ILP or the Labour Party and considered that an application to the International Federation of Trade Unions would be worth while, a view also expressed by Sidney Webb to Mrs Palmer. Although the International Federation normally accepted only applications for affiliation from national centres, he thought that in the special circumstances of South Africa an application from the ICU would be entertained. One was duly sent off in November. Jones agreed that the establishment of an informal committee in London to help the union would be a good idea.[37]

For some months the ICU remained on good terms with both liberals and Communists, with Ethelreda Lewis's literary articles in *The Workers' Herald* (whimsically signed 'Reader') appearing next to radical attacks upon much that she held dear. Mutual distrust, however, was growing between the union and the CP, which by then had a very strong contingent on the National Council – La Guma, Khaile, Gomas, Mbeki (who, though only twenty or so, had become Transvaal Provincial Secretary in July 1926, to enable Tyamzashe to devote his time to the Complaints and Research Department at Head Office) and a newcomer, R. de Norman, the Indian Chairman of the Cape Town branch. Champion, who as early as May 1926 was denying in Durban any connection between his organization and the Communists, was particularly uneasy about the relationship and, being into the bargain abnormally sensitive to criticism, was stung to fury, and no doubt to hatred of the Communist Party, in August 1926, by some mildly adverse comment that appeared in the Communist *The South African Worker*. Bunting was deeply suspicious of Champion and faintly contemptuous of Kadalie.[38]

The occasion for, though not the cause of, a breach between the ICU and the CP was the unauthorized acceptance by La Guma of the Party's nomination to its delegation to the Congress of Oppressed Nationalities (planned to take place the following year at Brussels). His alleged discourtesy prompted those leaders who were anxious for a show-down with the Communists to place on the agenda of the next National Council meeting a request for the formulation of a definite policy governing 'the Union's relation to other political orginisations, such as the Communist Party'. The National Council met on 16 and 17 December at

Port Elizabeth, to which Kadalie and Champion proceeded after a tour that took them to Bloemfontein and through the Eastern Province, to celebrate Kadalie's recent legal victory. The meeting, attended by only thirteen of the nineteen Council members, was a stormy one, with Kadalie throwing a tantrum as a result of an altercation with La Guma. At one point the meeting broke up, and when it resumed after a short interval, a resolution was moved by Alex P. Maduna, himself a renegade from the Communist Party,[39] seconded by A. W. G. Champion, requiring union officials who were members of the Communist Party either to relinquish their membership or to resign office in the ICU. An amendment moved by Thomas Mbeki that 'no official be expelled by reason of his being a communist' was rejected and Maduna's motion carried by six votes (including Maduna, Champion, Kadalie, and Tyamzashe) to five (La Guma, Khaile, Gomas, Mbeki, and probably B. C. R. Mazingi), with presumably two abstentions. Refusing to resign from the Party, four of the five Communists on the National Council were summarily expelled from the union, and the meeting came to an abrupt close. De Norman, who was not present, submitted with an ill-grace, and Mbeki recanted.[40]

The Communist version of events claimed that the real reason for the expulsion was that the Party members were an increasing embarrassment to 'reactionary, bureaucratic and corrupt elements' in the ICU, as they pressed for a more active and forthright policy, stricter control of finance, and a curb on the National Secretary's power.[41] This allegation is not without substance and the weightiest piece of evidence showing that Communist officials were more concerned than their colleagues about financial irregularities and constitutional improprieties is a report drawn up by La Guma in March 1926, upon a tour of inspection he had made of the ICU branches.[42] Estimating conservatively a loss during the preceding year of between five and six hundred pounds owing to 'Inefficiency, Dishonesty, and Unconstitutionalism on the part of Branch and other Officials', but admitting that a high level of administrative competence could hardly be expected from untrained and inexperienced branch officers, the General Secretary made some severe criticisms that extended to a number of the Provincial Secretaries – certainly Maduna and Mancoe, but not Champion, whose administration was in fact commended – and were particularly unsparing of the National Secretary himself, who was taken to task, not for financial offences, but for his failure to observe proper constitutional procedures in his leasing of the Workers' Hall. 'It seemed that a dictatorship is in embryo,' reported La Guma. There is some evidence that in the latter part of 1926 he was becoming dissatisfied, too, with Champion's high-handed management of the Natal finances and that the latter in turn was resentful of La Guma's attempts to assert central control.[43]

One cannot doubt the truth of these strictures. Although at conferences and at meetings of the National Council Kadalie was subject to a restraint which sometimes made him behave in a petulant and puerile way, between meetings of these bodies he had a more or less free hand, constrained only by the need to gauge accurately what the rank-and-file of the organization would accept or tolerate. It is also true that about La Guma, Gomas, and Khaile, the officials who preferred to leave the ICU, no word of scandal is heard, and the same cannot be said about Maduna, who moved their expulsion, Champion, who seconded it, and Kadalie, whose consent made it possible. Some significance might be seen in the fact that La Guma was succeeded as General Secretary by Sam Dunn, who was sent to prison in 1928 for theft of ICU funds, Khaile as Financial Secretary by William Smith, who absconded with £25 in 1928, and Gomas as Provincial Secretary by James Dippa of the Eastern Province, reinstated after having been suspended for neglecting his duties, to be replaced in turn by the conformist de Norman.[44]

Another piece of evidence that supports the Communist case is that, during the National Secretary's ban, the General and Financial Secretaries were urging a policy of boldness. They wanted to call a general strike by way of protest and to restore ICU morale. Kadalie took the view that the movement was not ready for such drastic action, and he noticed that the militant La Guma himself was not keen to take charge of 'the army which was about to be disintegrated by the enemy', but 'confined himself to Headquarters'.[45] It is difficult to accept wholly uncritically the claim of the Communists that they were the voice of conscience, urging greater militancy, financial purity, and democracy. Both Kadalie and Champion had a good record of vigorous, if spasmodic, action against misuse of funds, and no one was better placed than the Communist officials themselves to stamp out dishonesty at branch level, seeing that La Guma as General Secretary was responsible for general administration and Khaile was Financial Secretary. They did not take their disapproval of the arrogant irresponsibility of Kadalie and Champion to the point of resignation.

Kadalie and Tyamzashe left Port Elizabeth immediately after the National Council meeting for Johannesburg, where they arrived on 21 December.[46] Consequently they missed the rival gatherings held by the ICU and the expelled Communists at Korsten on the following Sunday. The latter, who demanded reinstatement and a campaign of passive resistance against the pass laws, seem to have drawn the greater sympathy, perhaps because Kadalie was not there to use his influence.[47] The Communist Party next issued an indignant manifesto 'to the Native workers and oppressed peoples of Africa', denying any intention of subverting the ICU. At a meeting, also in December, in Johannesburg, where the Party had a militant, though not numerous, following, the audience could scarcely be controlled by the ICU leaders, who were compelled to accept a motion from the floor to submit the National Council's decision to the next conference for ratification. Kadalie mounted an attack upon Communism, especially upon its White leaders, and was subsequently accused by Bunting of a crude appeal to racial prejudice in order to make his policy acceptable. Despite attempts, however, to rouse the branches against the leadership, few responded and the confidence of the bulk of the membership in Kadalie and Champion remained unshaken.[48]

Kadalie, then and later, insisted that the Communists were ejected because they were overbearing and, over a period of eighteen months, had been 'prying deeper and deeper into the internal affairs' of the union, as a counter-manifesto of January 1927 put it.[49] That Black organizations resented and resisted White patronage is beyond dispute,[50] and at the end of 1926 the ICU leaders felt their freedom of action more threatened by the didacticism of the left than by the earnest advice of the centre, just as later the liberal yoke in turn became too heavy to bear.

The Communists claimed that the expulsion of the ICU officials aroused widespread indignation and that 'the whole of the ICU machinery' was thrown 'into a state of chaos'.[51] On the whole, however, it seems that the CP was damaged more than the ICU. The latter without doubt lost some able officials and it is clear that there was regret at the departure of Gomas,[52] but the union's triumphant progress that had just begun proceeded unimpeded, its leaders even claiming that the breach had brought advantages.[53] It was the Communist Party that was 'left fairly high and dry'.[54]

Notes

1. His ideas were expounded in his book *South Africa; White and Black – or Brown?* The Conference was reported in *The Workers' Herald* 28 April and 15 May 1926.
2. Kadalie, C., *My Life*, 81–3; H. D. Tyamzashe, loc. cit., 9–11.
3. There is some uncertainty about Gomas, who was far from 'lunatic fringe' and who was also described as a Die-hard.
4. Kadalie was generally in hot water on that particular day. Later on he was 'pulled over the coals' by A. M. Jabavu for 'leaving the House without the Chairman's permission'. He was perhaps not the autocrat that the Communist Party subsequently alleged him to be.
5. *The Workers' Herald* 28 April 1926; Kadalie, C., *My Life*, 86; President, Senior Vice-President, National Secretary and General Secretary to Branch Secretaries 22 April 1926 (F 1926/8); Cowley and Cowley to A. W. G. Champion 15 June 1926 (F 1926/15); C. Kadalie to A. W. G. Champion 22 July 1926 (F 1926/34). When the case was eventually heard, the Native Affairs Department changed its defence and argued that Kadalie's claim fell, not under Ordinance 28 of 1902, but under Proclamation 35 of 1901, the Coloured Persons Exemption Proclamation, and, therefore, that his application was irregular. This argument was upheld by Acting Justice I. Grindley-Ferris, who dismissed the application for a court order. An application by Kadalie's solicitors for exemption from costs was also rejected (South African Law Reports (1927), Transvaal Provincial Division, 1927 TPD, *Rex versus Harmsworth*, 862–9). On appeal, in 1928, Kadalie at last won his case with costs (Findlay and Niemeyer to C. Kadalie 1 August 1928, B/UCT; Kadalie, C., op. cit., 102, which has the dates muddled).
6. A. W. G. Champion to C. Kadalie 12 May 1926 (F 1926/11); A. W. G. Champion to J. La

Guma 14 May 1926 (F 1926/12). Cf. also C. Kadalie to A. W. G. Champion 17 May 1926 (F 1926/13).

7. *The Workers' Herald* 15 June 1927.
8. C. Kadalie to A. W. G. Champion 22 July 1926 (F 1926/34).
9. C. Kadalie, J. La Guma, and E. Khaile (presumably in their joint capacity as National Council Executive Bureau) to ICU Branches 30 July (F 1926/37).
10. H. D. Tyamzashe.
11. A. P. Maduna perhaps.
12. *The Workers' Herald* 15 June 1927. Cf. also *The Workers' Herald* 14 September 1926 and Kadalie, C., *My Life*, 91.
13. *The Workers' Herald* 14 October 1926; C. Kadalie, *My Life*, 92–3.
14. Champion, A. W. G., *The Truth about the ICU*, 17–19; Kadalie, C., *My Life*, 91–5. Kadalie was defended by Roy Hathorn, K.C. (National Council Executive Bureau to National Council Members 21 October 1926, F 1926/46), not Hawthorn, as Kadalie says.
15. *The Workers' Herald* 14 September 1926; A. W. G. Champion to C. Kadalie 30 October 1926 (F 1926/38a); Union of South Africa, *Debates of the House of Assembly*, 1926, Col. 1280–1281; Central Archives: Department of the Interior 10/A/1787 Acting Secretary for the Interior to the Commissioner of Police 30 August 1922.
16. Roux, E. R., *Time Longer than Rope*, 161.
17. *The Workers' Herald* 15 December 1925 and 14 August 1926.
18. The letter was published in the issue of 15 June, 1925 with a bitter editorial comment. There was an attack on Phillips in the next issue with the caption 'A Case of Satan Reproving Sin'.
19. *Ilanga lase Natal* 1 February 1924.
20. *The Workers' Herald* 15 August 1925.
21. E.g. *The Workers' Herald* 9 January 1925.
22. Palmer, M., 1957, *The History of the Indians in Natal*, Cape Town, vii.
23. W. Holtby to E. Lewis 24 August 1926, (B/Wits).
24. Her best known novel is *South Riding*.
25. Brittain, V., and Handley-Taylor, G., 1960, (eds.), *Selected Letters of Winifred Holtby and Vera Brittain, 1920–1935*, London, 97, 101, 116, 136, 137.
26. Brittain, V., *Testament of Friendship*, 155.
27. Lewis, E., Memorandum on the ICU and White helpers, 22 January 1927 (B/Wits); E. Lewis to General Smuts 4 January 1927 (B/Wits).
28. Memorandum on the ICU.
29. J. D. Krige to E. Lewis 18 and 30 November 1926 (B/Wits); E. Lewis to Lord Olivier 2 April 1928 (B/UCT); *The Workers' Herald* 14 August 1926.
30. Lewis, E., The Church and racial problems (B/Wits).
31. *The Workers' Herald* 20 July 1923.
32. The National Council Executive Bureau to the Members of the National Council 21 October 1926 (F 1926/46); C. Kadalie to W. Holtby 10 September 1926 (WH).
33. C. Kadalie to W. Holtby 10 September 1926 (WH); C. Kadalie to E. Lewis 1 October 1926 (B/Wits); *The Workers' Herald* 15 November 1926.
34. Partha Sarathi Gupta, 1975, *Imperialism and the British Labour Movement, 1914–1964*, London and Basingstoke, 121–3.
35. W. Holtby to E. Lewis 24 August 1926 (B/Wits).
36. C. Kadalie to A. Creech Jones 6 October 1926 (WH).
37. C. Kadalie to W. Holtby 10 September 1926 (WH); W. Holtby to C. Kadalie 8 October 1926 (B/Wits); A. Creech Jones to W. Holtby 8 October 1926 (WH); C. Kadalie to A. Creech Jones 1 December 1926 and 8 February 1927 (WH); fragment of letter from M. Palmer probably to W. Holtby (c. January 1927) (B/UCT).

38 National Council Executive Bureau Report July 1926 (F 1927/3); A. W. G. Champion to C. Kadalie 12 May 1926 (F 11926/11); Roux, E. R., *S. P. Bunting*, 73, 75; *The Workers' Herald* 15 May and 14 August 1926.

39. *The Workers' Herald* 15 June 1927.

40. Johns, S. W., III, Trade Union, political group, or mass movement? The Industrial and Commercial Workers' Union of Africa, in Rotberg R. I. and Mazrui, A. A., 1970, eds., *Protest and Power in Black Africa*, New York, 1970, 722–6; Roux, E. R., *Time Longer than Rope*, 163–4; *The Workers' Herald* 14 September 1926 and 12 January 1927; H D. Tyamzashe to A. W. G. Champion 21 December 1926 (misdated 1927) (F 1927/136)/; H. D. Tyamzashe, loc. cit., 20–1. It is difficult to tell who were the six absentees, but they included Gumbs, de Norman, and 'Mote and probably Johnson. Jabavu left before the crucial debate. In Gumbs's absence the meeting was, strictly speaking, unconstitutional, because the President's attendance was necessary for a quorum (ICU, *Revised Constitution, As Amended by Conference at Johannesburg, 1925*, Cape Town, 1925, Section 9). The meeting was chaired by Tyamzashe (*The Workers' Herald* 15 June 1927). 'Mote gave his support to the motion later (C. Kadalie to A. W. G. Champion 28 December 1926, F 1926/67).

41. *The Workers' Herald* 12 January 1927; Roux, E. R., *Time Longer than Rope*, 163–4; Johns, S. W., loc. cit., 723 725.

42. General Secretary's Report of Inspection of Branches 6 March 1926 (F 1926/6).

43. Statement of Samuel Wilfred Dunn to P. C. Cochran, Magistrate 26 November 1926 (F 1927/122), 15–16.

44. *The Workers' Herald* 15 June 1927; W. G. Ballinger to W. Holtby 8 August 1928 (B/UCT).

45. *The Workers' Herald* 15 June 1927.

46. H. D. Tyamzashe to A. W. G. Champion 21 December 1926 (misdated 1927) (F 1927/136).

47. C. Kadalie to A. W. G. Champion 29 December 1926 (F 1926/68).

48. *The Workers' Herald* 12 January 1927; Roux, E. R., *Time Longer than Rope*, 165–6; S. W. Johns, Trade union, political pressure group, or mass movement? 726. Kadalie's own version of the Johannesburg meeting was somewhat different – 'I gave them what they deserve' (C. Kadalie to A. W. G. Champion 28 December 1926, F 1926/67).

49. *The Workers' Herald* 12 January 1927.

50. Cf. ICU Manifesto of 1923 (*Imvo zabantsudu* 9 October 1923).

51. Roux, E. R., *Time Longer than Rope*, 165.

52. There was apparently no regret at the departure of La Guma, who was very much the office-bound bureaucrat (*The Workers' Herald* 12 January 1927), a view supported by Mr Gomas's recollections (Interview 18 May 1970).

53. The 'opposition of the Communist Party helped us a great deal to consolidate our ranks' (*The Workers' Herald* 10 December 1927).

54. Roux, E. R., *Time Longer than Rope*, 203.

CHAPTER 8

The Great Expansion, 1926-1927

'When Noah sailed the ocean blue,
He had worries the same as you.
For weeks and weeks he drove the ark,
Before he found a place to park.

'When oft man's power and strength and all
Seems but to fail and faint away,
The mighty hand salvation brings.
When hills and vales and waters sank,
God spake to Noah to build an ark.
Out of a burning bush God said
to Mose [sic] "*Go lead thy men away*".
As he was bid he did not doubt
And saved the Israelites from doom.
As it was in the aged past,
So it is in the present day.
For years untold the son's [sic] *of man,*
The Africans of Native birth
Have been oppressed and called, "Jim Fish";
Kicked like dogs and called the brutes;
Sent to jail without fair trial;
With badges of oppression heaped;
Dismissed from farms before time's due;
Taken for beasts and shot to die;
Bribed and tipped to wreck their own;
Enslaved under disguise and taxed
To swell the coffers we know not
And feed the orphans of strange men.

'To Champion son of George God spake:
"Go lead thy men". He left the mines
To lead the world-wide ICU
Ere since he has worked unflinchingly
And is the terror of the day.
Etc.'

(ICU poem, c. 1928)

Of the twenty-seven ICU branches known to have been founded up to 1925 some twenty, almost three-quarters of the total, were in the Cape Province. Even at the time of the 1925 Conference, after the transfer of the headquarters to Johannesburg and after nearly two years of activity in the Transvaal and Natal and longer in the Orange Free State, approximately two-thirds of the thirty or so branches then in existence were still in the Cape. Transvaal by then had eight, perhaps ten, branches, but in Natal the movement had spread no further than Pietermaritzburg – and that only recently – from Durban, while the Orange Free State boasted a solitary branch in Bloemfontein. In appearance the union seemed to remain dominated by a single province. However, that two-thirds of the branches in early 1926 were still situated in the Cape of Good Hope obscured the essentially unsatisfactory situation of the ICU there. If anything it was deteriorating, as is made clear by the General Secretary's report of his tour of inspection at the beginning of 1926.[1] East London seemed to provide the only exception to the general malaise, being described as 'easily the foremost Branch of the Organisation as far as active membership, systematic administration, and efficiency is [*sic*] concerned'. The report on Cape Town is ambiguous, but leaves the impression that all was not well there: it 'has encouragingly increased its membership, though at the cost of consistent effort owing to the strong and numerous counter-attractions and propaganda of other organised bodies . . .' Kimberley 'is practically defunct', Port Elizabeth 'in a deplorable state'. Of the small branches Adelaide, which in 1925 had displayed a most remarkable zeal, was in the throes of a minor financial scandal that was one of the factors leading to the suspension of the Provincial Secretary, James Dippa; Somerset East was 'on the decline'; Bedford was 'defunct'; and King William's Town was 'in the unenviable position of having a monthly income just about sufficient to discharge its monthly liabilities'.

It appears from La Guma's report that the most promising branches early in 1926 were Johannesburg – 'one of the most important Branches of the Organisation' – and Durban – 'a stronghold of the Organisation in Natal . . . progressing famously'. The situation in Bloemfontein was less satisfactory. 'Matters are taking a decided upward trend and with careful supervision by the responsible officials Bloemfontein can be expected to regain its former prestige within the year'. Clearly this was an optimistic forecast of the future progress of a branch that had had its trials – the scandal associated with the April riots and the embezzlement charges against Elias and Mancoe.

In the months following the General Secretary's report, the period during which Kadalie was under ban and the ICU was in the doldrums, Bloemfontein did not, it would appear, justify La Guma's optimism, and even the Rand was disappointing. Kadalie attributed the drop in support to the fact that he was cooped up in Johannesburg, but this would not account for the lukewarmness of Johannesburg itself, which was noticeable even before the ban.[2] It is apparent that the union was living – ban or no ban – a hand-to-mouth existence, dependent upon current income and with no reserves.[3] The only consolation during the period of stagnation was the increasing prosperity of the branch in Durban, from which Champion reported in May 1926 that the membership was 'going very high'.[4]

Kadalie's letters during the months of his ban were one long complaint about money – falling revenue and mounting debts.[5] Funds were so short that 'dependable branches' were authorized to meet liabilities from what they could collect themselves, by-passing Head Office.[6] This appealed so little to James Dippa that he sued the union for arrears of salary. It was for this piece of disloyalty, as well as for the Adelaide scandal, that he was suspended. There was also the charge that he was so busy with a land settlement company of which he was secretary that he was neglecting his ICU duties.[7] He was replaced by Maduna who was moved from the Orange Free State.

One reason for financial stringency was the stubborn refusal of the Cape Town members of the National Council to consent to the transfer of the union's fixed deposit of £400 from Cape Town to Johannesburg, where it was needed as a security against an overdraft. It was impossible to get a quorum for a National Council meeting in Johannesburg because the President and the other Cape Town members refused to budge. Eventually, with the prior agreement of the non-Cape Town members, La Guma was sent from Johannesburg and Champion from Durban to make a quorum in Cape Town and, apparently, after some persuasion these two got Gumbs to sign the necessary documents. By the end of July the union had an overdraft of £268.[8] It gave only temporary relief.

The National Secretary relied increasingly upon Durban. 'I desire you,' he wrote in July 1926 to Champion, 'that you make special efforts to raise a considerable sum of money and must be banked [*sic*] before the end of the month . . . But what is desired is that you as a comrade whom one can rely upon, is whether you can raise a substantial sum, either by loan or otherwise which must be credited against Head Office of the Organisation.'[9] In September he wrote: 'While thanking you for the banking made to-day according to your telegram, I shall be glad if you will make special effort to raise another £50 . . .'[10] When Kadalie challenged the Government's ban in Natal, the legal charges were borne very largely by the Durban branch.[11] An appeal to members to make donations to cover the cost of his defence seems to have brought in only small sums from the branches. Durban, then, was comparatively wealthy, but there were limits to the demands that could be met. There were occasions when the Natal Provincial Secretary lost patience, since there were calls enough in the city itself upon the revenues of the branch. In October he complained that 'officials are more concerned with clean up to date offices with all modern conveniences more than the rights of their fellow workers'.[12] This was not rebellion, but a fit of pique. The feeling that Natal was bearing an unfair burden remained buried, but it came to the surface again in 1928. In the meantime Head Office's appetite for money continued unappeased. In December Kadalie was still asking Durban to 'help us with funds'.[13]

That Durban became the bastion of the ICU in 1926 and disposed of an income that no other branch – even Johannesburg – could match, may be attributed to the tireless efforts of A. W. G. Champion, who, though Provincial Secretary of Natal, unconstitutionally ran the Durban branch in person. An indefatigable correspondent, possessed of a genius for making himself unpleasant to those in authority and for fastening upon and exploiting grievances, Champion was for ever sending off letters ingratiating at one extreme, hectoring at the other, to government officials (including the Chief Native Commissioner of Natal), the Durban Native Affairs Department, members of the Durban Joint Council of Europeans and Natives, and employers, demanding attention and redress of grievances.[14] He took the view that the Native Affairs Department of the municipality worked hand-in-glove with the employers, whose interests were always upheld against the complaints of Black workers,[15] while the Joint Council he contemptuously dismissed as 'a non-Corporation Department of the Municipal Native Affairs'.[16] Litigious by disposition and equipped with no mean knowledge of the law himself, the Provincial Secretary had frequent recourse to the courts. He had many undoubted successes.

'It may be necessary,' Champion wrote in later years, 'to put down on record some of the important cases that were placed by the ICU in the hands of Messrs Cowley and Cowley, solicitors of Durban, for the ruling of the Courts. These cases had to be taken to the Supreme Court and even the Appelate Division . . .'[17] There follows a list of successes, including the right to establish the African Workers' Club in Durban; the removal from the pass that a Black employee was obliged to carry of the so-called character column, where an unfavourable comment by an employer (who might, for example, object to ICU membership) could ruin the chances of further employment; the abolition of the night curfew for Black residents; the ending of compulsory disinfecting of Blacks (known as 'bodily dipping of natives') entering Durban; the exemption of Black women from the pass system; the restraining of the police from summarily demanding the production of passes; and the discontinuation of the practice in the magistrate's court of trying in batches Blacks charged with similar offences and of using policemen as interpreters. Besides the major cases listed there was a host of small ones,[18] arising from clashes between individuals and the police or employers. Most of the minor cases seem to have concerned the dismissal of workers without pay in lieu of notice.[19] Large sums of money went to Cowley and Cowley.[20] As Champion put it in the early days of his association with the firm, 'Our Legal Advisers charge money for every word they give and for every letter they receive and read.' However, he continued, 'Any how this firm is the only firm in Natal that is friendly with the natives.'[21] There can be no doubt that Cecil Cowley incurred considerable odium among his White fellow citizens and suffered loss of ordinary business. Champion paid him a glowing tribute at the

Seventh Annual Conference of the ICU in Durban in April 1927.[22] Kadalie, from the very beginning, was distinctly cooler.[23] During the whole of 1926, he later alleged, though probably with some exaggeration, the firm received over £2 000 from the branch at Durban, and perhaps as much again in 1927.[24]

While Champion was active with his lawsuits in Durban, two other energetic officials, Keable 'Mote, who had replaced Maduna as Provincial Secretary in Bloemfontein, and Thomas Mbeki, Provincial Secretary of the Transvaal, were busy, delivering fiery speeches[25] and courting arrest.[26] Since they tilled a less fertile corner of the vineyard than did Champion and lacked his instinct for the promising lawsuit, their successes were less solid and their contribution to the ICU purse less lavish than his. The impression is inescapable that both men – each termed at one time or another the 'Lion of the North' – modelled themselves on Kadalie, without, however, having his intelligence or subtlety of intellect. There is something in what C. R. Swart, the Nationalist MLA for Ladybrand,[27] who was shrewd enough to see that Kadalie was no fool, had to say of 'Mote in 1927 during the debate on the Native Administration Bill: 'a worthless young native who apes everything Kadalie says'.[28] Nevertheless, he and Mbeki had much success in drumming up support. In the four months from October 1926 to January 1927, 'Mote opened nine branches in the Orange Free State and Mbeki fourteen in the Transvaal.[29]

In January 1927, the ICU was claiming a membership of 57 760.[30] This was an advance of 17 760 on its previous claim, of March 1926.[31] Although Durban branch accounted for more than half the increase, it is clear that after Kadalie's successful appeal in October 1926 the union escaped from its lethargy and many new branches were founded, though it is unlikely that his flouting of the ban had much more to do with the ICU's revival than the imposition of the ban had with its stagnation. There are two extant branch lists for 1927. The first, a list of those which transferred money to Head Office in the period May-October 1927,[32] contains 66 names. The second list,[33] which gives the names of those branches that transferred money to Head Office during the period January–December 1927, adds a further 22. Whereas two-thirds of the branches in April 1926, had been in the Cape Province, now, although the Cape still had nineteen of the branches – which are more or less equally shared among the provinces (Natal 24, Orange Free State 22, and Transvaal 23) – in terms of income to Head Office, it was the least important province. The financial support given to Head Office by the branches, province by province, was as follows in 1927: Cape Province £441/9/8 (3,6%); Orange Free State £1 052/4/2 (9,1%); Transvaal £3 062/19/8 (26,1%); and Natal £7 138/8/6 (61,0%): Total £11 695/2/0.[34]

The Cape Province never escaped from that decline that had been noticed by James La Guma on his tour of inspection early in 1926. 'What is wrong with the Cape?' asked *The Worker's Herald* of 6 April 1927. Recalling the past strength of the ICU there, it continued, 'But of a sudden, the Cape has made a halt, I was almost tempted to say, it is dead.' The writer (probably Clements Kadalie) seemed to think that the cause really lay in the negligence of officials, including Provincial Secretaries and other members of the National Council, and in an outbreak of tribalism. 'About three or four members of the National Council run their districts by appealing to tribal jealousies.' A new policy and new men were called for. The sick man of the ICU failed to respond to treatment. In his report of November 1927,[35] A. W. G. Champion, then Acting National Secretary, described the Cape as 'very slack', Port Elizabeth as 'dead'. On the same occasion, a meeting of the National Council, R. de Norman, Provincial Secretary for the Western Province, 'gave his reasons for Cape Town being slack, among them the collection of National Levy [*sic*] on the promise that a Hall would be built for Cape Town but instead a Hall was provided for Johannesburg'. It is evident that by 1927 the ICU had lost a good deal of support in the docks.[36] The assumption may safely be made that the union never recovered, in the city of its birth, from the removal of Head Office to Johannesburg in 1926. There is good reason to suppose that the use to which the ICU funds were put in 1926 rankled with the Cape Town members as late as 1928.[37] Perhaps, besides, the movement became too Black for a membership that was largely Coloured.[38]

The decline in importance of the area where the ICU gained its first support was accompanied by a pronounced shift from town to country in relative significance. Until 1926 the organization had a discernible urban bias. By the end of 1925 each of the eleven biggest towns in South Africa (measured by size of European population) had an ICU branch – Johannesburg, Cape Town, Durban Pretoria, Port Elizabeth, East London, Bloemfontein, Pietermaritzburg, Germiston, Kimberley, and Benoni. In addition to these branches, almost two-fifths of the total, another six were situated in towns with a White population of more than two thousand. The evidence of branch location is confirmed by the 1925 Report of the Commissioner of Police: 'A few educated natives have been busy in the towns making inflammatory speeches . . . It is noteworthy that these pseudo-enlightened natives confine their attention to the towns, probably because they would get very little sympathy or encouragement from the kraal natives.' Indeed, giving evidence before the Economic and Wage Commission of 1925, the union stated explicitly that most of its members were 'drawn from urban and de-tribalised Natives and also from the Coloured workers'.[39]

While it is not true that the ICU in its early years was exclusively urban – for the Eastern Cape branches probably had a strong, even predominant, agricultural membership – by mid-1927 the rural support had been greatly enlarged and extended to the other provinces of South Africa and, in so far as new support emerged in the Cape Province, it too was among country dwellers. Contemporary observers were well aware of the change that overtook the ICU. 'While the movement was confined to the towns comparatively little notice was taken of it,' wrote a correspondent in *The Times* of 10 October 1927. 'With its spread among the farm labourers it caused a great stir.' Only a third of the hundred odd branches known to have existed in 1927 were in largish towns (those with a

White population of more than 2 000), and most of those urban branches drew a proportion of their support from the surrounding countryside.[40]

It is scarcely surprising that, once the ICU had broken out of the Cape and established a footing in Durban, Johannesburg, and Bloemfontein, it should permeate the countryside and become a rural protest movement. It is not easy, however, to determine the precise nature of the rural support for the union, since not all Blacks in the farming areas had the same grievances. The rural population fell into three categories – subsistence farmers on land not owned by Whites, supplementing their income with wages earned away from home; squatters and share-croppers on White-owned land, who farmed independently upon payment in cash or kind to the landowner; and labourers receiving wages in cash or kind and/or receiving the right to grow some crops and keep some cattle on their employer's land. The second group tended to fade into the third. Frequently the man who was pledged only to a relatively short period of labour service each year, say three months (as was usual in the Orange Free State and the Transvaal), was termed a squatter, while the man who was pledged to an extended period, say six months (the usual period in Natal), was termed a labour tenant.[41] These different categories and sub-categories had their proper grievances. At the same time there were burdens common to all. Among them was the poll tax, which, as the goad that drove many unwilling Blacks into employment and kept many others in debt servitude to farmers who paid it for them,[42] was resented. Until 1925 the tax was much more burdensome in the Orange Free State and the Transvaal than in the Cape and Natal, an injustice that was righted by the Natives Taxation and Development Act of 1925, which equalized it in the four provinces. It might be supposed that this Act promoted the cause of the ICU in the Cape (in so far as it did spread there) and Natal, where the tax was levelled upwards, but it seems unlikely that it added significantly to the general discontent.[43]

Although the unfairness of such an ungraduated tax is manifest, it still cannot be compared as a source of unrest with the widespread, indeed almost universal, shortage of land. The ideal of most Blacks was landed independence, an ideal strengthened by the closing of avenues to economic and social advancement in the towns by the industrial colour bar and territorial segregation. Land hunger was undoubtedly acute in the 1920s and gained a new importance in 1926–1927 as a result of the publication and discussion of the Natives Land Act (Amendment) Bill, which was part of General Hertzog's 'package deal' aimed at solving the 'Native problem'. The publication of the Bill had two quite contradictory effects: it heightened fears and it raised hopes. One of the aims of the Bill was to reduce squatting in the broadest sense of the term. If Africans were to be segregated in their own areas, they could gain admission to European areas only as wage labourers, not as independent or quasi-independent farmers raising their own crops and keeping their own cattle. There was, however, a more rational and more worthy motive as well. Squatters and labour tenants were neither good farmers nor good labourers as a rule. With their obstinate attachment to cattle as a mere measure of wealth, they overgrazed the land and they gave their services grudgingly and inefficiently. However, whatever the motives behind the intention, the object was indubitably to reduce labour tenancies and squatting.

The Land Amendment Bill aimed at completing the process begun by the original Natives Land Act of 1913, the purpose of which had been to put a stop to Black cash and share cropping tenancies in White areas and to restrict independent Black farmers to 'scheduled land' (tribal land already reserved for Blacks together with land to be set aside by some future arrangement). It is clear that the 1913 Act failed to put an end to what was called 'Kaffir farming' on White-owned land. In the Cape Province the restrictions placed by the Act on Black landholding were declared *ultra vires* on the ground that they were in conflict with the property qualifications for the franchise, while in the Orange Free State the offending tenancies were left to run out and in the other two provinces White landlords were even permitted to renew them.[44] Moreover, a good deal of illegal squatting, condoned by the Native Affairs Department, went on.[45] The Chief Native Commissioner, Natal, estimated in 1927 that in his province alone there were then still 185 000 to 200 000 Blacks paying rent on European-owned land, 95 000 of them on land owned by Whites but not farmed by them.[46]

The treatment and conditions of service of labour tenants varied very widely. Some received no wages at all, but only land (for example, in the northern Transvaal, northern Natal, and Zululand); others could earn as much as nearly £30 for a 300-day working year (in 1928–1929).[47] The amount of land provided also varied a great deal, as did the length of service required. Another variation was in the demands made upon the services of the tenant's family. Yet another was in the degree of humanity displayed by employers. Cases of cruelty were reported in the press not infrequently. 'In this country how many Africans,' asked *The Workers' Herald*, 'are being ill-treated on the farms month after month, plus receiving sjamboks from European farmers but the world knows nothing about it?'[48] Many farmers were reluctant to bind themselves to written contracts and tenants complained that promises were not honoured.[49] 'Slavery' was the word often on the lips of Blacks when speaking of labour tenancies, and sometimes perhaps this was not an exaggeration.[50]

Despite the disadvantages of labour tenancies Blacks preferred them to wage labour, and they were unwilling to move off White land. The reserves were for the most part grievously over-populated in relation to what the poor farming methods employed there could produce, and, in any case, labour tenants were frequently living on the ancestral land that had been taken from them and was the only home they had ever known. If anything, the trend since the 1913 Land Act had not been towards the reserves, but away from them, into the under-utilized White farms.[51] Now, however, the situation of the labour tenants was deteriorating and the very existence of the tenancies under threat. In 1926 the

Masters and Servants Law (Transvaal and Natal) Amendment Act brought the labour tenancy contract within the scope of the Masters and Servants Laws of these two provinces, and this was obviously not done with the interests of the tenant in mind.[52] Now the Land Amendment Bill intended to lengthen the period of labour service from 90 to 180 days and impose new obligations upon the tenant's family, without giving the protection of a registered contract except in the case of tenancies longer than 180 days.[53] What was more, labour tenancies, as well as cash and share-cropping tenancies, were to be reduced in number and Black farmers forced to become a rural proletariat or be pushed back into the over-crowded reserves or driven into the towns. Here was a new grievance in the making, though there are indications that farmers were beginning to turn labour tenants off their land anyway because of their reluctance to accommodate large numbers of cattle.[54]

If the proposed Bill added to fears, it also brought hopes. For it promised to 'release' more land for Black purchase, and undoubtedly many thought they would be beneficiaries of land redistribution. In Natal, just as White farmers were frightened that they were going to be expropriated, so landless Blacks looked forward to holding farms of their own. If pessimism could cause restlessness, so could optimism.[55] There is no reason to suppose that the ICU was directly responsible for raising such hopes. It does not seem to have given particular emphasis to a demand for land, though the land question naturally came up in the speeches of its officials. There is no evidence at all to support the suggestion that propagandists made rash promises of land to their eager followers.[56] An examination of speeches that must have reached mainly rural audiences reveals that they were composed largely of general complaints about the political and economic situation of Blacks, demands for higher agricultural wages, vague talk of the recovery of freedom and ill-defined threats of the dire consequences of government policy, but certainly no explicit promises of land. If they had a common theme, it was the virtues and value of organization, of building the ICU into a large and powerful body.[57]

One wonders what it was that the thousands of farm workers who flocked to pay their enrolment fees and collect their red membership cards expected to get. Perhaps they were simply buying a promise of a better life.[58] It is difficult to believe that they appreciated the aims and methods of trade unionism. However, if the finer points of industrial organization were lost on them, they knew where the shoe pinched. Everywhere farmers complained that their labourers were getting 'more and more cheeky', and cheekiness seems to have taken the form chiefly of a demand for higher wages.[59] The steady increase over the years in the cost of living had imposed a growing burden that was not much relieved by the deflation that began in 1920. The new protectionist legislation introduced by the Pact Government, at least partly in the interests of White labour, pressed hard upon people whose slender means were depleted by the higher costs of blankets and other imported goods.[60] However, it was not so much because they had to pay more for things that they were accustomed to buy that Blacks were in greater difficulties, as because they were compelled to buy a much wider range of commodities as their habits and tastes were modified by contact with a different civilization.[61]

It was among the wage labourers and labour tenants that ICU propaganda gained most response. While it is true that subsistence farmers depended to some degree upon cash earnings, dissatisfaction with the amount of money that could be earned was, curiously, in their case an industrial rather than a rural problem, since they derived their cash income from contract labour in the mines, factories, railways, and docks. The ICU was affected only to the extent that it had a following in such industries, and since its influence within the compounds was in fact marginal, the union had little contact with the Blacks from the 'territories'. Within these 'territories' themselves it encountered the conservatism of people and chiefs. The ICU leaders had an understandably ambiguous attitude towards the traditional rulers. On the one hand, chiefs were thought to be relics of the past, out of touch with modern conditions, reactionary, and subservient.[62] On the other hand, there remained a considerable fund of respect for them, the ancient rulers of the people and the custodians of their traditions. Undoubtedly the ICU would have preferred winning their support to earning their displeasure. Kadalie expressed the ambivalent ICU attitude in his report for 1925. He considered it 'of vital importance that we should get in touch with the territories, for is it not there that the Chamber of Mines has a reservoir of cheap and docile labour? The sooner we educate the chiefs and their people that our trade union movement in urban areas does not suggest disloyalty to constituted Government or any disloyalty to the chiefs themselves, but is calculated on a 'bread and butter' struggle – for ourselves, our women and children – a holy and noble struggle – we shall then be nearing our goal to economic emancipation . . .'[63]

There were instances, here and there, of chiefs adhering to the ICU. Chief Diniso Nkosi of Barberton in the Transvaal was responsible, according to Thomas Mbeki, for bringing into the union 1 900 members at one go. This chief took with him to the 1927 Conference at Durban the greetings of nine other chiefs from his part of the country.[64] Elsewhere the chiefs, either because of pressure from the authorities or because of their personal distaste for glib young men from the towns, were suspicious and hostile. The Paramount Chief of the Zulus, Solomon ka Dinuzulu, denounced the union in August 1927, much to the approval of the Rev. J. L. Dube's *Ilanga lase Natal*,[65] which complained that the ICU leaders gobbled up money and fostered racial hatred. Chief Swayimana of New Hanover District, Natal, was more explicit. 'I heard,' he said, 'that there are people who go about to see what they can pick up. They are thieves and have got their knowledge from other thieves. Who the original thieves were I do not know'.[66] New Hanover was one district where there was no ICU branch, and it is significant that the union as a rule failed to gain a firm footing in the reserves. This failure may have been due to the attitude of the chiefs or to the persistence of communal land holding or to the absence of large numbers of men working on contract. Whatever the reason, there was only one branch in Zululand, at Eshowe;[67] none in the Transkeian Territories apart from the one at Kokstad in Griqualand East;[68] none, except briefly in Middledrift, in the Ciskei reserves of Middledrift, Keiskamahoek, Glen Grey, and Herschel; and only late and ephemeral branches in the districts of Harrismith, where the Witzieshoek reserve was situated, and Thaba 'Nchu, where the other small Orange Free State reserve was. Nor did the ICU penetrate into the northern Transvaal – Pietersburg, Pilgrim's Rest, Potgietersrus, and Zoutpansberg – where Blacks pursued on White-owned land a way of life that dated back to before the European conquest and where incomes were supplemented, not by work on White farms, but in the mines or domestic service.[69]

In Basutoland, where Keable 'Mote began proselytizing in October 1927, it is said that Chief Jonathan Malapo Moshoeshoe gave him 'full permission to organise' and that seven branches were opened.[70] Since almost the whole of the Protectorate fell under customary tenure, the ICU protest there must have been different in character from that in the Union of South Africa and may have been political rather than economic. It was evidently a nine days' wonder. In contrast, the expansion into Southern Rhodesia was more spontaneous and made a deeper impression. While its appeal was felt primarily in the towns, notably Bulawayo and Salisbury, the movement also had an impact upon the countryside, especially among the landless. The Southern Rhodesian Government was alarmed, expelled the ICU organizer sent by Kadalie, and, in order to facilitate control, sought additional powers that gave rise to some ineffective criticism in the House of Commons.[71]

In its rapid spread throughout South Africa the ICU was not without rivals. The African National Congress, in July 1927, toyed with the idea of setting up for its members an African Labour Congress, obviously modelled on the ICU, that would sectionalize workers according to their trade. In Natal the Social and Economic Workers' Union of Africa was founded in August 1927, at Pietermaritzburg. The Transkei was pre-empted by a more serious competitor, the ingenious and romantic Dr Wellington, *alias* Elias Buthelezi, a former pupil of Lovedale. Representing himself as an American, he propagated the doctrines of the Universal Negro Improvement Society, though he seems to have been a free-lance.[72]

Dr Wellington was not merely anti-White, but also anti-missionary. Since the ICU, too, was widely suspected of being both, some missionaries and other churchmen warned their people against joining the union or dismissed ICU members from their employment.[73] The well-known Catholic missionary, Fr Bernard Huss of Mariannhill in Natal, was alleged to have referred to the ICU in the course of a newspaper interview as a 'deadly threat to the peace of the country'. Although he subsequently claimed that he had been misreported and that he had 'frequently emphasised and defended the good points of the ICU', he was not spared the taunts of *The Workers' Herald*, which called him a 'political parson', who would be spending his time 'more profitably, nobly and Christianly by agitating for the abolition of the Pass Laws, and all other iniquitous legislation affecting both European and non-European workers of South Africa, than by rushing into print with foundationless and unworthy political rigmaroles'.[74]

The farmers, of course, clamoured for action by the authorities. The ICU itself admitted that 'a few inexperienced young organisers of the ICU are not very circumspect in their choice of language'. However, there is much truth in its claim that the farmers did 'not so much object to the alleged improper expressions of certain ICU organisers. These farmers are against the movement as a whole, whether its organisers are reasonable or unreasonable men.'[75] Not all ICU speakers were wild men. 'I can vouch for the fact that there was no sedition or insulting language made use of,' said one police witness of an ICU meeting in October 1927.[76] 'My text,' said the Branch Secretary of Vredefort, OFS, 'was: "This is the Hour of Peace and Fair Wages to all Workers in South Africa."'[77] 'I am trying with all my level best,' declared the ICU man at Ixopo, Natal, 'to use moderation and diplomacy when Europeans are present, even if they are absent, because I know that they send in the "watch dogs" to attend out meetings.'[78]

As early as June 1927 farmers' associations passed resolutions calling upon members to take action against labourers who belonged to the ICU.[79] At a congress specially summoned in August to consider 'the ICU danger', the Natal Agricultural Union resolved to take measures (possibly in the form of a Farmers' Vigilance Association) for the protection of farmers 'against unjust and unreasonable action of trade union organisations and communistic bodies', to send a deputation to wait on the Prime Minister and to request a probihition of meetings unauthorized by a magistrate.[80] There was large-scale eviction of tenants and even reports of huts being burnt down.[81] Not unnaturally the Government was not in favour of eviction, but preferred to use a new weapon then at hand, the recently passed Native Administration Act, which was at least partly intended to fulfil the purpose of the abortive Sedition Bill. In August 1927, the Secretary for Native Affairs warned the ICU that the Act would be brought into operation on 1 September and that it had better exercise restraint.[82] At the local level it was common for Native Commissioners to order ICU organizers out of their districts[83] and for municipalities to close their locations to union officials or to prosecute them for contravention of location regulations.[84] The sort of harassment to which branches were subjected can be seen from a report made in 1928 by the secretary of a Transvaal district that included Volksrust and Wakkerstroom. Members were evicted, prosecuted, and denied passes, and the police rigorously enforced the pass laws. 'This persecution,' the report continued, 'culminated in large sums of money being spent in defending and assisting victimised members in order to keep their confidence in the Union. During March of this year, the evictions reached the climax, just in the critical time of the year. Large numbers of families were forced to leave their crops and filled the public roads. Funds were much crippled. The Municipalities of both the towns restricted entrance into their locations of natives ejected from farms; and things grew from bad to worse, since these families had nowhere to live in the districts . . .[85]

Farmers were not uniformly hostile and self-righteous. 'Farmers had themselves to blame,' declared one at an Orange Free State agricultural congress at the end of September 1927, 'if natives complained that they were treated like slaves.'[86] Nor was the ICU agitation without positive effect. The Reitz farmers in July 1927 not only recommended eviction, but also proposed the drawing up of a uniform scale of payment.[87] The Orange Free State farmers composed a resolution to be submitted to the South African Agricultural Union congress calling for 'a uniform system of contracts with labourers'. Clearly what the farmers had in mind was the *worst* conditions of service that would find general acceptance among employers, since the resolution went on to suggest that 'in various areas, districts or circles conferences should be held to fix a uniform *maximum* wage for labourers for the different farming operations'.[88] Nevertheless, it can be assumed that a uniform system of contracts and even a uniform maximum wage would have given many labourers better terms than they were getting at the time. At all events the ICU welcomed the resolution.[89]

White resentment sometimes erupted into violence, especially in Natal. At Bergville soldiers broke into the ICU office and burnt books and papers.[90] Ae Pietermaritzburg on New Year's Eve 1927 the windows of the ICU's club wert smashed, but it was members of the club who were arrested by the police – for breach of the peace.[91] At Greytown, Weenen, and Kranskop, in March 1928, the union's offices were burnt. The rage of the White mob is said to have been aroused by the desecration of the Greytown cemetery in February 1928, by one Gwaza, thought to be a member of the ICU. The alleged culprit was in fact a renegade from the ICU who had attempted in the previous year to form a rival union, the Northern Trade Native Union [*sic*].[92] ICU officials were sceptical of his guilt. One thought it impossible 'for one man to pull down approximately 100 tomb stones in one night – or, rather, in a few hours' time', and he evidently suspected White provocation in the shape of a 'Black-hand gang'. He further complained that the police were dilatory at Greytown in providing protection for the ICU office.[93] What added to the indignation of the union was that the Weenen arsonists were sentenced to an absurd one pound fine.[94]

The invasion of the countryside paid the ICU enormous short-term rewards in both membership and income, but it saddled the union with insoluble problems that remained after there was no more money to part with. As the District Secretary of Volksrust and Wakkerstroom put it, 'The above branches are supported by agricultural workers whose labouring conditions and wages are such that they cannot pay their dues regularly weekly or monthly. The only period during which farm squatters handle money at all is between the months of July and September, after gathering their scanty crops.'[95] The ICU income of 1927 was to a considerable degree a non-recurring levy on peasants who wanted immediate relief. To use an appropriate metaphor, it was a windfall.

Notes

1. General Secretary's Report of Inspection of Branches 6 March 1926 (F 1926/6).
2. Ibid.
3. J. La Guma to C. Kadalie 5 February 1926 (F/Copies of Letters (1926/44).
4. A. W. G. Champion to J. La Guma 14 May 1926 (F 1926/12).
5. C. Kadaile to A. W. G. Champion 17 May and 22 July 1926 (F 1926/13 and 34); National Council Executive Bureau to ICU Branches 30 July 1926 (F 1926/37).
6. National Council Executive Bureau to ICU Branches 30 July 1926 (F 1926/37); National Council Executive Bureau Report, July 1926 (F 1926/38).
7. National Council Executive Bureau to Members of the National Council 28 October 1926 (F 1926/48).
8. National Council Executive Bureau Report July 1926 (F 1926/38).
9. C. Kadalie to A. W. G. Champion 22 July 1926 (F 1926/34).
10. C. Kadalie to A. W. G. Champion 2 September 1926 (F 1926/43). The money was needed for legal expenses in connection with Kadalie's attempt to obtain a certificate of exemption from the operation of the pass laws.
11. National Council Executive Bureau to Members of the National Council 21 October 1926 (F 1926/46); National Council Executive Bureau Report, July 1926 (F 1926/38); Expenditure Durban Branch, August and September 1926 (F 1926/41 and 44); J. La Guma to A. W. G. Champion 5 November 1926 (F 1926/52).
12. A. W. G. Champion to C. Kadalie 21 October 1926 (F 1926/45).
13. C. Kadalie to A. W. G. Champion 29 December 1926 (F 1926/68).
14. A. W. G. Champion Letter-book 1925-26 (Wits CP) and F/Copies of Letters (1926) *passim.*
15. A. W. G. Champion to J. D. Taylor 15 February 1926 (F/Joint Council File/6).
16. A. W. G. Champion to Secretary, Durban Joint Council 22 June 1926 (F/Joint Council File/4).
17. An undated fragment of an apologia in autograph, from internal evidence 1929 or 1930 (Forman Collection, identified only as '4').
18. An account of Cowley and Cowley of 31 January 1927 (Forman Collection) lists 69 cases, mostly against employers, including Durban Corporation.
19. Cf, for example, A. W. G. Champion to Registration Officer, Native Affairs Department 12 February 1926 (F Copies of Letters (1926)/54).
20. Sums paid to Cowley and Cowley (in round figures) – March 1926 – £73 (J. La Guma to A. W. G. Champion 4 May 1926, F 1926/64b); April, 1926 – £20 (ibid.); August, 1926 – £29 (Expenditure of Durban Branch, August 1926, F 1926/41); September 1926 – £100 (Expenditure of Durban Branch, September 1926, F 1926/44); October 1926 – £189 (Expenditure of Durban Branch, October 1926, F 1926/49); November 1926 – £100 (General Funds Accounts, Durban, April 1927, F 1927/16b); December 1926 – £91 (Accounts submitted by Cowley and Cowley, Forman Collection); January 1927 – £445 (Account of Cowley and Cowley 31 January 1927, Forman Collection); March 1927 – £200 (General Funds Account, Durban, April 1927, F 1927/16b); April 1927 – £327 (ibid.).

21. A. W. G. Champion to C. Kadalie 12 May 1926 (F 1926/11).
22. *The Workers' Herald* 17 May 1927.
23. C. Kadalie to A. W. G. Champion 17 May 1926 (F 1926/13).
24. Proposals for Curtailing Expenditure at Head Office, Report to the National Council by the General Secretary (C. Kadalie), n.d. (probably January 1928).
25. Cf. articles by them in *The Workers' Herald* 27 March 1926.
26. In July 1926, Mbeki was arrested and charged with entering the location and organizing a procession in Middelburg, for which he was fined £3 (National Council Executive Bureau, Report, 1926, F 1926/38). 'Mote was one of the first to be arrested under the Native Administration Act of 1927 (T. D. Mweli Skota, op. cit., 214).
27. Later Minister of Justice, later still first State President of the Republic of South Africa.
28. Union of South Africa, *Debates of the House of Assembly*, 1927, Col. 3009.
29. *The Workers' Herald* 15 February 1927.
30. C. Kadalie to Secretary for Labour 19 January 1927 (B/Wits).
31. Investigation and Report; the Natal Provincial and Durban Offices of the ICU 4 April 1928, Annexure F (F 1928/24).
32. Statement showing Head Office Income and Expenditure 1 May to 31 October 1927 (F 1927/107).
33. Branch Transfers and Requisitions, Year ended 31 December 1927 (F 1927/107).
34. Ibid.
35. Minutes of the National Council November, 1927 (F 1927/124), p. 13.
36. Ibid., 14.
37. Undated and untitled memoir of W. G. Ballinger (*c.* 1953) (B/Wits).
38. An examination of the names of those subscribing to the National Levy seems to show that the majority of the Cape Town members were Coloured men and women (*The Workers' Herald* 1925 *passim*). Afrikaans speakers were not catered for in *The Workers' Herald* after the first five issues in 1923, and the Conferences of the union were conducted almost exclusively in English.
39. Union of South Africa, *Annual Departmental Reports No. 6, Covering the Period 1925-1926* (UG 6 – 1927) – Report of the Commissioner of Police for the Calendar Year 1925, 72-3; *The Workers' Herald* 2 April and 15 May 1925; *Evidence to the Economic and Wage Commission*, 2, 19.
40. *Evidence to the Economic and Wage Commission*, 29; Union of South Africa, *Report of the Select Committee on the Subject of the Union Native Council Bill, Coloured Persons Rights Bill, Representation of Natives in Parliament Bill and Natives Land (Amendment) Bill* (S.C. 10 – 1927) – '*The Select Committee on the Subject of Native Bills*', 23.
41. Cf. the evidence of J. C. Gilfillan of the Transvaal Agricultural Union to the Select Committee on the 'Native Bills' (ibid., 203).
42. Cf. Union of South Africa, *Report of the Native Economic Commission 1930–1932*, 195.
43. Cf. Union of South Africa, '*The Select Committee on the Subject of Native Bills*', 39.
44. Robertson, H. M., 'The economic condition of the rural natives' in Schapera, I., 1934, ed., *Western Civilisation and the Natives of South Africa; Studies in Culture Contact*, London, 144.
45. Union of South Africa, '*The Select Committee on the Subject of Native Bills*', 118.
46. *The Natal Witness* 24 November 1927.
47. H. M. Robertson, loc. cit., 153.
48. *The Workers' Herald* 27 March 1926.
49. *The Workers' Herald* 31 December 1928.
50. Cf. evidence of R. D. Doyle of the Transvaal Agricultural Union to the Select Committee on the 'Native Bills', 209–10.
51. H. M. Robertson, loc. cit., 152–4.

Holtby, A. & McWilliam, J. eds., *Letters to a friend* (London, Collins 1937). Reproduced with the permission of her literary executor, Paul Berry.

Mabel Palmer – Killie Campbell Africana Museum, Durban

52. In its passage through the House of Assembly it was criticized by members of the Labour Party (Union of South Africa, *Debates of the House of Assembly*, 1926, Col. 1282–1286.
53. Union of South Africa, '*The Select Committee on the Subject of Native Bills*', 151.
54. Cf. ibid., 43.
55. Cf. evidence of W. Elliot of the Natal Agricultural Union to the Select Committee on the 'Native Bills' (ibid., 100, 102).
56. 'For one shilling initial membership and 3d. per week, farms were promised to all and sundry.' Ballinger, W. G., 'Iseeyou', *The Nusas*, November 1928, 21.
57. Cf. speeches by Simon Elias and Keable 'Mote in the Orange Free State (*The Frankforter* 3 February, 1927) and by Alex Maduna at Graaff-Reinet (unidentified newspaper cutting, *c*. June 1927, B/UCT). Cf. also Coka, G., The story of Gilbert Coka of the Zulu tribe of Natal, South Africa, in Perham, M., 1936, ed., *Ten Africans*, London, 206.
58. Cf. *The Times* 10 October 1927.
59. Union of South Africa, *Debates of the House of Assembly*, 1927, Col. 5747, 5749.
60. Union of South Africa, '*The Select Committee on the Subject of Native Bills*', 179.
61. Cf. evidence of Dr A. W. Roberts of the Native Affairs Commission to the Select Committee on the 'Native Bills' (ibid., 20).
62. *Cape Times* 22 April 1925.
63. *The Workers' Herald* 28 April 1926.
64. *The Workers' Herald* 17 May 1927.
65. 12 August 1927.
66. Union of South Africa, *The Select Committee on the Subject of Native Bills*, 385.
67. This would not preclude individual membership. According to Champion, the people defied the Paramount Chief (A. W. G. Champion, *Mehlomadala*, *My Experiences in the ICU*, Durban, n.d., *c*. 1929, 2, translation (*Old Eyes*), 1, B/UCT). Cf. *The Times* 10 October 1927
68. Attempts to organize the Transkei (cf. A. W. G. Champion to T. B. Lujiza 12 October 1927, F/Undated/47) do not seem to have enjoyed any success.
69. H. M. Robertson, loc. cit., 143; Union of South Africa, '*The Select Committee on the Subject of Native Bills*', 167, 205.
70. *The Workers' Herald* 18 January, 1928.
71. C. Kadalie to the Prime Minister of Southern Rhodesia 22 December 1927 (Forman Collection); Gann, L. H., 1965, *A History of Southern Rhodesia*, London, 269-71; Ranger, T. O., 1968, *Aspects of Central African History*, London, 228-230; Partha Sarathi Gupta, 1975, *Imperialism and tne British Labour Movement*, *1914-1964*, London and Basingstoke, 125; Charles van Onselen, op. cit., 209-18; Palmer, R., 1977 *Land and Racial Domination in Rhodesia*, London, 227-9.
72. A. C. Jones to C. Kadalie 14 December 1927 (WH); ICU of Africa, Administrative Report 20 June 1929 (B/Wits); *The Workers' Herald* 15 September 1927; *The Churchman* October 1927; Champion, A. W. G., 'My second visit to the Cape Province' (n.d. Forman Collection).
73. *Ilanga lase Natal* 24 June 1927; *The Workers' Herald* 28 July 1926; ICU News Letter 5 December 1928.
74. *The Workers' Herald* 15 September and 15 October 1927.
75. *The Workers' Herald* 15 September 1927.
76. *The Natal Witness* 29 October 1927.
77. *The Workers' Herald* 15 September 1927.
78. Branch Secretary, Ixopo to A. W. G. Champion 25 August 1927 (F 1927/46b).
79. *The Star* 18 July 1927.
80. *The Star* 19 August 1927.

81. Lewis, E., The Geneva spirit, an appeal for the native trade union (B/UCT), published in *The Star* 16 November 1927.
82. *The Star* 19 August 1927.
83. Telegram D. Labase to ICU Head Office 16 August 1927 (F 1927/40). Labase had been given twenty-four hours' notice to leave Barberton.
84. *The Workers' Herald* 18 January 1928; Minutes of the National Council November 1927 (F 1927/124) and January 1928 (F 1928/1).
85. Mazibuko, L. A., Report on Volksrust and Wakkerstroom, attached to the News Letter of 5 December 1928, and also published in *The Workers' Herald* 31 December 1928.
86. *The Natal Witness* 1 October 1927.
87. *The Star* 18 July 1927.
88. A. W. G. Champion to Secretary, South African Agricultural Union Congress 28 October 1927 (F 1927/99a).
89. Ibid.
90. Minutes of National Council November 1927, 15 (F 1927/124).
91. A. W. G. Champion to M. Palmer 4 January 1928 (misdated 1927) (F General Letters/78).
92. Union of South Africa, *Report of the Commissioner of Police for the Year 1928-1929* (UG 13 - 1930); Chief Native Commissioner, Natal to A. W. G. Champion 17 November 1927 (F/Misc.).
93. *The Workers' Herald* 12 May 1928.
94. *The Star* 27 March 1928.
95. Mazibuko, L. A., Report on Volksrust and Wakkerstroom, ICU News Letter 5 December 1928.

CHAPTER 9

In Darkest Europe, 1927

'Perhaps another person would have hesitated to penetrate so deep into the heart of Europe unaccompanied, but for me I left my fears behind in Africa to tell the story of a New Africa in the making.'

(Clements Kadalie in his Autobiography)

Ethelreda Lewis had hopes that the expulsion of the Communists by the National Council in December 1926 and the application for affiliation to the International Federation of Trade Unions, would soften the attitude of the Government towards the ICU, and she did not delay to point out to General Hertzog the turn for the better in the union's affairs. 'It is surely better,' she wrote to the Prime Minister, 'to have Kadalie, with his undoubted power over fifty thousand natives, on the side of reasonable trade union ambitions for the black man than to leave him as a useful catspaw to men of the Moscow type, who within the last twelve years have done untold harm to South Africa by means of the native . . . And to find an individual amongst the natives who is willing to follow the path of decent and, so to speak, powerful moderation, and to turn his back, at no small personal risk, on the violent principles in the exertion of which the white communist party had hoped to use him as a lever, is surely nothing less than the stepping-in of Providence at a critical moment.' Providence, she thought, might be assisted by Hertzog's 'helpful and active sympathy', which would be best shown by 'certain modifications in the Native Bills . . . modifications dear to the heart of every native'. An interview with the Prime Minister was sought to apprise him more fully of her work with the ICU.[1]

Mrs Lewis followed this letter up with one the next day to General Smuts, informing him of her action and asking him to impress upon the Prime Minister the importance of her request, should that be necessary. She drew his attention to the change that had come over Kadalie, 'giving up gaudy feathers for a sober garb,' and his consequent need for unobtrusive support. Smuts did nothing except acknowledge her letter.[2] In the acknowledgment she received from Hertzog through his Private Secretary, the Prime Minister, while promising to give her views 'every consideration', was doubtful quite what was expected of him.[3] 'Some approving message or kindly notice,' answered Mrs Lewis.[4] The Prime Minister met her suggestion with a firm, but courteous, refusal.[5]

By this time the ICU's application to the IFTU had been accepted. This, however, availed it little when it proceeded to take a further step aimed at forcing the attention of the outside world on the wretched conditions endured by Black workers in South Africa. The National Council of the union at its meeting of

December 1926 came to the decision, overshadowed by the controversy surrounding the expulsion of the Communists, to put forward Kadalie as a candidate for government nomination as a delegate representing 'organised non-European workers' at the next International Labour Conference. An application was sent off to the Secretary for Labour on 19 January 1927. In due course this Department replied, asking such searching questions about the union and its finances that one wonders whether its purpose was to elicit information or to nonplus the National Secretary. Kadalie remained unperturbed and the information was duly furnished.[6] Predictably, after a protracted delay, the Department rejected the request. The Secretary for Labour, C. W. Cousins, gave as its reason that it could not regard the ICU as 'the most representative Industrial Organisation in South Africa'. To the International Labour Office, however, he put forward a different explanation, arguing that the ICU was not 'so constituted as to enable the Department to afford its recognition under the Industrial Conciliation Act' and that it did not appear to be 'an established industrial organisation in the sense in which such organisations are ordinarily regarded'.[7]

The rejection of the National Secretary's candidature for nomination was one of the topics discussed at the next, the Seventh, Annual Conference, held at Durban that year. This got off to a disappointing start. When he was approached to perform the opening ceremony, the Mayor, after first pleading absence from the city, finally declined the invitation on the ground of his disapproval of the preamble to the ICU Constitution. In the end the Conference was opened by Kadalie. One of the first things it did was to telegraph fraternal greetings to the South African Trades Union Congress, then in session at Cape Town, and to call for a 'united front against a common enemy – namely, the arbitrary and unlimited power of capitalism'.[8] If the ICU leaders thought that the affiliation of their union to the IFTU would bring about recognition by and alliance with the White labour movement, they were being excessively optimistic. Although their overtures were not spurned, they were received with great caution. C. F. Glass moved the despatch of fraternal greetings and a meeting between the executives of the two organizations, and this motion received support from the Communist trade unionists. It was, however, disliked by most of the other delegates and a compromise cut the motion into two parts, the first part – the reciprocation of fraternal greetings – being accepted, the second part being held over for discussion until after consultation with the Cape Federation of Labour Unions.[9]

Whatever support the ICU received from the White labour movement came from the very members of that movement who were most suspect to the authorities and the general public. It was Glass, later to become Mrs Lewis's *bête noire*, who, after the expulsion of La Guma and Khaile, was brought into Head Office to audit the union's accounts and to prepare the financial statement required by the Department of Labour when Kadalie's name was put forward for the International Labour Conference.[10] It was not, however, Glass's bookkeeping that attracted unfavourable attention, but his oratory. He and W. H. Andrews created a furore in the press and the House of Assembly by their radical speeches at an ICU rally.[11] Mrs Lewis was particularly incensed.[12]

The Glass-Andrews affair was an unpropitious prelude to the ICU's Durban Conference. This found, however, the union, with its expanding membership and rising income and the promise of a new and rewarding policy, ebullient and confident. The proceedings opened on Good Friday, 15 April, and there were in attendance no fewer than two hundred delegates.[13] J. G. Gumbs presided. In welcoming them to his own city Allison Champion launched into a characteristically extravagant attack upon the Mayor. In the course of a belligerent speech he touched upon the ICU's relations with the labour movement in South Africa and abroad, calling – somewhat infelicitously – upon the South African Labour Party – 'these traitors' – to 'throw away their arrogance and link up with the true ideals of labour'.

On the first full day of business, Saturday 16 April, there was a brief discussion of the Non-European Conference to be held at Kimberley in June of that year, to which the ICU was invited by the African People's Organization to send representatives. It was decided to send, as the ICU was 'essentially a Trade Union Organisation' and the convenors of the proposed conference were 'recognised as agents of certain political parties', only observers, 'to watch that those well-known political agents do not use that Conference for their self-interest'. After making this decision, the delegates applied themselves to the main business of the morning, a debate on the refusal of the Minister of Labour to nominate Kadalie as a delegate to the International Labour Conference. In their speeches Mbeki and Maduna stressed the necessity of sending 'a full-blooded Native' to Geneva. It was not that the Blacks objected to being represented by a White delegate simply because he was White, but – as Maduna put it for the benefit of what he called 'our European friends' – because 'the white man is selfish, knows nothing about the grievances and sufferings of the Natives in this country'. The Conference therefore decided 'to instruct its National Secretary, Mr Clements Kadalie, to proceed to Geneva to submit the claims of the Non-European workers who are the victims of merciless exploitation of both capitalism and the white labour policy of the Pact Government, and with this object in view this Congress instructs its National Secretary to carry on an extensive propaganda throughout Europe, if necessary, including the United States of America.'

During the course of the debate on Geneva, on the Saturday afternoon, there intervened the curious episode of S. M. Pettersen, a local socialist and organizer of the racially-mixed Seamen's Union,[14] who was on good terms with Champion and had thrown whatever influence he had in the docks and elsewhere upon the side of the ICU. Pettersen, who was neither reticent nor self-effacing, wanted to be accepted by the Conference as a fraternal delegate from the Durban dockworkers, and his request was supported, in the absence of Champion through illness, by Clements Kadalie. Considerable opposition was manifested by the delegates, either because Pettersen was White, or because, despite his denials, he was thought to be a Communist, or because he was thought to be intrusive, or because they did not much care for him personally. There can be little doubt that there was a strong feeling against the Communist Party, not because of its aims, but because of its methods, suspected as it was of trying to manipulate the union in the pursuance of interests that were not directly its own. It was this very same Conference that welcomed A. F. Batty, the 'Father of the ICU', as White and as alien as Pettersen, but one whose role during the early days had been by no means domineering. Kadalie's motion was rejected by a majority of one – 36 to 35.

Immediately afterwards, in a debate on the Government's four Native and Coloured Bills, Kadalie hotly attacked the White race for its greed and hypocrisy, and he advocated a one-day protest strike should the Bills become law. The Ginger Group wanted stronger action. A counter-motion was moved by Mbeki and supported by Maduna. 'Are you going back to the masses and ask them to pray, or will you go back and tell them to depend on their numerical powers?' asked Mbeki. Resuming the debate on Easter Monday, in a fiery speech that won loud applause, he called for a general strike, and when Kadalie rose to repeat his support for a day of protest, some of the delegates remonstrated with him: 'No, no, no, that is too mild, chief.' Apparently nettled, the National Secretary retorted, 'All right, if you want to lead a bloody revolution I am going to follow you, but, mark you, if I do follow you, I am going the whole hog. I am not a religious fanatic, as I ceased to pray in 1910 and will not pray again until we are a free people by fair means or by foul means.' Nevertheless, though he suggested that 'instead of prayer, let us have a militant day' – whatever he meant by that – he was unwilling to go further and accused the Ginger Group of 'juggling with high-sounding and empty phraseology'. When the Conference divided, fifty votes were cast for Kadalie's motion, seventeen for Mbeki's. Those who spoke against extreme measures regarded them as premature and unrealistic and the speeches that favoured them as braggadocio. 'I know that the very people who speak so loud now about a strike,' said H. K. Binda of Kroonstad, 'will creep under their grandmothers' beds when the thing comes to a head.'

On Easter Monday also there was the usual debate on the iniquity of the pass laws, a staple of ICU conferences. That year Kadalie attacked them on novel grounds – that the revenue for passes was used for the support of the country's universities, largely White preserves. He suggested a strong deputation to the Government, followed, in the inevitable absence of relief, by a challenge in the law courts, 'even to the House of Lords'. Only if that failed should other – unspecified – means be resorted to. At the end of the debate, however, a somewhat stiffer counter-motion by de Norman was passed in preference to Kadalie's original motion. The National Council was instructed 'to appoint a deputation to interview the Government and demand the immediate abolition of all pass laws, and if no satisfactory reply be received to organise a Passive Resistance Movement throughout the Union'.

The main business of the morning of Tuesday 19 April was a debate on the position of Communists within the organization. Kadalie opened it with the accusation that the Communist Party had done nothing to help him when he was banned and only wanted to stir up trouble. He was echoed by Maduna of the Ginger Group, who dwelt upon the Party's interference in the union's internal affairs. De Norman, on the other hand, spoke against severing ties with the Communists, pointing out that the National Secretary had been responsible in the first place for their penetration of the ICU and claiming freedom of political affiliation for members. An acrimonious exchange followed, with Champion calling upon de Norman to 'speak out like a man' and say whether or not he was a member of the Party. In the end a recommendation by the National Council that 'ordinary members of the organisation be not allowed to identify themselves in any way with the Communist Party' was passed overwhelmingly.

On Tuesday afternoon the last major debate of the Conference took place, on the minimum wage question. It was a desultory discussion, with the Conference uncertain whether it was a topic suitable for debate or best left in the hands of the National Council. Random facts about wages were mentioned and suggestions of what constituted a fair minimum wage. The figure decided on for the final resolution was eight shillings a day. With justice Kadalie pointed out that they discussed this question each year, but they got no further, and he gave his support to making full use of the Wage Act and appealing to the Government to include agricultural labourers within the scope of that Act. De Norman, who concurred, thought that such an appeal would meet with a sympathetic response.

The remaining business was short. On Tuesday afternoon the only item on the agenda was the Native Administration Bill, which was condemned without discussion as 'anti-British and an unjust interference with free speech and the liberty of the subject', a 'retrograde undemocratic and criminal manufacturing measure'. The Conference then met again briefly in public session on Wednesday morning before going into committee for a discussion of internal affairs. By then many delegates seem to have left already, because there were only 46 votes cast in the last division of the Conference. A motion to give moral support to the Indian and Coloured tailors then on strike in Durban was narrowly defeated. Champion opposed it on the ground that the men were not members of the ICU and had in fact resisted its attempts at organization. Kadalie, who thought that it was their duty 'to sympathise with these men, whether they were members of the union or not, so long as they were not scabs', was unable to sway the opposition.

Three weeks after the Durban Conference ended, on 13 May 1927, Clements Kadalie set sail for Europe from Cape Town in the *Windsor Castle*. In London the Black-Red (as she called him) was welcomed by Winifred Holtby, who took him to the headquarters of the Independent Labour Party, where he met Fenner Brockway, its political secretary. The following day he left for Geneva,[15] where he spent two weeks attending the International Labour Conference. He issued a memorandum stating the claims of his union to choose the South African workers' delegate and he addressed the Workers' Group, and appeared in the photographs of its members. However, by his own account, he was cut out, at the insistence of the South African delegation, of the photograph taken of the British Empire delegations, and he received no official recognition.[16] The Credentials Committee of the Conference in its report (11 June) upheld the contention of the South African Government that the ICU claim could not be considered because the union was not registered. When Corneille Mertens, the Belgian workers' delegate, protested, the reporter of the Committee shifted his ground somewhat from one technical point to another. The ICU's complaint against the South African Government was essentially a protest at the nomination of a White workers' delegate instead of one chosen by itself. In fact, however, owing to a dispute between the two White trade union federations in South Africa, no workers' delegate had been nominated at all. Therefore the complaint fell away. Mertens demanded a vote on the report, which, however, on a show of hands, was accepted by the Conference, thus bringing to a close all the official notice taken of the ICU. Kadalie seems to have received no assistance from the British Workers' delegates, and it was Harold Grimshaw, the head of the Colonial Division of the International Labour Office, who took him under his wing. With his help Kadalie drew up a letter to the Director, pointing out that the South African TUC and the Cape Federation were also unregistered and requesting that the ICU's protest be included in the official record. Kadalie, in conclusion, asked for an assurance that the decision of the Credentials Committee had not been based on racial grounds. He obtained an interview with the Director, Albert Thomas, whom he thought sympathetic to his case.[17]

On 13 June the Indian workers' delegate, V. V. Giri, moved a resolution that the Conference should draw the attention of countries 'in which the white people are the ruling class, but in which the natives and the coloured people are either the majority of the population of that country or form a substantial portion of the population, to the desirability of the representatives of the native and coloured workers attending the International Labour Conference as part of the delegation from these countries'. He cited the case of South Africa. A South African delegate, B. J. Pienaar, pointed out 'that the mode of representation is laid down, I believe, in the Treaty of Versailles. It has nothing to do with the proportion of races. The method laid down in the Treaty has always been followed in South Africa. If the coloured, or other workers are not sufficiently represented, they have only themselves to blame. We can only follow the law as laid down in the Treaty of Versailles, and that we have done.'[18] Grimshaw drew from this statement the conclusion that, should Black unions become strong enough, the South African Government would not be able to overlook them in nominating the workers' delegate.[19] The question, however, never arose.

On the eve of Kadalie's departure from Geneva Grimshaw summed up the effects of his appearance there. 'He has been well received, particularly, of course, by the Workers' Group, and has undoubtedly made a favourable impression and secured a personal success. I have heard very favourable comments on the modesty and moderation of his proposals and procedure, and this in spite of the fact that an attempt was made to prejudice his case and to discredit him personally.'[20]

The favourable impression created by Kadalie at Geneva drove the Department of Labour to a realization that the Government had to come to terms with the Black industrial labour movement in order, if for no other reason, to meet criticism from overseas, where, as Thomas Boydell, the current Minister of Labour, expressed it with some understatement, 'a viewpoint different to that in this country is more and more gaining ground'.[21] First news from Geneva came from one of the delegates, W. Freestone, who, in a letter to the Secretary for Labour, described the Conference's reaction to Kadalie and the embarrassment he had allegedly caused the Director of the ILO and Deputy Director, Harold Butler. 'The event of the week so far as South Africa is concerned is the arrival of Clements Kadalie. His appearance created a mild sensation chiefly on account of the shiny blackness of his skin. Socially I hear he has proved to be successful, many of the delegates from European countries and their womenfolk finding him very interesting and appealing. The notion that we are deliberately refusing to dispense even-handed justice appears to have considerable sway here and our explanations are not at all satisfying the ideas and minds of the average European whose knowledge of the Native has been gleaned from Missionary reports and sermons along with an occasional interview with solitary Natives. Since his arrival here Kadalie has interviewed M. Thomas and Mr Butler as well as other officers and members of the Governing Body. They appear to find him a difficult subject and scarcely know what to do with him, or about him. On Friday he turned up (without invitation) at a reception given by Mrs Butler to a number of members of the League of Nations Union, and of course was immediately seized upon by the female portion of the visitors who appeared to greedily swallow all the stuff he was willing to supply. Mrs Butler was most unhappy about it.'[22] 'I feel quite sure,' Cousins commented, 'that the Government has not appreciated yet the importance of setting in motion an authoritative exposition of its attitude to the Native population and its system of Native administration.'[23]

It seems odd that eighteen months after Hertzog's Smithfield speech and a year after the publication of the Native Bills the Secretary for Labour should still require an authoritative exposition of the Government's attitude to the Native population and its system of Native administration. How the Nationalist wing of the Pact Government viewed the position of the Black population in the country was being made all too clear in the Native Administration Bill then before Parliament. For Hertzog and Roos, the Minister of Justice, that Bill was to serve a dual purpose. On the one hand, replacing the Sedition Bill which had been withdrawn in deference to Labour susceptibilities, it permitted control of Black agitators without trespassing on the rights of White trade unionists; on the other, it 're-established and resurrected the diminishing tribalism among Africans'[24] with a view to ensuring that the National concept of two irreconcilable cultures, a superior and an inferior, remained correct. Kadalie was well aware of what the Nationalists were up to. 'The present Government,' he wrote to Miss Holtby, '. . . desires the Native population of South Africa to return to their old state of barbarism, and the advances they are now making, economically, politically and socially are annoying the Government extremely. What they desire is that the natives shall be controlled by native chiefs, a manifest absurdity in these days of democracy.'[25]

The Bill proposed to give the Government wide powers enabling it to restrict severely the movement and gathering of Blacks[26] and to banish from any named locality those guilty of offences that were left to the executive to define.[27] Its most notorious clause, Clause 26, which applied to Whites as well as to Blacks, empowered 'the Governor-General to make regulations to prohibit the dissemination by any person of doctrines subversive of peace and good order among the Natives of the Union. The acts which may be prohibited by such regulations shall include those done with an intention . . . to promote feelings of hostility between different races in the Union.'[28] In a letter of protest to the Secretary for Native Affairs, Major J. F. Herbst, the Secretary of the IFTU (requested by a telegram from the ICU to intervene[29]) described these clauses as extremely vague and capable of admitting of an interpretation which would be highly prejudicial to trade union activities.[30] It was not, however, only the ICU that was unhappy about the so-called sedition clauses of the Bill. The Labour Party and the SATUC, too, raised objections, particularly with respect to Clause 26, with the result that the Prime Minister was compelled to agree to a Select Committee and the withdrawal of the offending clause. The other objectionable clauses, however, remained and part of Clause 26 itself slipped back in as Clause 29 (1), the hostility clause – 'Any person who utters any words or does any other act or thing whatever with intent to promote any feeling of hostility between Natives and Europeans shall be guilty of an offence and liable on conviction to imprisonment for a period not exceeding one year or to a fine of £100, or both.' Furthermore, a new clause, presumably aimed at Kadalie and 'Mote, was introduced, which provided for the deportation of any Black born outside the Union of South Africa should he be convicted of any offence under Clause 29 (1).

In July the Bill became law. The White labour movement of South Africa might have eased its conscience, but the Act, in its final form, remained very ominous for Black trade unionism and evoked further protest from the IFTU.[31]

Confronted with criticism from abroad, the Secretary for Native Affairs took up the defence that the Act had nothing to do with trade unionism and, pressed by the Department of Labour for 'a clear and concise statement of the native position . . . in order to rebut misrepresentations', insisted that it was directed against 'unscrupulous and fanatical agitators, who, for their own ends or profit, do not hesitate to promote racial strife and promote doctrines subversive of all order and good government, heedless of the consequences to their misguided followers'. Among such unscrupulous and fanatical agitators Herbst counted Kadalie and Mbeki, and he did not consider the ICU to be a legitimate trade union. 'Apart from any other consideration,' he wrote to the Department of Labour, 'the Government is not satisfied that the finances of the Industrial and Commercial Workers' Union of South Africa . . . are properly accounted for or administered. No annual report containing a satisfactory statement is issued by this body . . .'[32]

It is plain that the views of the Labour and Native Affairs Departments were at variance. Two and a half months before Major Herbst's diatribe against the ICU the Secretary for Labour wrote to his colleague of the Native Affairs Department stressing the need, in view of the prestige that Kadalie had acquired at Geneva in the eyes of South African Blacks and in view of the impending visit to South Africa, at the invitation of the Government, of the Deputy Director of the ILO, to formulate a policy on the question of 'Native industrial organization' in order, 'if possible, to guide and direct the movement into channels in which reasonable action can be assured and friction and trouble be averted'. It was essential, he went on, that Butler should get 'a proper comprehension of the difficulties of Native Administration in South Africa' because, whatever he reported would be 'distributed to the Governments and all Industrial Organisations throughout the world'. He concluded by suggesting an inter-departmental consultation.[33]

At the beginning of September Cousins drew up a memorandum[34] for the benefit of his minister setting out in very guarded terms the trend of policy, as he saw it, of the Department of Labour in its dealings with the Black in industry in general and the Black labour movement in particular. To him, looking back to the establishment of the Department in July 1924, the pressing problem which it had been set up to deal with seemed simplicity itself – 'turning the tide which had set adversely to the employment of white labour in the opposite direction'. The primary function of the new department had been 'to use all the opportunities afforded by legislation and by administrative methods to further the interests of the white population and to widen the opportunities for white labour in the Union'. While it had been recognized that, for all practical purposes, part of the Coloured population was indistinguishable from the White community, Blacks had been regarded as wholly the concern of the Native Affairs Department. After a time, however, the permanent officials had begun to wonder whether in fact that was an appropriate body to deal with the interests of Blacks in towns. The Black, the memorandum went on, 'is not *de facto* covered advantageously at the present time by any of the industrial legislation. Indeed, he is suffering displacement and he is further being taught to believe that differentiation is taking place on the ground of colour and race, and that the European fears him, fears particularly his competition in industry, and is endeavouring by legislative methods to rule him out of industry.'

It was because of the discrimination experienced by Blacks, the Secretary for Labour acknowledged, that the ICU was formed and gained strength. While it could not be registered, it could not be ignored, given its formidable membership claims, its recognition by the IFTU, and the sympathy displayed by the British trade union movement. One difficulty was that not enough was known about its operations and influence. Although he did not go so far as to make recommendations, Cousins hinted at the sort of change that he himself thought acceptable.[35] There was no reason, he thought, why the Wage Act should not be used for the benefit of Blacks as well as Whites. He even envisaged, though his memorandum does not baldly say so, an amendment to the Industrial Conciliation Act to bring within its scope all Blacks by a change in the definition of employee or by de-proclaiming certain areas proclaimed under the Transvaal Urban Areas Pass Act of 1909. If that were done, Blacks would, whenever an industrial agreement was negotiated, have to be represented, perhaps by an official of the Native Affairs Department, perhaps even by a trade union, possibly a parallel union, a Black branch of a White union. If anything does emerge from the mandarin prose of the Secretary for Labour, it is the recognition that Black unions were an inevitable development and must be accepted and guided, above all steered away from politics and race antagonism.

In the ensuing weeks the question of the place of Blacks in industry was discussed by a conference representing the Departments of Labour and Native Affairs and the Native Affairs Commission, which was held at the end of October 1927 at Cape Town under the chairmanship of C. W. Cousins and, after a month's adjournment, had a final day's session at Pretoria. Its deliberations were inconclusive. There was no voting, but the chairman gained the impression that the conference was not averse to the use of the machinery of the Wage Act on behalf of 'such natives as those for whom the Bloemfontein Native Wages Commission endeavoured to get a minimum wage fixed', in other words those engaged in occupations – other than farming and mining – where the question of civilized standards did not arise. In those cases where it seemed appropriate for the Wage Board to intervene on behalf of Blacks, it would be desirable, the conference thought, for an additional member or members to be appointed to the Board in consultation with the Minister of Native Affairs.[36] This was as far as very tentative agreement would go. The Native Affairs Department, represented by Major Herbst and Major Cooke (the Director of Native Labour), refused to commit itself on the question of bringing Blacks within the scope of the Industrial Conciliation Act. The Department of Labour, in contrast, considered that it was undesirable to extend the operation of the Wage Act to Blacks without at the same time including them within the scope of the other Act, and it is not difficult to see why. Every time the question of Black wages came up for determination, the responsibility for a decision would be thrown on the Minister of Labour. The Wage Board could not itself make any recommendation if it felt unable to recommend a wage 'suited to civilised requirements' and, in such circumstances, it was incumbent upon the Minister to instruct the Board to recommend a wage 'suited to the conditions'. Should, however, Blacks be subject to the procedures of the Industrial Conciliation Act, then the more difficult cases, those involving Blacks in racially mixed occupations, would fall to the industrial councils established under the Act. A further objection raised by the Department was that the inclusion of Blacks in the working of the one Act and not the other 'would definitely operate against the slower but more healthy process allowing the development of Native participation in industries which the Department knows to be essential.'[37]

While all this activity was going on in Cape Town and Pretoria Kadalie was continuing his European tour. On his return to London in mid-June he rented an office at the ILP headquarters, employed a typist, and 'worked enormously'. 'Everyone,' wrote Winifred Holtby to Mrs Lewis, 'seems to be liking Kadalie. I personally have been delighted by his behaviour. Of course, one never knows how long these things last, and he is clever. But certainly his manner, to me for instance, is an absolute contradiction of the saying in South Africa that if you treat a native man like a human being he takes advantage. I have spent hours with him, in his office, in his hotel, in the Penn [*sic*] Club. Never has he by look or word transgressed the laws of courtesy and profound respect, and his manner with the labour leaders and so on whom he encounters, is admirable with its mixture of deference and dignity. He seems to get on well with his typist, a competent, but quite young girl, who takes him perfectly for granted and whom he treats as any other gentleman would treat his typist. I feel sometimes that it is too good to last and that we shall find a fatal flaw somewhere.'[38]

By his own account the six weeks Kadalie spent in Britain until he left for a second visit to the Continent at the end of July were very full ones, passed 'in a glare of publicity'.[39] Fenner Brockway and Winifred Holtby arranged for him a programme of speeches, talks with labour leaders, and encounters with the influential. He visited the headquarters of the Labour Party, the Trades Union Congress, and the Co-operative Movement, some trade union offices, and the House of Commons, where he spoke to the Commonwealth Group of the Labour Party and met, among others, George Lansbury, J. R. Clynes, and Arthur Henderson. The Imperialism Committee of the ILP arranged two weekend schools at which Kadalie spoke. After three weeks in London he made a tour of Scotland, the North of England and the Midlands, meeting people and addressing dozens of gatherings.[40]

The first week of August was spent at the Congress of the IFTU in Paris, where he urged the International Federation to bring into its ranks the workers of Asia and Africa in the interests of the workers of Europe itself. After an interval in London, at the end of August, he went to Amsterdam and to Utrecht, where he addressed railway workers, then to Berlin as guest of the German Federation of Labour.[41]

Back in England, after an unpleasant experience in London trying to find a hotel that would take a Black man,[42] Kadalie travelled north to Edinburgh to attend the Conference of the TUC. In spite of his hopes he was not accepted as a fraternal delegate lest this should irritate the White labour movement in South Africa. However, he was cordially received and was introduced to Ramsay Macdonald.[43] Returning to London, he raised, in the course of discussion with his English sympathizers on the future of the ICU, the question of obtaining the services of an experienced trade unionist who would spend some months in South Africa to give advice on 'the technical side of industrial organisation'. This, he thought, would have the additional advantage of bringing about 'improved relations with white labour in South Africa, as of course the English organiser would go out with fraternal greetings to the white unions and labour movement'. He was, however, a little apprehensive about Champion's reaction to the idea of importing a White man to tell Black men how to run their affairs. The suggestion was taken up with enthusiasm by Winifred Holtby, Creech Jones, and Fenner Brockway, who thought that the best arrangement would be to presuade a British trade union to lend an official, since that would relieve the ICU of the expense of engaging an expert. Miss Holtby thought (as did Kadalie) that Creech Jones himself would have been ideal – 'so sane and moderate and tolerant', but there was never any real chance of his going.[44]

The question of an adviser was one of the topics discussed at a wide-ranging conversation between Kadalie and Creech Jones on 14 September. Jones had in mind a rather longer period – at least a year – for the adviser to stay with the ICU, and he also thought that the union could do with 'first-class secretarial assistance on the staff side', a woman with 'considerable courage as well as determination'. He urged the National Secretary to take advantage of his stay in Britain to study carefully the methods and constitution of British trade unions and to seek advice from lawyers on the precise legal position of the ICU, what it could do and what it could not do. On his return home, he should ensure that there was a constant flow to his English friends, to the IFTU, and to any German sympathizers whose support he could enlist, of information for publication in the European press. Kadalie should eschew as far as possible political activities, especially those that might be interpreted as unconstitutional. Nevertheless, there must be an attempt to secure political redress and Creech Jones, a little naïvely, thought the best plan would be for the ICU, if it could do so in good conscience after the debate on the Native Administration Bill, to seek affiliation to the South African Labour Party. Kadalie, who was keen on trying to raise

£3 000 to establish a printing press, was tactfully advised to aim at a more modest objective, a small press costing three or four hundred pounds.[45]

Winifred Holtby, too, tried to dissuade Kadalie from setting his heart upon such a luxury and made it clear that he had no hope of raising so large a sum of money in England. Then, after very sensibly pointing out that, with the passage of the Native Administration Act and the eviction of farm labourers, the ICU would need to conserve its resources, she touched delicately on the subject of Kadalie's personal extravagance. 'I have heard,' she declared, 'some criticism, not from one quarter alone, and always from people ready to help you, of the lavishness of your expenditure. I know that some items of this have been necessarily heavy. You have had to travel and to get secretarial help and to print pamphlets. But while on the one hand we have been asking for financial help for your work . . ., on the other we have seen you able, apparently, to manage without yourself, as representative of the ICU, practising economy . . . because I felt that there was just sufficient truth in what is said . . . to be important, I thought that you might forgive my frankness for the sake of such small service as I have been able to do your cause . . .' Like Creech Jones, Miss Holtby advised him to concentrate on industrial issues and to secure political reform by way of affiliation to the South African Labour Party. If that should spurn the ICU's advances, then external pressure could be brought to bear through the Labour and Socialist International and the British Commonwealth Labour League. She did not make it at all clear how the ICU was to keep out of politics when most of the disabilities afflicting Black workers had a political origin: and she herself admitted some substantial exceptions to the general rule of political detachment, accepting the reasonableness of participation 'in the political struggle on specific points, say the Pass Laws, the Native Administration law, and the native franchise'.[46]

At the end of September, on Creech Jones's advice, [47] the National Secretary left once more for the Continent, this time to Austria, where he was the guest of the Austrian Trades Union Congress. He stopped over at Geneva, where he obtained the advice of Harold Grimshaw on a new constitution for the ICU drafted by Jones. In Vienna he was presented to the Mayor. He left the Austrian capital on 7 October to be the guest for the second time of the German Federation of Labour on another visit to Berlin. From Berlin it was back to London. Altogether Kadalie, who thought it was his 'duty to show Europe that we did not neglect the social side in our onward march to a higher civilisation', seems to have had a jolly time in Austria and Germany.[48]

One of Kadalie's chief preoccupations during his weeks in England was mobilizing opinion against the Native Administration Act. The liberal barrister, Holford Knight, was consulted, and he condemned it; a memorandum setting out the background to the Act was submitted to the Labour Party Conference at Blackpool in July; letters were sent to Walter Citrine of the TUC and Arthur Henderson of the Labour Party, who, on making inquiries, were assured by their

South African counterparts that the original Bill had been substantially altered to meet the objections to it; and at a rally in London on 13 October Kadalie was joined on the platform by Fenner Brockway, Winifred Holtby, and a canon of Westminster.[49]

In the meantime disqueting news was coming from South Africa, culminating in an alarmed telegram from Mrs Lewis, who had a profound mistrust of Champion, urging Kadalie not to proceed with a proposed lecture tour of the United States, but to return home as soon as possible. The tour had, in fact, already been cancelled from New York, much to Kadalie's chagrin. An invitation from a Communist organization in Berlin to visit the USSR was not taken up, presumably on the advice of his English friends and on account of Mrs Lewis's urgent summons.[50] On 28 October the National Secretary set sail on the *Balmoral Castle*. He took with him the promise of a number of scholarships in England and Denmark, the possibility of getting an English adviser, the sympathies of many well-wishers, and a great deal of advice. Everyone took care to impress on him the need for moderation. Typical was the earnest warning of Charles Roden Buxton: 'I am sure you feel that very great responsibility which rests upon you now, and how absolutely essential it is to avoid injuring the prospects of the ICU at this critical state in its development. I know you will exercise the greatest care in accuracy of statements, in moderation of policy, and in strictness with regard to accounts. Your opponents will be on the watch for any failure in these points, and will make the very most of it, if it occurs.'[51] By October 1927, the ICU had indeed reached a critical stage in its development, but it was a crisis of existence that was already beyond remedy.

Notes

1. E. Lewis to General Hertzog 3 January 1927 (B/Wits).
2. E. Lewis to General Smuts 4 January 1927 (B/Wits).
3. Private Secretary of the Prime Minister to E. Lewis 18 January 1927 (B/Wits).
4. E. Lewis to General Hertzog 27 January 1927 (B/Wits).
5. Private Secretary to E. Lewis 3 February 1927 (B/Wits).
6. Kadalie, C., Facts for the International Labour Conference (B/Wits). The letters exchanged between the ICU and the Department of Labour are to be found in the Ballinger Collection, University of the Witwatersrand.
7. Secretary for Labour to Director, ILO 1 April 1927; International Labour Office, *International Labour Conference 10th Session*, Geneva, 1927, Vol. I, 17.
8. The proceedings of the Conference were reported in *The Workers' Herald* 17 May 1927.
9. *Cape Times* 18 April 1927.
10. C. Kadalie to Executives and Members of the ICU 13 January 1929 (B/UCT); National Secretary to Registrar of Trade Unions and Employers' Organizations, Department of Labour 3 February 1927 (B/Wits).

Ethelreda Lewis – Africana Museum, Johannesburg

W.G. Ballinger, *The Workers' Herald* 18 August, 1928 – University of Cape Town, Ballinger Collection

11. *The Star* 6 April 1927.
12. Cf. 'A letter to the Press which a member of the Pretoria Joint Council signed his name to and got into the papers recently' (B/Wits). It was published in the *Cape Times* 19 April 1927 over the name of F. S. Livie-Noble.
13. Or so it was claimed. The largest number of votes cast throughout the Conference was seventy-one.
14. He was later a Nationalist senator.
15. Kadalie, C., *My Life*, 103–6; Brittain V., and Handley-Taylor, G., (eds.), op. cit., 167.
16. Kadalie, C., Facts for the International Labour Conference (B/Wits); C. Kadalie to A. W. G. Champion 27 June 1927 (F 1927/24).
17. ILO, op. cit., 261; C. Kadalie to Secretary-General of the International Labour Conference (alias the Director of the ILO) 11 June 1927 (F 1927/18; WH); C. Kadalie to W. Holtby 11 June 1927 (B/UCT).
18. ILO, op. cit., 336.
19. H. Grimshaw to F. Brockway 15 June 1927 (B/Wits).
20. Ibid. The South African delegates, according to Kadalie, claimed that the ICU had only 6 000 members and that Kadalie was not a British subject, but came from the Belgian Congo (C. Kadalie to Mrs E. Lewis 13 June 1927, B/Wits).
21. Central Archives: Department of Labour 4002/1103 Part 2 T. Boydell to C. W. Cousins 17 July 1927.
22. Central Archives: Department of Labour 4002/1103 Part 2 C. W. Cousins to T. Boydell 30 June 1927.
23. Ibid.
24. Tatz, C. M., op. cit., 43.
25. 8 September 1927 (B/UCT).
26. Chapter VII, Clauses 24, 25.
27. Chapter II, 4 (c).
28. Chapter VII, 26 (1) & (2).
29. Secretary for Native Affairs to Secretary, IFTU 4 May 1927 (B/Wits).
30. Secretary, IFTU to Secretary for Native Affairs 28 June 1927 (B/Wits).
31. Report No. 32 of the IFTU, Amsterdam 8 September 1927, quoted in Central Archives: Department of Labour 4003/1103/1 Secretary for Labour to Secretary for Native Affairs 19 October 1927.
32. Secretary for Native Affairs to Secretary, IFTU 25 July 1927 (B/Wits); Central Archives: Department of Labour 4003/1103/1 Secretary for Labour to Secretary for Native Affairs 19 October 1927 and Secretary for Native Affairs to Secretary for Labour 26 October 1927. It is strange that one government department in a minute to another should refer to its own views as those of the Government.
33. Central Archives: Department of Labour 4002/1103/2 C. W. Cousins to J. F. Herbst 9 August 1927.
34. Central Archives: Department of Labour 4002/1103/2 Secretary for Labour, 'Natives under the Industrial Code' 2 September 1927.
35. His discussion explicitly excluded Black labour in the mining industry.
36. Central Archives: Department of Labour 4002/1103/2 Chairman's Report on the Conference 25 November 1927.
37. Note appended to the chairman's report.
38. W. Holtby to Mrs Lewis 3 and 27 July 1927 (B/Wits). One wonders what 'fatal flaw' Miss Holtby feared to find. Kadalie is alleged to have had an affair in England with Dorothy Woodman of the Union of Democratic Control (W. G. Ballinger to A. Fenner Brockway 15 May 1929, B/Wits). For requests for money see C. Kadalie to A. W. G. Champion 13, 27, and 28 June (F 1927/19, 24, and 26).

39. Kadalie, C., *My Life*, 114.
40. C. Kadalie to A. W. G. Champion 7 July (F 1927/28) and to E. Lewis 10 August 1927 (B/Wits).
41. Kadalie, C., *My Life*, 119–20; C. Kadalie to A. W. G. Champion 7 July and 1 September 1927 (F 1927/28, 53).
42. A. Creech Jones to C. Kadalie 15 September 1927 (WH).
43. Kadalie, C., *My Life*, 136–7.
44. W. Holtby to Mrs E. Lewis 8 September 1927 (B/Wits); C. Kadalie to A. Creech Jones 30 November 1927 (WH).
45. A. Creech Jones to C. Kadalie 15 September and 21 October 1927 (WH).
46. W. Holtby to C. Kadalie 7 September (1927) (B/UCT). Kadalie does not seem to have been offended (C. Kadalie to W. Holtby 8 September 1927, B/UCT).
47. A. Creech Jones to C. Kadalie 15 September 1927 (WH).
48. C. Kadalie to W. Holtby 1 October 1927 (B/Wits); Kadalie, C., *My Life*, 129–33.
49. Kadalie, C., *My Life*, 126–7; C. Kadalie to W. Holtby (together with the memorandum to the Labour Party) 21 July 1927 (B/UCT). The opinion of Holford Knight has survived, dated 14 September 1927 (B/Wits). Cf. also circular letter from C. Kadalie entitled 'Martial law in South Africa', n.d. (B/UCT); C. Kadalie to W. Citrine 22 August 1927 (B/Wits); W. Citrine to C. Kadalie 24 August 1927 (B/Wits); A. Henderson to C. Kadalie, n.d. (B/Wits); C. Kadalie to A. Henderson 26 August 1927 (B/Wits).
50. E. Lewis to W. Holtby 26 September 1927 (Wits ICU); C. Kadalie to A. P. Randolph 12 September 1927 (F 1927/58); Society for the Promotion of Cultural Relations between Russia and Foreign Countries to C. Kadalie (telegram 22 September 1927, F 1927/69).
51. Kadalie, C., *My Life*, 139–40. For Kadalie's home-going see W. Holtby to E. Lewis 28 October 1927 (B/Wits); A. C. Jones to C. Kadalie 8 November 1927 (WH); C. Kadalie to A. C. Jones 30 November 1927 (WH).

CHAPTER 10

The Great Contraction, 1927-1928

'It is no use wasting time about the shortcomings of Kadalie. He has done what no man ever did and has reached a place where he has failed as a man. He has a clean record. He is the only black man who has led his people for ten years enjoying their confidence . . . Today Kadalie has soldiers but no officers. He is a Field Marshal without Generals. He must fall and that is the end of him.' A. W. G. Champion 26 June 1928

'A bankrupt, discredited, chaotic association of incompetent natives with a few struggling defeated officials who had never been able to handle money or to protect themselves from the truly scandalous exploiting of their money by white men out only to line their pockets; unable, too, to save their organisation from the appropriation of funds by dishonest native officials.'

(Ethelreda Lewis's appraisal of the ICU, July 1928.)

There is ample evidence that, by Kadalie's return from Europe, the ICU was past its prime and that the grandiose plans for reorganization which he had conceived during his absence were futile. The loss of support may have had something to do with the inability of the union to take advantage of industrial unrest that occurred during the winter of 1927 – a token strike of 1 500 dock workers in Durban on 16 June in protest against the arrest of poll-tax defaulters; a strike at the end of June of four and a half thousand coal miners in Natal for higher wages; and a strike of four hundred-odd contract labourers at the Kazerne railway goods shed in Johannesburg on 7 July, also for higher wages. All were spontaneous and short-lived. Although the ICU was suspected of being behind the coal strike, it is difficult to see why, because it was prevented by the mine managements from openly penetrating the labour force.[1] That strike can scarcely be accounted an ICU failure. It is the inept handling of the Durban dispute that is most surprising and of the Johannesburg one that is most inexcusable. One would have expected a more vigorous policy from Champion as Acting National Secretary. It is evident, however, that he was ill-at-ease in Johannesburg. 'There is nothing so difficult,' he wrote at the end of his six months in office, 'for one who comes from a different place to another different place, like myself, who came from Durban as a Provincial Secretary to the Head Office in Johannesburg and to manage people who have their own lines of policies.'[2] He apparently spent a good deal of his time in Durban, where, however, he missed the June dock strike. There the senior ICU official was Sam Dunn, the amiable but lethargic Acting Provincial Secretary.

During Champion's protracted absences from Johannesburg the Head Office was left in the charge of H. D. Tyamzashe, the Complaints and Research Secretary, who was an able journalist but a weak labour leader. Ineffectual and, in any case, all too likely to give way to pressure from Mrs Lewis, he advised the Kazerne workers to go back to work and congratulated himself on the moderation of his policy.[3] The strikers ignored the advice and were forthwith dismissed and replaced.[4] The episode showed the ICU in a poor light. Here were men, mostly members, whose grievance was unknown to their union until they were on the point of striking and who then evidently received no support and little sympathy. It was the employer, a labour contractor, who brought Tyamzashe into the dispute, and it is clear that his hand was strengthened by the ICUs disavowal of responsibility. It had neither the organization nor the ability to keep open proper channels of communication with its own members or to carry out purposeful negotiations with employers. Many members must have wondered what was to be gained from paying subscriptions to such an organization.

These urban events, however, were overshadowed by the rural problem, the plight of the ejected members of the union, in the latter part of 1927 and early 1928. The extent of the problem can only be guessed at. Eviction was evidently very common in Natal, and there were many cases reported in the Orange Free State.[5] Once again the experience of the two Transvaal branches, Volksrust and Wakkerstroom, illustrates the situation. In March 1928, 'evictions reached a climax . . . despair gained the place of confidence in the organisation and a general decline in financial strength inevitably followed'.[6] Confronted with a problem of such gravity there was little the ICU leaders could do. Champion, as Acting National Secretary in 1927, fell back on the only policy that he knew – recourse to the courts. Cecil Cowley obligingly opened a branch office at Ixopo on the strength of an ICU promise of sixty pounds' worth of business a month.[7] More to the point, the union obtained from the Supreme Court in Natal a ruling that tenants were not to be evicted before they had a chance to reap their crops, and damages were extracted from some farmers who had resorted to summary evictions.[8] The scale of the problem, however, was too immense for the ICUs resources.

In May 1927, before the evictions had started, but when there were complaints in Parliament and the press about the activities of the ICU, Champion wrote to the Prime Minister requesting an interview, so that he might hear at first hand the ICU case.[9] After a considerable delay the request was refused, though with the utmost courtesy.[10] In a new effort, at the end of July, the Acting National Secretary wrote to the Natal Agricultural Union, shortly before its special congress to consider the ICU question, asking it to let him attend to present his union's point of view.[11] Although he expressed willingness to accept a written statement, the Secretary would not permit attendance, and in the event the congress called for stern measures.[12] When in September Champion again wrote to the Prime Minister, asking for government help for tenants turned off the farms, a reply came from the Native Affairs Department almost two months later merely urging him to advise the displaced to make their difficulties known to the magistrates of the districts or to the local officers of the Department.[13]

At its August meeting at King William's Town the National Council decided to investigate the possibility of purchasing land for the homeless and to buy maize in bulk for re-sale at low prices to those in distress.[14] Land purchase was a desperate and unrealistic remedy, given the size of the problem and the ever-diminishing income of the ICU. As early as July 1927, there appears to have been insufficient money to pay Branch Secretaries,[15] and by the end of the year even Durban, the milch cow of 1926–1927, was drying up. Income reached its peak as early as April/May 1927, after which enrolment fees and subscriptions fell continuously.[16] The decline of Durban had a great deal to do with two great financial scandals that came into the open in November 1927. The first one had been in the making for many months and concerned George Lenono, a foundation member of the ICU, a Basuto and a clerk in the Native Recruiting Corporation. The story began in October or November 1926, when Lenono sent an unsigned letter to Kadalie, then in Durban, complaining about Champion's financial administration. At a subsequent interview with the National Secretary he asked why it was that certain funds belonging to Durban branch were banked in Champion's personal account and the property of the union held in his name. Kadalie, at that time on the best of terms with the Natal Provincial Secretary, to whom he owed the success he had had in flouting the ban upon his movement, simply passed the complaint on to Champion, who thereupon accused Lenono of speaking about him 'in private corners' and seeking to 'undermine his authority and lower his dignity in the eyes of Mr Kadalie'.[17]

In December 1926, the Communists were expelled and Lenono extended the range of his accusations to include Kadalie, suggesting that La Guma was dismissed for being too honest. Kadalie (once again informing Champion) wrote him a denial that was cordial, even jaunty, wishing him a merry Christmas. Lenono was not amused and claimed that he was being threatened, which was hardly true. Getting no satisfaction, he collected the correspondence together and had it printed, together with an introduction, as a pamphlet, with the aim of discrediting his enemies. It seems likely that Ncwana and Nyombolo of the old ICWU were behind this move. The essence of the pamphlet was the accusation that some of the officials of the ICU, notably Champion, were 'exploiting the less intelligent members of their race for their own personal interests'. Arriving in Durban with nothing, Champion, it was alleged, had acquired landed property and established businesses with ICU funds, which he alone administered and which he used as though they were his own money. Champion was so angry that he sued the pamphleteer for libel. This was in March 1927, but the case did not come on until November, just as Kadalie got back to South Africa.[18] The plea was dismissed, and the judge, Justice Tatham, made some caustic remarks about the financial adminstration of the ICU in Natal.

Champion had indeed, Justice Tatham found, used thousands of pounds of ICU money as though it was his own, some of it on trading schemes operating in his own name, all in flagrant violation of the union's constitution and normal accounting procedures, without any supervision by the ICU Executive Committee in Durban or authorization from Head Office. The same cavalier behaviour, he suggested, was evident in the founding and running of the African Workers' Club. Champion lined his own pocket at the expense of the members, whose only safeguard lay in a constitution that was consistently flouted, and the fact that Kadalie apparently condoned his conduct was little to his credit. The Durban leader, with his 'evasive answers and uneasy demeanour', was, to Tatham's mind, 'clever but untruthful'.

The Tatham judgment was not wholly fair. The truth of the facts that came to light is undeniable, though they were set out in a harsh, unsympathetic, and remorseless fashion. What is less certain is that it was fair to infer from his bizarre and naïve bookkeeping that Champion was 'exploiting the less intelligent members' of his people, and what is still less certain is that Lenono published his allegations 'honestly and without malice'. Opening his campaign with an anonymous letter, Lenono proceeded in a manner that conveys an impression of a mere search for vengeance, an impression strengthened by his association with the enemies of the ICU, Ncwana and Nyombolo, in the publication of his pamphlet. Subsequent demonstrations of loyalty to Champion indicate that many ICU members in Durban were convinced of his innocence, however damning the evidence appeared to be. Clearly Champion himself thought his integrity so manifest that his conduct would be vindicated as a matter of course, though he must have known the deviousness and equivocation of his administration would be brought to light. Among the White patrons of the ICU Mrs Palmer thought him innocent of actual dishonesty and even Mrs Lewis considered his offence relatively mild.[19]

No sooner had the Lenono case been decided against Champion than the second scandal erupted, involving the ex-Acting General Secretary, Sam Dunn. Apparently at the insistence of the members, Champion had suspended him from his post as Provincial Secretary in Natal on 2 August. Going through the books, Champion found a loss of £500. Dunn admitted to using £416, which had gone on a car for himself, a one-ton lorry, which he left with his brother in Zululand, furniture for his house, and clearing off some old debts; and he put forward a scheme that would, he said, bring in enough money to cover the loss. Champion was unimpressed and laid charges against him. He was arrested at Komatipoort in November when on his way to Lourenco Marques.[20] Charged with theft by conversion of £800, Dunn came up for trial on 14 December.[21] Some very damaging evidence of extraordinary laxity came out. Hundreds of pounds were often thrown carelessly into an open cash box, miscounted, and casually banked. To exculpate himself, Dunn alleged that 'the whole system of handling the finances was rotten to the core'. Provision in the constitution for death benefit was a fraud. Champion and Kadalie, 'the two autocrats', spent money as fast as it came in without any check. For good measure the accused went on to claim that the ICU was hostile to the White race and that a general strike was being plotted to lead, in the event of action by the Government, to 'a general upheaval all over the country'. Such evidence, offered under such circumstances, clearly has to be treated with care. Nevertheless the description of the financial arrangements confirm the impression gained from the Lenono affair. This did not save Dunn, who was found guilty and sentenced to a year's imprisonment.

Champion also fell into difficulties because the various business enterprises that he ran did not pay. These included the Vuka Afrika Company (a 'Native eating house') and the Natal Boot and Shoe Repairing Hospital.[22] He also ran a newspaper *Udibi Lwase Afrika,* which is unlikely to have been anything other than an additional drain on resources, if the experience of *The Workers' Herald,* with which it needlessly competed, is any guide. If Tatham was correct, these enterprises were subsidized by the ICU. They certainly collapsed with it.[23]

Shortly after the return to South Africa of the National Secretary the National Council met in Johannesburg from 18 to 25 November, in order to hear his report on his European tour and also Champion's report on his term of office as Acting National Secretary. The draft of the amended constitution that had been discussed in England with Creech Jones was accepted with only minor changes and it was decided to summon a special conference to Kimberley to ratify it. When nominations for the new posts were called for, there was some dispute about the appointment of Financial Secretary. Kadalie wanted C. F. Glass, but the appointment of a White to an official position encountered general opposition and the question was referred to the National Council Sub-Committee, a new body provided for under the not yet ratified new constitution. The Sub-Committee subsequently decided to appoint Glass in a temporary capacity, until the adviser expected from Britain was able to train a Black for the post. There was no dissent over the latter appointment, but some objection to bringing from Britain a White private secretary for Kadalie, who, to the apprehension of his English friends, wanted to import the typist he had employed in London.[24]

The National Council meeting produced a number of resolutions. It was agreed to set up a sub-committee to consider the purchase of a printing press and of the Workers' Hall and, in view of the legal opinion taken by Kadalie in England and of the sympathy aroused there, to test the Native Administration Act in the courts and, if necessary, to lodge an appeal with the Privy Council. It was further agreed to seek affiliation to the South African Trades Union Congress.

The last day and a half of the meeting was taken up with a survey of the state of the union. In his report on Natal Champion 'informed the house that the situation . . . in regard to members of the Union who were ejected was critical and that unless farms were purchased for them, they would all leave the Union'. The matter, however, was shelved, left in the hands of the National Council

Sub-Committee. The other provincial reports gave rise to not a little – to use a term commonly employed – backbiting, with charges and counter-charges of irresponsibility, drunkenness, indiscipline, extravagance, scandal-mongering, negligence, indolence, and incompetence. Perhaps the most extraordinary feature of the meeting was the inability of the National Councillors to come to terms with the financial situation. There was Kadalie asking for a private secretary, 'Mote for buildings to be put up on vacant stands leased at Bloemfontein, and Maduna for a hall for Port Elizabeth, while the whole Council discussed the possibility of buying a printing press and the Workers' Hall and accepting without protest a great increase in the size of the salaried staff. This absurd sanguineness was to persist into the new year.

The Kimberley Special Conference opened on Dingaan's Day, 16 December 1927, and was in session until noon of the 20th. Two hundred delegates attended, including a number of women and several chiefs. The Conference, like the previous one, was opened by Kadalie. The South African TUC, invited to send an official to do so, politely declined, and the Mayor of Kimberley was also unavailable, though his Deputy presided over a civic reception to the delegates on the evening of the first day. The proceedings went off, so *The Workers' Herald* reported,[25] 'with the spirit of seriousness, myrth [*sic*] and goodwill'. Yet there was cause for disquiet and a good deal of anger was displayed. On the third day newspaper reporters were asked to leave, ostensibly because their reports were inaccurate and biased, more likely in order that the ICU's dirty linen could be washed in decent privacy. *The Star* described the early debates as stormy, and there was indeed an undercurrent of dissatisfaction with the policy of seeking closer relations with the White labour movement. 'Are you a black man or a white man?' Kadalie was asked by an irate Coloured delegate from Cape Town. This was on the first day, an inauspicious preliminary to a debate upon affiliation to the SATUC.

Little business was done on that first day. On the second, Saturday 17, the President of the African National Congress, Rev. Z. R. Mahabane, attended to congratulate Kadalie upon his journey to Geneva and the ICU upon its success in gaining support and recognition. Calling for 'the unification of all sects and societies for the redemption of Africa', he suggested that the ICU and the ANC co-operate. His impromptu speech, which betrayed both impatience and toughness, was loudly applauded. In moving a vote of thanks, however, Champion took the opportunity of chiding Congress. Three-quarters of the delegates present, including himself, were, he said, members of the ANC, and yet that body engaged in an attempt to organize workers in rivalry to the ICU,[26] and had also given a home to the ICU officials expelled for refusing to resign from the Communist Party. Nonetheless, he welcomed co-operation.

On the Sunday morning the Conference was addressed by a Natal chief, Peter Dhlamini of Richmond, whose remarks initiated a debate on the farm question. While paying tribute to Kadalie as 'a God-sent' and declaring that the people in Natal, even though homeless, were still staunch members, he said that the union must raise money to help those who had been evicted from farms and that an approach must be made to the Government. Kadalie's reply was not much help: he assured the chief that the plight of the people in Natal and the Orange Free State had aroused indignation in England and that farms would be bought, but admitted that money was 'badly needed'. Champion, who spoke next and, as the union's leader in the distressed province, must have been particularly sensitive to criticism of the ICU's performance, was less than gracious. 'To-day,' he said, 'an ignorant Native chief had come to ask them point blank what they were going to do. They did not know whether this man was a spy, because the authorities were very clever and would naturally detail an assumingly ignorant (yet clever) person as a spy . . .' In conclusion he suggested that 'the enemy had succeeded to get 'good boys' into the inner councils of the ICU', perhaps a dig at Kadalie.

Champion seemed to be in favour of a resolution requiring a special levy (an impossible £5 on each member) to buy land. In a rejoinder Kadalie, although he 'admired Champion's speech' and 'must give credit to Comrade Champion for getting the Government to agree to the purchase of farms',[27] uttered some home truths about the ICU machine in Natal. There was no need, he declared for a special levy, since 'Durban branch alone had 56 000 members, and if each member donates only 1s. they would get £2 000 right away. He alleged that the branch offices in Natal were all overstaffed . . . The Head Office in Johannesburg was continually getting big accounts from Natal running into three figures. He urged that all the superfluous clerks in the Natal offices must be retrenched. He was sorry to say that the Natalians were not rendering any service to the organisation . . .'

It is obvious that the rural situation was causing alarm. As J. Mancoe put it: 'What was the good of revising the constitution when the people had no homes?' A Pietermaritzburg delegate related how he and a colleague 'had been sent to look into distress areas, and they discovered that there were hundreds of families actually starving. These families had offered to sacrifice their all if they could only be assured that farms would be purchased.' Lujiza insisted that the land question was crucial for the future of the organization and that something had to be done. Nothing constructive was. On the motion of Kadalie it was decided that the National Council Sub-Committee be authorized to use whatever money there was to buy farms and report progress by the end of February 1928. Ever optimistic Kadalie supposed that 'there was money lying at various branch offices'.

The Conference then resumed the debate on the draft constitution. It is apparent that it encountered fierce criticism, but that acrimony was aroused less by its provisions than by Kadalie's intention to introduce Europeans into officials positions. In defence he pointed out that a narrow racial attitude was inconsistent with the policy of identification with the international labour movement. The discussion raged all night, and it is clear Kadalie did not win his point, because the matter came up again at the National Council meeting of the following month. However, the draft constituion itself was accepted with only minor alteration.[28]

Since 1925 the ICU constitution had undergone two revisions, in 1926 and 1927, presumably, though there is no record of any debate on the subject, at the Sixth (Johannesburg) and Seventh (Durban) Conferences. While neither of these revised constitutions has survived, the nature of the changes made can readily be deduced.[29] The 1926 revision seems to have made changes only in wording. In 1927, however, there were two major changes, both of which had the effect of increasing the power and extending the autonomy of A. W. G. Champion. For, on the one hand, the offices of General Secretary (filled previously by J. La Guma and then Sam Dunn) and Financial Secretary (vacant after the expulsion of E. Khaile) were abolished and their duties transferred to a new official, the Assistant National Secretary, Champion; and, on the other hand, Provincial Secretaries were given power to use General Fund money, which hitherto had to be centralized, for certain specific purposes, this provision, too, strengthening the hand of Champion, who retained a tight grip on Natal affairs even after his promotion to Assistant, then Acting, National Secretary.

One of the important changes of the December 1927 constitution was the dropping of the innovations of its immediate predecessor. The office of Financial Secretary was revived and given more important duties, taking over, in fact, much of the work of the old General Secretary. The National Secretary was renamed the General Secretary (Kadalie) and the Assistant National Secretary the Organizing Secretary (Champion). The centralization of funds was reimposed. Two other major differences were, firstly, the dropping of the IWW-inspired preamble and, secondly, the introduction of proper sectionalization of members. Otherwise only a careful scrutiny of the printed 1925 constitution and a comparison of it with the printed December 1927 constitution[30] can show the differences, since they seem to be so slight. The objects of the union remained much the same as before and its government also remained largely unaltered except for the changes in the titles and functions of the chief officers noted above and for some strengthening of the power of the National Council. A larger number of Provincial Secretaries was envisaged and each of them was to be obliged to acquire 'specialised knowledge of one or more of the main industrial sections enrolled in the Union'. On the whole the new constitution was not revolutionary.

After approving the new constitution and deciding that the regular Conference should be held at Easter, 1928, the delegates left Kimberley on 20 December. They were in high spirits. The Johannesburg Branch Secretary produced a gramophone on the station and Kadalie and Maduna had 'a little "go" on the light fantastic' while they waited for the train, and there was much singing and cheering.[31]

The euphoria was short-lived. During the succeeding months a rift developed between Kadalie and Champion. There had been a long-standing grievance in Natal about money and dissatisfaction was brought to the surface, no doubt by the reversion in the new constitution to centralization of funds, but certainly by the Lenono case. The union had to decide whether or not to assume responsibility for the costs that had been incurred. Another source of friction was the proposed importation of an adviser from England. Kadalie was under great pressure from Mrs Lewis to hasten along the path of moderation and respectability. She, in the meantime, was busy negotiating for assistance from the Carnegie Trust of New York, which seemed favourably disposed to helping the ICU to purchase a sports ground, which, she hoped, would get its members away from the 'coroding preoccupation with their rights and wrongs'.[32] Her most pressing fear remained the Communists. For, it seemed to her, they were again infiltrating the ICU. It had apparently been only during Kadalie's absence that she had become aware of the connection of C. F. Glass with the union, and she was under the false impression that he had been brought in by Champoin. The fact that he had done some useful work on the tangled finances of the ICU did not weigh with her. She wanted him out and an honest adviser in.[33] Another source of worry was the ICUs worsening relations with the Government. The advice of Creech Jones to pursue a policy of restraint in public speeches was not allowed in any way to cramp the established oratorical style of the leaders. There were some arrests for breaches of the Native Administration Act, culminating in the arrest of Kadalie in April, for a speech made in Pretoria after the Easter Conference. A sympathetic magistrate acquitted the General Secretary in May, but his defence imposed an additional financial burden on the slender resources of the ICU.[34]

From the deliberations of the National Council at its meeting of January 1928 in Johannesburg it would be difficult to guess that it was discussing the policy of an organization fast sliding into bankruptcy.[35] Certainly there was some awareness of the financial problem. The General Secretary put forward proposals for curtailing expenditure and there was talk of raising funds to buy land for evicted farm workers by borrowing from the branches. Kadalie was urged to tour the Orange Free State to try and get money. It was obviously a forlorn hope. Abel Ngcobo, Sam Dunn's successor as Provincial Secretary of Natal, thought that his people would be willing to contribute towards buying farms and that they would like to discuss the matter with Kadalie, and this seemed a better proposition than touring the Free State, where, 'Mote said, only three branches had any reserve funds and where 'if we went to collect money now from the people they would require to know what had become of the 5/– collected for the Pass Laws', a reference to an earlier levy raised to campaign against those laws. Kadalie was most reluctant to undertake a tour, but, when the proposal was put to the vote, he found himself in a minority of one.

In spite of the acknowledged gravity of the financial situation there was still serious discussion of sending Kadalie to Geneva again in 1928, of providing him with a private secretary and each Provincial Secretary with a clerk, and of buying a car for Head Office. Moreover, there were still hopes of buying a printing press and the Workers' Hall, though discussion was again deferred. Several new senior appointments were made, including a Research Secretary. Two provincial Secretaries were assigned to the Transvaal (one of them Maduna, who took over North-East Transvaal) to replace Mbeki, first suspended, then dismissed, for habitual drunkenness.

Inevitably there was wrangling. Champion and 'Mote clashed early in the proceedings, and later there was a quarrel over a problem that had arisen at Kroonstad, where the residents of the location had been persuaded, either by themselves or by 'Mote, to resist a rise in rates, refusing to pay while the ICU contested the increase in the courts. When the case, after having been taken to the Supreme Court, was lost, the residents turned to the now impoverished union for assistance in paying arrears, and, unable or unwilling to meet the demands of the City Council, were being ejected from their houses, which were being pulled down.[36] Kadalie, Champion, and 'Mote all disclaimed responsibility for the fiasco. No help was offered to the distressed householders; it was simply agreed that the National Council Sub-Committee should investigate. Another source of dispute was Kadalie's proposal, as part of his plan for reducing expenditure, to insist on National Council sanction for major litigation. This encountered strong opposition from Champion, who said that it would be impossible under such circumstances to carry on in Natal. To the chagrin of the General Secretary (Kadalie), who denounced its unconstitutionality, exemption was granted to Natal. Then there was a row over the fixing of salaries for officers under the new constitution. Kadalie became enraged when the matter was referred to a sub-committee and the National Council adjourned to permit this to discuss the matter at once. He became more angry still over the appointment of a private secretary for himself. It was not that the appointment was rejected (and it was even agreed that he could have a White), but that the salary was fixed absurdly low in his view, and part of it was to come from a reduction in his own salary. Since it was too low for bringing a girl from England, the whole idea of importing secretarial assistance was given up.[37]

The major row was over the Lenono case. There was a preliminary skirmish over a libel suit brought by Rev. John Dube against Champion's paper *Udibi Lwase Afrika*. Kadalie opposed a request from Champion for permission to raise money in Durban to meet costs. He argued that, as *Udibi* was not the union's official paper, the case was entirely Champion's affair, and furthermore repudiated ICU responsibility for the costs of the Lenono case. Champion was deeply offended, declaring that he had acted in the interests of the union and that Kadalie had himself agreed to the action against Lenono and had indeed accompanied him to Cowley's office in connection with it. To add insult to injury Kadalie had already appointed, in the wake of the Tatham judgment, an auditor to go through the Durban books. Now Champion asked for and was granted two months leave. The National Council, against Kadalie's wishes, authorized the payment of the defendant's costs in the Lenono case, a little less than £220.[38]

Less than a week after the National Council meeting the Executive Council of the South African Trade Union Congress met with the executives of its affiliated unions to discuss the application of the ICU for affiliation.[39] Kadalie, by disregarding the advice of Creech Jones to escape from the belief that mere size was a sign of strength[40] and applying for affiliation on the basis of a membership of 100 000, had spoilt what chance there had been of acceptance. One hundred thousand Blacks would have swamped an organization dedicated to the protection of White proletarian interests. At the SATUC meeting an extreme point of view reminiscent of 1922 was advanced by the representative of the South African Mine Workers' Union. 'The native would undersell,' he said, 'the European even if the ICU became affiliated . . . The natives were savages, barbarians. Kadalie is not there to organize the natives for their own benefit but for the capitalists, which was indicated by the expulsion of the Communists from the ICU.' All those present, however, with two exceptions were in favour of consultation with the ICU, because it was thought to be realistic to come to terms with its existence. Subsequently the SATUC consented to, when consulted by the British TUC, the ICU's attendance at the 1928 Commonwealth Labour Conference, an invitation the ICU was in no position to accept.[41]

It appears that the South African Trades Union Congress, solemnly debating the wisdom of admitting the ICU into its ranks, was unaware that it was in fact a hollow shell. For some months yet the leaders themselves, national and local, were spared the truth – or could not face it. Before the collapse they staged one more of their much-loved set pieces, another African Labour Congress. The Eighth Annual Conference of the ICU, which was held in Bloemfontein at Easter 1928, heralded, so *The Workers' Herald* thought, the 'birth of a new nation'.[42] Early in the Conference Kadalie was blithely prophesying a membership of a million by the end of the year. One cause of optimism was the cordial relations that had been established with the African National Congress, which happened to hold its Annual Conference at the same time and place. A joint meeting of the Executive Committee of the ANC and the National Council of the ICU took place on the afternoon of Easter Monday 9 April. The outcome was an agreement to co-operate on opposition to the Hertzog bills and the pass laws. To facilitate this co-operation the ANC repudiated its association with the Communist Party. The good understanding then reached was almost the only solace the ICU derived from the Bloemfontein Conference, and even that source of comfort was illusory. In the succeeding months it was fully occupied with its internal problems.

The proceedings of the Conference were conducted in a hall placed at its disposal by the Anglican Bishop of Bloemfontein, who also consented to address the gathering. 'In a most humorous, yet Christianly speech' Bishop Carey said that 'he had been a labour man himself in England . . . He was a friend of the Bantu in their legitimate aspirations . . . But, he added, if their demands were unfair and unreasonable, he would resist them as strenuously as he would help them otherwise . . .' J. G. Gumbs, presiding for the last time – he died the following year[43] – urged the delegates to 'show by their behaviour that they were in deep thoughts'.

The Conference had before it an Economic and Political Programme for 1928 that had been drawn up by the General Secretary. It betrays the influence of C. F. Glass rather than that of Creech Jones, especially in its introduction: 'Opponents of the ICU have frequently asserted that the Organisation is not a trade union in the sense that the term is generally understood in South Africa, but that it is a kind of pseudo-political body . . . The new constitution . . . definitely establishes the ICU as a trade union, albeit one of native workers . . . At the same time it must be clearly understood that we have no intention of copying the stupid and futile "non-political" attitude of our white contemporaries. As Karl Marx said, every economic question is, in the last analysis, a political question also, and we must recognize that in neglecting to concern ourselves with current politics, in leaving the political machine to the unchallenged control of our class enemies, we are rendering a disservice to those tens of thousands of our members who are groaning under oppressive laws . . . At the present stage of our development it is inevitable that our activities should be almost of an agitational character, for we are not recognised as citizens in our own country, being almost entirely disfranchised and debarred from exercising a say in state affairs closely affecting our lives and welfare.'[44]

The Programme had ten points, concerned with wages, hours, illegal practices by employers, the franchise, the pass laws, land, free speech, propaganda, new recruits, and representation on public bodies. Its objectives were a minimum wage of £5 a month and an eight-hour day, the protection of farm workers against withholding of wages and seizure of stock by employers, the maintenance and extension of the parliamentary franchise for Blacks, suspension of the pass laws, extension of the 'Native reserves', the legalization of squatting, repeal of the provisions of the Native Administration Act restricting the right of free speech, the better information and deeper involvement of ICU members, the establishment of influence among workers 'to whom the ICU is scarcely known' – those in the gold and coal mines and the railways – and the re-establishment of influence among the dock workers, and the election of ICU candidates to the Cape Provincial Council. Its proposed methods were negotiation with employers, use of the machinery of the Wage Act, representations to government officials, petitions to Parliament, propaganda, frequent meetings, and demonstrations. The most militant proposal was the burning of passes in the event of a government refusal to accept a trial suspension of the pass laws.

Point 1 of the Programme – wages – was discussed on Easter Monday. Keable 'Mote began by giving his opinion that five pounds a month for farm labourers was a preposterous wage, which no farmer would ever pay, and cited farm workers in the north-eastern Free State who, on ten shillings a month, were as well off as town workers paid ten pounds a month, and, in some instances, were permitted to keep forty head of cattle each. This information met with some scepticism – 'Loud cries: "That's a confounded lie." ' – and the next speaker, from Natal, pointing out that in his province many farmers paid half a crown a month or even no wages at all, very sensibly remarked, in effect, upon the difficulty of making generalizations for the entire country. What did emerge from the debate was that the delegates could quote examples of farm conditions within their own experience, but that the Conference did not have before it a comprehensive body of statistics in the light of which a reasonable minimum wage could be determined. Opinion was divided between those who thought it was desirable for the ICU to make an unequivocal demand for a minimum wage so that White people would know exactly what the Blacks wanted, and those who argued that a minimum wage for agricultural workers was premature and that a demand for one would only lead to wholesale evictions. R. de Norman reminded the Conference that farm labourers and domestic servants were excluded from the working of the Wage Act and suggested that it was futile to insist upon an agricultural minimum wage before the scope of the Act was widened.

The next subject of debate was the merits of written contracts, whether their advantage as a safeguard for the employee was outweighed by the disadvantage of the restraints associated with them. Champion was against them, and they were also opposed by Mogaecho of Bloemfontein, who thought the best protection of the workers lay in the establishment of labour bureaux, and by John Mancoe of Winburg, who rudely, if irrelevantly, alleged that ICU secretaries wasted time in big towns – eating puddings, and the like – instead of going to the rural areas and organise [*sic*] the real workers of the country.' A motion supporting written contracts for farm labourers was carried.

The proceedings of the Conference were interrupted by a special meeting of the National Council to discuss, as it was given out, the policy of the union with regard to the parliamentary franchise and the next general election. In all probability, however, it was at this meeting that the case of Allison Champion was discussed and the strictures of Justice Tatham at the conclusion of the Lenono trial. By that time the report of the auditors engaged to examine the Durban accounts was in the hands of the National Council. The decision of the meeting was the suspension of Champion pending an inquiry into his financial administration (though it is clear that some leaders, notably Maduna, who subsequently took over Champion's job as Organizing Secretary, were in favour of immediate prosecution)[45], and this decision was upheld by the Conference, which went into private session for two days, Thursday and Friday 12 and 13 April. It must have been during this session, too, that the union endorsed the policy of bringing out an English adviser and agreed not to proceed with the appointment, as Financial Secretary, of C. F. Glass, who, however, remained in a temporary capacity. That policy was the result of pressure from Mrs Lewis.[46] Champion retired to his home at Inanda, a sick man.[47]

On Saturday morning the Conference continued in open session and a debate on the purchase of farms for evicted ICU members was opened by the General Secretary. He had little to say of comfort. Land was not easy to obtain. Several offers of farms in Natal and Zululand had had to be turned down because they were not within a 'Native area' and government permission for their purchase was withheld. This, however, was far from being the greatest of the ICU's difficulties: Of more importance was its bankruptcy. Although after the National Council meeting of January Kadalie had made a round of the branches and succeeded in raising a loan of £200, the only reasonably priced farm which, being within a 'Native area' (in the Harding district of Natal), was readily available required a deposit alone of £800 and a total expenditure of more than £2 000. Kadalie, optimistic as ever, 'was certain that the people themselves would substantially contribute towards the purchase price', but reports from delegates showed that the situation was beyond the remedy of the purchase of a farm or two. These spoke of thousands of evictions in the Orange Free State and Natal, of people 'homeless and starving'.

The only solution to the problem proposed by these delegates was that branches should be empowered to collect money themselves and buy land. The debate developed into a heated discussion on the constitutional propriety and practical desirability of branches of collecting money and entering into contracts. Champion came in for some criticism, and Kadalie, with some sarcasm, observed that, if Champion had achieved nothing while he was Acting National Secretary, it was not because he had spent his time cooped up in Head Office. As a compromise he suggested a land scheme fund administered by headquarters but with separate provincial accounts. This did not satisfy the Natal representatives (and also Simon Elias), who wanted provincial control of money raised for this purpose, and in the end it was they who carried the day. All land scheme funds were to be sent to Provincial Secretaries and administered by provincial committees. The delegates had taken leave of reality. President Gumbs spoke more truly than he realized: 'I think sufficient hot air has been thrown off.'

Considerable, and understandable, indignation was generated by the next item on the agenda, the damage done to ICU property by White hooligans in Weenen, Kranskop, and Greytown. Kadalie compared the trifling fines, ranging from one to five pounds, imposed on the culprits with the heavy bail demanded in the case of two ICU officials recently charged under the Native Administration Act, 'Mote and Dumah. He claimed that the union had lost £200 at Greytown, and 'a considerable sum of money, as well as personal effects and office furniture' at Kranskop. He went on to recommend a civil action for damages. One or two of the delegates, however, were not satisfied that the Head Office officials had acted with sufficient vigour. In response Kadalie pointed out that Head Office had in fact written to the Minister of Justice before the case had come up. A resolution was unanimously passed calling upon the Government to initiate an investigation. There followed a dispute between militants (Kadalie, Dumah, Mancoe) who wanted to re-open the raided offices at once and who volunteered to go and do it in the interests of 'freedom and Justice' and moderates who thought that nothing should be done until after the civil action contemplated by the National Council and that to 'adopt mob law in retaliation is very wrong, as two wrongs do not constitute a right'. There was some sarcasm at the expense of 'those willing to sacrifice their lives' and of those who clearly were not.

There was no meeting on Saturday 14 April. It was pouring with rain and no hall was available. The Conference, when it met for the last time on Sunday, was thinly attended. It discussed the pass laws and the use of municipal by-laws, to impede ICU activity. The usual divergence of view between extremist and moderate appeared. The Pretoria delegate expressed surprise that 'they were still talking about resolutions. In Pretoria they have already started to put words into action, and many of them have thrown away their passes.' The Port Elizabeth representative disagreed. They 'were going rather too fast,' he said, 'There should be no half-hearted measures in this matter, therefore they should first of all get the support of the whole country behind this movement. To hurry and fail is both dangerous and undignified.' Mancoe 'agreed that the rank and file were ready for direct action, but were only waiting for word from the leaders. Maduna told them last Sunday to do away with passes, yet they were now still discussing.' Delegates, however, were reminded by de Norman that they were pledged to co-operation with the African National Congress and moved that the National Council be authorized to meet the Executive Council of the ANC, and this was unanimously agreed to. As for the by-laws, Kadalie advised that the best remedy was to bring a test case. As he picturesquely put it, 'they were allowing too many of these ultra-vires phantoms to stalk rampant through the land destroying all signs of justice'. There was criticism from left and right. Finally the Conference passed without dissent a resolution in favour of a test case.

On Sunday evening there was some discussion of 'matters of internal interest', after which, with the singing of *Nkosi Sikelel'i Afrika* and the *Red Flag*, the Conference dissolved.

In the months following the Bloemfontein Conference the history of the ICU was turbulent. Although it is apparent that Kadalie, in aiding and abetting Champion's suspension, was unaware that he was stirring up a hornet's nest, it must have been clear to him that he was challenging a formidable opponent, and his reasons for committing himself to so risky a course of action are a matter of speculation. The most obvious reason, and not less likely to be true for being so, was that the ICU could not afford to give the impression that it condoned a defalcation of such proportions by one of its principal officers. However, it is also obvious that Kadalie had little choice but to accept the explanation thought up by his European supporters for the crisis facing the union. This is how Mrs Lewis saw the situation: 'A very great set-back was given to the ICU during Kadalie's absence at Geneva last year by the misdeeds of the man who took his place as secretary for the time being. It was this man Champion, a Natal native, who (1) introduced a very dangerous man into the office as book-keeper and general factotum, a Russian Jew of a virulent political type who has wasted no opportunities of working for his crowd, and discovering everything possible about the ICU. (2) He (Champion) used the ICU funds for his own purposes and ran up huge debts to lawyers as well, leaving the ICU in a very precarious financial state which Kadalie has had to struggle against ever since his return six months ago.'[48] If he chose not to put the blame at Champion's door, who or what else could be held responsible? When he sailed for Europe, he left behind an apparently prosperous and expanding organization; he returned to a dwindling membership and empty coffers. If the damage had not been done in his absence, if Kadalie had in fact been in a position to know quite well the real state of the ICU, then he had deceived himself and his friends, hardly an admission he would have cared to make. Another possible explanation for Kadalie's conduct was that he thought the time had come for a show-down with an over-mighty lieutenant, also not an implausible theory. For Champion undoubtedly regarded himself as something of a kingmaker. Champion's friends, however, advanced another explanation, among them Batty, who had gone to live in Durban and had apparently been working for Champion and drawing an ICU salary.[49] 'Kadalie is driven,' Batty thought, 'by the fear that the Government may call for an audit of all the Books at Head Office and we know what that would mean. Therefore, at all cost, Kadalie must confine the trouble to Natal.'[50]

It is not impossible that the General Secretary was hoping, by dropping Champion, to escape responsibility for the ICU debts contracted in Durban. Cowley, after collecting a considerable income from the union in 1926–1927, was no longer being paid and was dunning it. Kadalie prevaricated. Although he did not have a fraction of the thousand pounds that the lawyer was demanding, he gained time by quibbling about certain items on the bill and by promising payment and then going back on his promise. One of the heaviest charges was Champion's own costs in the Lenono case, and the easiest way of reducing the bill and delaying payment was to question the ICU's responsibility for them. In February 1928, Kadalie and Glass, accompanied by other officials, called at Cowley's office to discuss the outstanding account and ways of reducing future expenditure, and it was then that they repudiated responsibility for the Lenono costs, objecting at the same time to the payment of a substantial retaining fee, which Cowley claimed as compensation for not taking cases against the ICU.[51] Cowley was told that he must get the Lenono money from Champion himself, and this he promptly tried to do,[52] in spite of the fact that he entertained hopes of enlisting Champion's support in securing election to the House of Assembly to represent Africans in the event of the passage of Hertzog's 'Native bills' – 'even though I lose money by it'.[53] Champion, of course, had no more money than Kadalie. At the beginning of March 1927, his patience worn out, Cowley threatened to issue a summons if his bill were not paid.[54] Kadalie seemed to think – erroneously, as it turned out – that the ICU was safe from any legal action because it was 'an unincorporated body, capable in law neither of suing nor of being sued'.[55] Perhaps because he too was doubtful, Cowley stayed his hand for some months, and when the summons was issued, it was prudently issued against, not only the ICU, but also the trustees of the African Workers' Club – one of them Champion – which was the only institution connected with the ICU that had any assets.[56]

It was clearly not the intention of either the General Secretary or the Organizing Secretary to break off all relations, and Champion went ahead with preparations to present his defence before the proposed commission of inquiry into his administration.[57] From Inanda Champion got his wife to write to Kadalie, who replied sympathetically and at his most charming. 'I am deeply touched to know that Comrade Champion is laid up and that he is unable to do any writing . . . I hope, however, Providence will restore him his usual health.'[58] Meanwhile in Durban, during Champion's absence, the ICU members, incensed by the treatment meted out to their compatriot, embraced his cause with enthusiasm. On 19 April Durban branch held an emergency meeting from which William Smith, the Financial Secretary, who was in the town with de Norman, both members of the commission of inquiry,[59] and Abel Ngcobo, the Provincial Secretary for Natal, were excluded, on the ground that they had not spoken up for the Organizing Secretary in the National Council. Resolutions were passed demanding the auditing of Head Office books and expressing confidence in Champion's honesty and integrity.[60]

At the end of April Kadalie set out for Durban to try and pacify the angry supporters of Champion. Apparently his nerve failed him on the way and he stopped short at Pietermaritzburg, whereupon the Durban members who had assembled to meet him, impatient from their long and fruitless wait, sent a car to fetch him from his bed in the middle of the night. After a stormy and unprofitable meeting, during which he had the utmost difficulty in gaining a hearing, Kadalie was allowed to go at daybreak upon promising to attend a resumed meeting in the evening. He did not go back, but fled to Pietermaritzburg, then to Johannesburg. The adjourned meeting was subdued and, although some speakers talked of secession, the majority was against it.[61] One result, however, of the confrontation with Kadalie was the resurgence of the tribal feeling that the ICU had been largely successful in suppressing. 'We are angry, terribly angry,' declared one speaker, 'but let us show Kadalie we Zulus are gentlemen, and will not be interfered with by a man from Nyasa [*sic*].'[62]

A few days later, at its weekly meeting, Durban branch delivered an ultimatum, demanding that the National Council meet in the city within fourteen days, reinstate Champion, and abandon the commission of inquiry, failing which 'drastic measures' would be taken.[63] The next Sunday, 6 May, Champion was brought from his sickbed to witness a demonstration in his support.[64] Two weeks later Durban seceded. Champion, in a letter to Kadalie, professed ignorance of this plot; he said that he had gone to Durban on Sunday 20 May to address the members, but, discovering what was afoot, had declined to speak; and asked for 'an advice', complaining that since the Conference he had received no information at all, from either Head Office or the Natal Provincial Office, and that the only news he had heard had been from the papers and from Smith and de Norman.[65] His complaint was unjustified, for, at the end of April, he had been sent a copy of the accountants' report on the Durban books.[66] Meanwhile Champion's White friends were unsparing in their advice. A. F. Batty was urging him not to 'take this set-back lying down', 'to defeat the diabolical plot up North', while Mrs Palmer was exhorting him to submit to the inquiry in the interests of clearing his name and reputation, and to appreciate the dilemma of the Conference, which, in the circumstances, could not have acted otherwise than it did. She regarded secession as 'disastrous . . . a serious decline in the importance and influence of the Union', especially if Champion consented to lead the dissident branch; for 'such a proceeding, though it might be immediately gratifying to you, would in the end destroy your prestige with the white people and with many of your own people.'[67]

Ignoring the advice of Mrs Palmer, Champion accepted the position of General Secretary of a separate Natal organization, the ICU yase Natal. It is easy to see his point of view. 'I was responsible,' he declared, 'for the biggest contribution to the funds of the ICU. My activities in Natal were responsible for the magnitude of the ICU in 1926 and 1927. We had funds enough to send Mr Kadalie to the Geneva Conference and we supported him with over £800 while he was overseas . . . I had caused the freedom of Mr Kadalie when the Government had put a ban against his free movements, but when he came back from Europe he turned up [*sic*] against me . . .' This was broadly true. Other charges the Natal leader made did not have the same substance. Writing to Kadalie in May, he accused him of levity – while the offices of the ICU at Greytown were burning, Kadalie was 'forcing girls in the Hall to dance on a gramophone [*sic*]' – and fraternizing with the outcast Lenono. At the same time he suggested that the appointment of an auditor to investigate the Durban accounts was an act of revenge 'to damage my character more than the Judge had done'. The motive for the alleged revenge is, however, obscure.[68]

Before the final breach an attempt was made to effect a reconciliation. A settlement was patched up, which provided for Champion's reinstatement, the ending of secession, and provincial autonomy in financial matters, but it was never implemented and it is unlikely that Champion ever intended to take Durban back into the ICU, even if he could have. For his part Kadalie was unhappy about provincial autonomy, which he regarded as a retrogressive step and openly attacked in July 1928.[69]

The success of Champion in defying Kadalie was probably the most important reason for the hatching of a plot in June 1928, to oust him. The conspirators, calling themselves the Clean Administration Group, issued a Manifesto complaining that 'ever since the inception of the Union no financial statement had been given to the Congresses or published'[70] and promising reform. The Group included Maduna, Doyle Modiakgotla, the Provincial Secretary for Griqualand West, and 'Mote and possibly C. F. Glass. The scorn of Champion, who was implicitly included in the condemnation, knew no bounds. 'To me the Clean Administration Group stands in a position of Satan trying to reprove sin . . .'[71] De Norman, himself disaffected, was just as contemptuous. 'These fellows,' he wrote to Champion, 'I do not in the least trust, because they are no better than their chief. The publication, all the same, of the Manifesto by his friends will be a revelation to many of the "great" Man's friends (Europeans), some of whom regard him as an Angel. I am now auditing the books of the Head Office and . . . the matters to be disclosed in this Audit will astound many people . . . I do not know whether I will be able to complete the Audit, as the Office Furniture may be attached any day and we might have to get out . . . It seems to me that the lead given by Natal will be followed by Free State and the Transvaal . . . No money is coming from any quarter and there is not a penny in the bank. Wages, as you are aware, have not been paid for some time and accounts are remaining unpaid. It seems there is no other option but for the closing of the Head Office. One thing, however, the so-called left wingers agree with us is that *Kadalie must go*. But of course there [*sic*] motives are different. Under the guise of Clean Administration, they are office seekers . . . One can safely say that Kadalie, as far as Public Life is concerned *is finished*.'[72]

Such was the ICU just before the arrival of the adviser from England, W. G. Ballinger.

Notes

1. *The Natal Witness* 28 and 29 June 1927.
2. Fragment of draft of Acting National Secretary's Report to the National Council 17 November 1927 (F 1927/118).
3. *The Workers' Herald* 15 July 1927.
4. *Cape Times* 9 July 1927.
5. *The Natal Witness* 23 June 1927; *The Workers' Herald* 18 January and 12 May 1928.
6. Report on Volksrust and Wakkerstroom, ICU News Letter 5 December 1928 (B/UCT).
7. C. Cowley to Provincial Secretary, ICU 15 November 1927 (F 1928 – *sic* – /21 f).
8. Fragment in A. W. G. Champion's hand in the Forman Collection, UCT.
9. A. W. G. Champion to General Hertzog 27 May 1927 (F 1927/14).
10. Private Secretary to the Prime Minister to A. W. G. Champion 14 June 1927 (F 1927/20).

11. A. W. G. Champion to Secretary, Natal Agricultural Union 31 July 1927 (F/NEUF)
12. Secretary to A. W. G. Champion 8 August 1927 (F/NEUF).
13. E. R. Gathorne to A. W. G. Champion 14 November 1927 (F 1927/119).
14. Minutes of National Council November 1927 (F 1927/124); A. W. G. Champion to K. 'Mote 3 November 1927 (F/General Letters/173).
15. Branch Secretary, Vryheid to A. J. Phoofolo 27 October 1927 (F 1927/96); Branch Secretary, Ladysmith to National Secretary 3 November 1927 (F 1927/110); C. D. Modiakgotla to A. W. G. Champion 9 July 1927 (F/General Letters/4).
16. Investigation and Report – Natal Provincial and Durban Offices of the ICU 4 April 1928, Annexure F (F 1928/24).
17. G. Lenono to C. Kadalie 15 November 1926 (F 1926/53a); Lenono, G., 1927, *The ICU Funds: Mr Allison Champion, Provincial Secretary ICU (Natal) and the ICU Funds*, (Durban).
18. Telegram from A. W. G. Champion to C. Kadalie n.d. (F/Undated MSS/30). Gumbs was in Durban for the trial.
19. Investigation and Report: Natal Provincial and Durban Offices of the ICU 4 April 1928, Annexure B, Mr Justice Tatham's judgment in the Champion v. Lenono case (F 1928/24): M. Palmer to A. W. G. Champion 20 December 1927 (Forman Collection); E. Lewis, ICU, 12 December 1927 (misdated 1928) (Wits ICU).
20. *The Natal Witness* 11 and 21 November 1927.
21. *The Natal Witness* 15 December 1927.
22. Unidentified fragment attached to a list of delegates attending the ICU Conference of December 1927 (F 1927/134).
23. Cf. C. Cowley to A. W. G. Champion 15 May 1928 (F 1928/36).
24. Minutes of the National Council (F 1927/124); A. C. Jones to C. Kadalie 8 November 1927 (WH); C. Kadalie to A. C. Jones 30 November 1927 (WH); Champion, A. W. G., *Mehlomadala*, 4 (translation, B/UCT, 2).
25. The Conference was reported in its issue of 18 January 1928.
26. He was referring to the African Labour Congress.
27. This was credit wrongly attributed. Although Champion had certainly negotiated with farmers for the purchase of land, the Government was unsympathetic. Cf. A. W. G. Champion to C. L. Dube 26 October 1927 (F/General Letters/158); *The Workers' Herald* 12 May 1928; Central Archives: Department of Labour 4003/1103/1 Secretary for Native Affairs to Secretary for Labour 26 October 1927. The Chief Native Commissioner was especially unsympathetic after the Lenono case (Chief Native Commissioner to Cowley and Cowley 9 February 1928, F 1928/7).
28. Champion, A. W. G. *Mehlomadala*, 22 – English section; *The Workers' Herald* 18 January 1928.
29. Cf. Investigation and Report: Natal Provincial and Durban Offices of the ICU 3 April 1928 (F 1928/23), 3–4.
30. Industrial and Commercial Workers' Union of Africa 1928: *Constitution and Rules; Revised and Adopted by Special Congress at Kimberley 16th to 21st December, 1927*, Johannesburg.
31. *The Workers' Herald* 18 January 1928.
32. £750 a year for five years was made available to the Associated Joint Councils, but Dr C. T. Loram made sure that none of it reached the ICU (C. T. Loram to E. Lewis 8 February, 1928, B/Wits; F. P. Keppel, Carnegie Corporation, to E. Lewis 30 September 1930, B/Wits).
33. Telegram E. Lewis to W. Holtby 27 March 1928 (B/Wits); E. Lewis to Lord Olivier 2 April 1928 (B/UCT), in which she altered the phrase 'a group of savages' to 'a group of uneducated natives'.
34. King v. Clements Kadalie. Con. Section 29(1) Act 38 of 1927, 22 and 29 May 1928 (B/Wits).

35. Agenda of the National Council, First Session of 1928 (F 1928/2); Minutes of National Council 6–9 January 1928 (F 1928/1)
36. *Cape Times* 21 January 1928; Minutes of National Council November 1927 (F 1927/124); Minutes of National Council, January 1928 (F 1928/1).
37. A Creech Jones to C. Kadalie 8 February 1928 (WH).
38. C. Cowley to C. Kadalie 17 February 1928 (F 1928/21c); A. W. G. Champion, *Mehlomadala*, 5 (translation, B/UCT, 3). The Dube libel case was settled out of court (A. M. Ngcobo to A. W. G. Champion 30 January 1928, F 1928/5).
39. South African Trade Union Congress, Minutes of Meeting of the National Executive Council with the Executives of the Affiliated Unions 15 January 1928 (B/UCT); A. Creech Jones to C. Kadalie 27 February 1928 (WH).
40. A. Creech Jones to C. Kadalie 21 October and 8 November 1927 (WH).
41. The South African Labour Party withheld its consent (Partha Sarathi Gupta, op cit., 123).
42. The Conference was reported in *The Workers' Herald* 12 May 1928.
43. M. Rousseau to A. W. G. Champion n.d.; A. W. G. Champion to M. Rousseau 23 July 1929 (F 1929/23a & b).
44. Economic and Political Programme for 1928 (F 1928/64; *The Workers' Herald* 12 May 1928).
45. ICU News Letter 19 October 1928.
46. E. Lewis to F. Keppel 19 May 1930 (B/UCT). According to Champion (*Mehlomadala*, 4, translation, B/UCT, 2) Kadalie wanted to keep Glass, which is probably true.
47. Some suspected poisoning (N. J. Mcunu to A. W. G. Champion 25 April 1928, F 1928/30).
48. E. Lewis to Lord Olivier 20 June 1928 (B/Wits).
49. W. Smith (?) to A. W. G. Champion 29 August 1927 (F 1927/50).
50. A. F. Batty to A. W. G. Champion 18 April 1928 (F 1928/26).
51. A. W. G. Champion to C. Kadalie 11 February 1927 (F 1927/3).
52. C. Cowley to A. W. G. Champion 17 February 1928 (two letters – F 1928/9 & 10) and to C. Kadalie 17 February 1928 (F 1928/21c).
53. C. Cowley to A. W. G. Champion 17 February 1928 (F 1928/9).
54. Telegram C. Cowley to ICU, Johannesburg 8 March 1928 (F 1928/22i).
55. C. Kadalie to C. Cowley 16 March 1928 (F 1928/19).
56. Summons, Supreme Court of South Africa, Natal Provincial Division, between Cecil Cowley, Plaintiff, ICU, first defendant, and trustees of certain landed properties purporting to belong to the African Workers' Club, 2nd defendants, 8 May 1928 (F 1928/34).
57. A. W. G. Champion to C. Kadalie 14 April 1928 (F 1928/25).
58. C. Kadalie to Mrs R. Champion 20 April 1928 (F 1928/28).
59. R. de Norman to A. W. G. Champion 26 June 1928 (F 1928/51).
60. *The Natal Advertiser* 20 April 1928.
61. *Natal Mercury* 27 and 28 April 1928; *The Natal Advertiser* 28 April 1928; *The Natal Witness* 28 April 1928.
62. *Natal Mercury* 27 April 1928.
63. Resolutions proposed by General Meeting held in Durban Thursday 2 May 1928 (F 1928/32).
64. Champion, A. W. G., *Mehlomadala*, 8 (translation, B/UCT, 5).
65. A. W. G. Champion, to C. Kadalie 22 May 1928 (F 1928/39). To Mrs Palmer also he disclaimed any knowledge of the impending secession (A. W. G. Champion to M. Palmer 23 May 1928, F 1928/40).
66. C. Kadalie to A. W. G. Champion 23 April 1928 (F 1928/29).
67. A. F. Batty to A. W. G. Champion 18 April 1928 (F 1928/26); M. Palmer to A. W. G. Champion 21 May 1928 (F 1928/38); cf. also M. Palmer to A. W. G. Champion 6 June 1928 (F 1928/43).

68. Champion, A. W. G., *Mehlomadala*, 21 (English section); A. W. G. Champion to C. Kadalie 14 May 1928 (F 1928/35).
69. *Natal Advertiser* 15 June 1928; telegram C. Kadalie to A. G. W. Champion 21 June 1928 (F 1928/50); Manifesto of 9 July 1928 (B/UCT).
70. Memorandum of W. G. Ballinger, n.d. (B/Wits).
71. A. W. G. Champoin to President and Members of the National Council 26 June 1928 (F 1928/53; B/UCT). 'Mote is identified as the 'man who betrayed his own men during the Bloemfontein riots', Glass among 'others who did not care to have their names known including white renegades who have failed both in the Communist Party and trade Union Congress'. Champion mentions a fifth, 'a man who should be arrested because he stole the ICU Funds', perhaps Simon Elias.
72. R. de Norman to A. W. G. Champion 26 June 1928 (F 1928/51).

CHAPTER 11

The Adviser, 1928-1929

'The ICU with all its shortcomings must boast of being the pioneer trade union that pioneered the trade union movement in South Africa under the leaderships [sic] *of Messrs. Clements Kadalie and Allison Champion and that when there was a disagreement there came to South Africa William Ballinger who made a mess of the whole thing.'*

A. W. G. Champion, *c.* 1929

'I still cannot help thinking that it was a good day's work for Africa when Kadalie asked for a White adviser. You have paid the price. You have been falsely suspected by Natives and Europeans alike. Your work has been belittled, ill-rewarded, underpaid. You have been frequently let down by your own collegues, and must often feel that your task was not only impossible but unnecessary. Yet I have no doubt at all that things in Africa today, bad as they are, are better than if you had not gone there.'

Winifred Holtby to W. G. Ballinger, 1932

'Ballinger did not manage to save the ICU and I think you can argue without fear of libel that he was not the best man for the job. But even if he had been an angel I don't think he could have saved it. The causes of the collapse were too general to be laid at the door of any one man.'

E. R. Roux, 1944

After a search of several months for a suitable Adviser to the ICU, the choice finally fell upon W. G. Ballinger. William Ballinger, who had been born in England, but whose family had moved to Scotland when he was a child, was then thirty-four, much the same age as Kadalie. He had come up the hard way. His father died when he was a boy and his first job was on the coal 'screes', sorting out coal from slate and stone. In time, however, he learnt a trade in the blacksmithing department of the railway workshops, where he joined the Amalgamated Society of Engineers. A dedicated trade unionist and a member of the Independent Labour Party, Ballinger was an excellent example of those Scottish socialists, hardworking, self-denying and of humble origin, who had made such a notable contribution to the British labour movement. After attending Workers' Educational Association extra-mural classes at Glasgow University, he took up a scholarship at the Folk High School of Elsinore, working his way to Denmark on a tramp steamer. It was through a WEA tutor, W. H. Marwick, that Ballinger first heard of the appointment with the ICU.

He was put in touch with George Aitken, a former missionary in Africa, then connected with the Union of Democratic Control in Glasgow, who recommended him to Miss Holtby as a man of 'grit, adaptability, and considerable experience in industrial, municipal and electioneering work'. At that time the future Adviser was acting as the agent of the Rev. James Barr, MP for Motherwell, and was Secretary of the Motherwell Trades and Labour Council and a town and parish councillor.[1]

To begin with Creech Jones had reservations about Ballinger's suitability, feeling that his trade union experience was not sufficiently long, varied, and senior, but after interviewing him at Manchester in March 1928, he decided to support his application. Miss Holtby was favourably impressed. 'I like very much,' she wrote, 'the tone of the letters we have had from him.' Kadalie expressed satisfaction with the choice, but was slow in confirming the appointment, chiefly, no doubt, because of shortage of money. May came before the ICU finally made the appointment, for a year with a possible extension to two.[2]

It was made quite clear to Ballinger that he was not destined for a sinecure. In letters to him and in a conversation with him at her London home, Winifred Holtby left him in no doubt that the very existence of the ICU was in the balance and that he was in for a difficult time, without, however, expressing any lack of confidence in Kadalie. She assured him that he would have the assistance of the Johannesburg Joint Council. It appears that he had already heard a disquieting report from a veteran and much respected socialist who had been shocked by Kadalie's behaviour on his visit to Scotland the previous year – his preoccupation with money and his comfort; but nothing he heard from Miss Holtby was sufficient to put him off. Like many socialists of the ILP persuasion he had pronounced secular missionary proclivities, and his profound sympathy for the lowest ranks of the working class and his distaste for the 'Labour Aristocrats' are beyond doubt.[3]

Before the new Adviser could sail two obstacles had to be overcome. One was the inability of the ICU even to pay his passage. Creech Jones was scrupulously anxious not to have the fare paid by sympathizers lest this should be interpreted as limiting Kadalie's freedom of choice, but eventually it was paid by Miss Holtby, who was later reimbursed by Mrs Lewis.[4] The surprising thing is that the appointment was proceeded with at all, given the ICU's dire financial straits. Kadalie was being less than honest, or at least wildly unrealistic, in promising a salary of £350 a year plus 'organising expenses', when he knew perfectly well that the ICU was bankrupt, but, though evasive in letters to England that referred to its difficulties, he was most anxious to get an adviser, presumably in the desperate hope of a miraculous rescue of his union from its plight.[5] Temporary assistance came from 'A Friend' – almost certainly Mrs Lewis, who promised £230 in monthly instalments towards the Adviser's salary, on the interesting condition that payments would cease if any leader or official of the

ICU were convicted under Section 29 of the Native Administration Act, under which, of course, an action was then pending against Kadalie himself.[6]

The second obstacle was the difficulty in persuading the South African authorities to admit Ballinger into the country. He sailed at the end of June third class on the *Kildonan Castle*, but on his arrival in Cape Town was served with a notice deeming him a prohibited immigrant, presumably because of the Nationalist ministers' view of the ICU rather than on account of any damning information about Ballinger's background.[7] Told that he had three days in which to appeal against this decision, the new Adviser was given a temporary residence permit.[8] The next move was made by the Minister of the Interior, Dr D. F. Malan. Since, as a member of a coalition government that included the Labour Party and was therefore indirectly dependent upon the support of the White labour movement, he could scarcely expel a trade unionist who enjoyed the backing of the Trades Union Congress of Britain, he avoided a scandal by granting the newcomer a three months' permit that required him to report his movements to the police, but at least allowed him to take up his duties. When it later became clear that the ICU Adviser was no firebrand, but rather the protégé of the Johannesburg Joint Council and the eminently respectable liberal establishment, Dr Malan gave way to the representations of the South African TUC to the extent of granting Ballinger a temporary permit which did not require periodic renewal or reporting to the police. The deeming order, however, remained in force, leaving Ballinger in a limbo where he was left undisturbed until his residence status was questioned twenty-two years later. At the Orange Free State National Party congress in October 1928, the Prime Minister, seeking to ally the fears of his followers, spoke of Ballinger as a moderating influence.

Kadalie, borrowing the train fare from Mrs Lewis, travelled down to Cape Town to meet his new Adviser. What he thought of him at the time can only be guessed at, since the sole record of his first impression dates from the period after the two had fallen out. Ballinger's own comment was: 'K. is a very likable chap and has a fund of good commonsense', a view that he was later to modify. Together they called on the local branch offices, where Ballinger found 'Financial transactions appalling; routine slipshop'. He also found morale low, animosity towards himself and resentment against Kadalie. In fact, Cape Town not long afterwards seceded. This was an inauspicious start and a portent that was soon to be confirmed by a brief stop-over at De Aar, where once more the Adviser was appalled by the apparent ignorance of, or indifference to, the elementary rules of bookkeeping. In Johannesburg he was welcomed by a contingent of supporters and well-wishers, a reception that was chiefly notable for the hopes expressed by prominent representatives of South African liberal opinion. Addresses of welcome were delivered by Howard Pim and Rheinallt Jones, Chairman and Secretary of the Johannesburg Joint Council. To welcome him at the ICU headquarters there were five writs from creditors demanding a total of £451 and only £100 in the bank, which presumably was still there only because it was on fixed deposit and the deposit receipt had been lost. In the succeeding weeks his horror deepened. 'ICU affairs,' he wrote early in August, 'are in a deplorable position . . . It is too early to say whether the organisation can be saved. I can only say, if it is, it will be a miracle.' A week later, however, he had cheered up a little. With five hundred pounds he thought he would be able to pull through.[10]

Shortly after their Adviser's arrival in Johannesburg the members of the National Council pledged themselves to support the reorganization of the Head Office in the way proposed by him and also the reorganization of the union on the model of the Transport and General Workers' Union of Britain, and furthermore 'to in every way assist in carrying out the instructions of our Adviser sanctioned by the National Council Sub-Committee'. They urged rank and file to pay their subscriptions; and exhorted Branch Secretaries to honour their constitutional obligation to centralize these subscriptions and raise additional money by means of a half-crown levy. 'Mistakes have been made in the past, they admitted, but they have not been wilful, they have been largely due to our inexperience.'[11]

The problems Ballinger faced in the succeeding months were immense, if not insoluble: bankruptcy, persecution of rural members, secession, strikes, administrative chaos, and petty quarrels.[12] Above all there was the shortage of money, with fewer than a dozen branches paying their way,[13] and there was the dunning of creditors – printers, lawyers, unpaid officials.[14] So desperate were his straits that in September he toyed with the idea of going in for illicit diamond buying and even went so far as to discuss this with Dr Lewis. His wife's dismay was unbounded, her self-righteousness outraged. Such a project would be a betrayal of friends in England and South Africa. 'Most of all,' she went on, 'it would be a betrayal of myself, who have worked for two and a half years under almost hopeless conditions to make friends for the ICU, who have made myself a laughing stock to many people because of it, and who have spent as much time on the work as if I had written a couple of books which might now be of considerable commercial value to me. It is not merely a question of cash, it is my own unwritten work that has been my greatest sacrifice to this native cause.' Under threat of cutting off further financial help, she extorted a written assurance of good behaviour.[15]

Though rather against the better judgment of Creech Jones, who thought that a trade union which had to rely on external subventions was not worth supporting, money was made available from England, where an appeal to trade unions, among other bodies, secular and religious, and individuals, had a modest success, and from the International Federation of Trade Unions, which was persuaded by Walter Citrine of the British TUC to make a grant (of £100). Such sums fell ludicrously short of the ICUs needs and also had the effect of changing Ballinger's relationship with the union. He was not merely the Adviser; he was paymaster, doling out to officials small amounts of money and paying bills, partly from his own salary, and practising rigid economies. His control and supervision extended to every part of the organization. Within a month of his arrival he had put a stop to unnecessary telephoning, made the new Financial Secretary (Geddes Nolutshungu) directly responsible to himself, taken over the Research Department, separated the running of *The Workers' Herald* and the Workers' Hall from the rest of the union's administration, undertaken personal instruction of 'propagandists', and pressed forward with consultations with the South African TUC.[16]

Ballinger's policy aimed at turning the ICU from an 'unwieldy mass organisation to united industry group organisation'. With this end in view he proposed (though this was not implemented) the abolition of the provincial divisions and the grouping of branches in smaller areas, and he pushed ahead with the sectionalization of the membership already envisaged by Kadalie. Major financial reforms were introduced. Above all a stamp system for subscriptions was adopted from the ILP. Branch Secretaries indented for stamps from Head Office, issued them in return for subscriptions, and centralized the funds raised from their sale. At the same time an attempt was made to complete registers of paid officials and of members. To tighten up financial controls Howard Pim, the head of a firm of accountants, was persuaded to audit the accounts monthly, the old books being closed and new ones opened. Several branches were visited in the Orange Free State and Transvaal and their books inspected. Ballinger fulminated against the incompetence and corruption, both local and central, that were brought to light. A number of officials were dismissed, including Simon Elias for embezzlement – for the second time.[17]

Apart from being very difficult to carry out at a time of disintegration and instability, such measures, admirable as they were, had little chance of succeeding because of the chronic shortage of trained and efficient officials. To remedy this, Ballinger sounded W. H. Andrews on the possibility of White trade union supervision of ICU branches and the Principal of Lovedale, James Harrison, on the possibility of recruiting officials from among the students there and at Fort Hare, but the union collapsed before anything could be done on those lines.[18]

It can readily be imagined how this consorting with the bourgeois respectable struck the Communist Party, by then altogether disillusioned with Kadalie. In September 1928, E. R. Roux gave his assessment of the situation to Dr Norman Leys, a former Medical Officer of Health in Kenya and a well-known critic of colonial rule, with whom he was on terms of mutual respect but ideological disagreement. Leys was connected with the Holtby-Jones group and had met Kadalie in England. 'The important thing to realise', Roux explained, 'is that Kadalie is as much a rogue as any of the others . . . The ICU (the Transvaal section or part of it) seems to have been taken over by the Chamber of Mines representative (Howard Pim), Rheinallt Jones (another anti-socialist, though I believe an honest negrophile of conservative type) and the ILP – rather a strange collection . . . I am in favour of disbanding the ICU as speedily as possible by appealing to all honest members to join the Communist Party . . .' The latter was by then proceeding with its own unionization plans, operating through the South African Non-European Trade Union Federation. The official Communist policy, however, was to penetrate and take over the ICU.[19]

Mrs Lewis urged Ballinger to concentrate on Johannesburg and the Rand, to abandon Natal and withdraw from the rural areas. An obligation remained, however, to those distressed farm workers who had trusted the ICU. Therefore an attempt was made to arrange talks with the farmers. In September 1928, Ballinger and Kadalie met the executive of the Farmers' Union of Volksrust, which agreed to let Ballinger address its annual conference on 20 October. At the time this was regarded as a great victory, but subsequently the invitation was repudiated by the rank-and-file, and Ballinger was not given a hearing. In any case the farmers' battle was won. The ICU had nothing to bargain with. Totally without funds, it was in no position to withhold labour. Ballinger endeavoured to maintain some contact with the countryside, but the strength of this link depended wholly upon the devotion and altruism of unpaid representatives. In truth the farm labourers' revolt had faded before the Adviser's arrival.[20]

Despite the Volksrust disappointment and the struggle against debt the ICU still seemed lively and to have a chance of recovery. Some money was coming in and there was still a measure of support. Officials, among them Ballinger and Kadalie, conducted vigorous tours in an attempt to revive interest. *The Workers' Herald* (unpublished in June and July) was brought out again; a weekly news letter (*Weekly News*) started; a meeting arranged between the Trades Union Congress and the ICU National Council; conferences of branch secretaries held in Natal, the Transvaal, and the Orange Free State; the claims of the Johannesburg shop workers for higher wages pressed; and an insurance scheme proposed to cover members for death benefit. Perhaps the most hopeful sign for the future was the long awaited Wage Board determination of September 1928, fixing a minimum daily wage of 3s.6d. for unskilled workers in Bloemfontein.

In October the union became involved in two industrial disputes, one at Onderstepoort, near Pretoria, concerning the workers at the government veterinary laboratory and farm, the other the workers at the Johannesburg post office. The first dispute was caused by 95 members of the ICU who wanted their claim for higher wages to be presented by officials of their union, with which, however, the Director of Veterinary Services declined to deal. The five members of a deputation that tried to interview him were dismissed, precipitating a strike. The police were called in, arrested 26 strikers, and marched them off to Pretoria, where they were charged under the Masters and Servants Act. All but five were fined ten shillings and subsequently dismissed from their employment. Ballinger enlisted the support of the Trade Union Congress, which took up the matter with the Minister of Agriculture, but to no avail, and the strikers failed to get their jobs back. Mrs Lewis devoted her efforts to trying to extract from General Hertzog a promise of a more sympathetic attitude towards Ballinger and the union. In a letter during the Onderstepoort trouble she requested him to grant the Adviser an interview, pleading at the same time for understanding and promising an end to agitation among farm workers. The inducement she offered was familiar: 'Mr Ballinger's work here is meant as a wedge between the native and the Moscow agitator and he might have some hopes of success if he could count on Government support instead of Government enmity.' A few days later the request for an interview and freedom from police surveillance was repeated, though with greater simplicity, by the Rev. Ray Phillips and J. D. Rheinallt Jones of the Joint Council. The request for an interview was once again courteously refused. Although Hertzog regarded Ballinger as a moderating influence, he could not agree that the ICU was a proper trade union.[21]

In her letter to the Prime Minister Mrs Lewis expressed the hope that, if he met Ballinger, he would be won over to the extent of satisfying 'the ICU in their reasonable ambitions to act as mediators in such matters as a wages dispute such as that at Onderstepoort . . .' So far was Hertzog from doing this, that shortly afterwards he rid himself of one of his ministers for having gone too far towards recognizing the ICU. This minor political crisis originated in the dissatisfaction of the Black workers at the Johannesburg post office with their wages and conditions of work and in their wish to be represented by the ICU in negotiations with their employer. Once more Ballinger obtained the support of the Trades Union Congress, and the Minister of Posts and Telegraphs, Walter Madeley of the Labour Party, at the end of October agreed to receive the TUC Secretary, W. H. Andrews, with an ICU deputation. At the last moment, under pressure from the cabinet, he withdrew the invitation to the ICU, though not to Andrews. Ballinger, however, decided to present himself with Kadalie and two other ICU officials at the time already arranged. Keeping close behind Andrews, they got into the postmaster's office, where the interview was to take place, before anyone realized what was happening. Once they were in, Madeley could not bring himself to turn them out. In the face of his apparent defiance and unimpressed by the argument that he had dealt, not with the ICU, but with the TUC, the Prime Minister demanded his resignation and, as this was refused, reconstituted his cabinet without Madeley, whom he replaced by another Labour Party man, H. W. Sampson.[22]

ICU sympathizers acclaimed the cabinet crisis as a signal victory. 'How thrilling,' wrote the Rev. Shearly Cripps, a great admirer of Kadalie, 'the news about Mr Madeley has been! May God defend the Right!!! . . .'[23], whatever he meant by that. While undoubtedly the expulsion of Madeley was the outcome of a conflict of views within the Government upon the desirability of encouraging Black trade unions and, more particularly, upon the character and worth of the ICU, the clash of principles was obscured by squalid intrigue within the Labour Party. The ICU blundered into a domestic political argument that was concerned with the relations between the South African Labour Party and its parliamentary representatives and that had much to do also with struggles for office.[24] The rank-and-file of the ICU displayed little interest in the incident.[25] While it is true that the postal authorities agreed to discuss grievances with an *ad hoc* deputation of workers[26] and a number of small improvements were introduced into the working conditions at the post office, Madeley's successor persisted in the Government's refusal to negotiate with the ICU.[27]

The post office dispute coincided with a renewed attempt by the ICU Head Office to come to terms with Natal, where, in Durban and perhaps elsewhere too, the ICU proper and Champion's breakaway union ran rival offices. At the beginning of July Champion, invited to meet the expected Adviser, as well as the National Council Sub-Committee, belligerently declined to do so, refusing to be 'jimcrowed in any way', but, after Ballinger had rejected – since he was so busy – a counter-invitation to travel to Pietermaritzburg or Durban, he changed his mind and asked, with misplaced optimism, for his fare to Johannesburg. In September he agreed to attend a conference in Bloemfontein, though still maintaining an aggressive attitude of self-justification. Ballinger, for his part, though privately expressing the view that Champion had 'lined his pockets' and should be forced to 'disgorge', in his early letters to the Natal leader did not go beyond reproaching him for not having submitted to the commission of inquiry and urging him to consent to a round table conference to discuss reunification. After three months of correspondence, however, he lost patience. In a letter sent at a time when strains were beginning to appear in his relationship with Kadalie, he complained of Champion's 'strange medley of cordiality, threats and arrogant presumption' and concluded, 'The written evidence is dead against you, but you are not the only delinquent.'[28]

Eventually Champion agreed to meet Kadalie in Durban. The meeting, in November 1928, proved abortive. At the end of the month Champion was accusing Ballinger of being a Communist. The latter, in turn, tried unsuccessfully to persuade the police to institute proceedings against Champion for misappropriating union funds. In the meantime the Cowley suit against the ICU had been heard, the union's properties sold, Cowley recompensed, and Ballinger's optimistic expectation of recovering something for the parent body confounded.[29]

In the early period of their partnership Kadalie and Ballinger appeared to get along famously, each complimenting the other in letters to Winifred Holtby and Creech Jones. From the beginning, however, Ballinger had nothing but contempt for Kadalie's closest companions, Tyamzashe and Maduna. Before long the latter, accusing Ballinger of being a dictator, took himself off to Durban to ingratiate himself with Champion. As the months went by the relationship with Kadalie himself began to deteriorate. Not only did Ballinger determine policy, he also in private reproved Kadalie for 'his drinking and immoral habits'.[30] Kadalie was increasingly restive. Compelled to account for every penny he spent, humiliatingly dependent upon his own Adviser for an allowance, and suffocated by the help that came from the hitherto reviled liberal community of Johannesburg, he found his position of subordination less and less endurable and his pent-up feelings more and more difficult to hold in. In mid-October 1928,

Group of I.C.U. members and 'police force', Durban – Documentation Centre, Sanlam Library, University of South Africa

A.W.G. Champion on his return to Durban in 1934. On his left is C. Kadalie – Documentation Centre, Sanlam Library, University of South Africa

Workers of the I.C.U. clothing factory, Durban – Documentation Centre, Sanlam Library, University of South Africa

Mrs Lewis chided him in her accustomed cloying style for his disparaging the Joint Council and for excusing his moral lapses by claiming that he was 'no worse than Benn Tillett', the well-known British trade unionist. Addressing him as 'Comrade Kadalie', she pointed out how vital the substantial aid coming from the members of the Joint Council was for the continued existence of the ICU and begged him not to let Ballinger's apparently officious manner obscure the value of his work. Kadalie should not, she suggested, excuse himself as an average sensual man, but exercise some self-control, if only for a year. 'Don't think of yourself as weak and wicked,' she wrote, 'or "no worse than Benn Tillett". But think of yourself as wasteful, unbusinesslike, a man who lets chances go by, just for want of a little self-sacrifice . . . This money aspect: even the great Mussolini is not paid more than £350 a year for his enormous services to his country. And in that he shows true greatness, however critical we may be of his methods. You are asking at this critical period for a sum to live on that comes not far short of that . . . you cannot expect me – no gentleman would expect me – to go on getting money from overseas, from men and women who trust you and your leadership, and not tell them the true facts of the case . . . that their money is going to be spent on personal expenses of officials, even luxuries, rather than really building up the cause.' Mrs Lewis signed her letter 'Yours fraternally, "Reader".'[31] Not long afterwards William Ballinger confided to Creech Jones, 'Kadalie is very peculiar these days. He resents being out of the limelight. He has lost much of his popularity. Many regard him as being a wasteful and unreliable official. It is a tragedy to watch him going down the path of debauchery.'[32]

At the end of October the General Secretary paid a visit to the Transvaal diamond 'diggings'. There, unable to contain himself any longer and perhaps infuriated by Mrs Lewis's letter, he launched out, in a speech at Lichtenburg, into a bitter attack upon the Prime Minister, who, he suggested, should be deported. The White liberals were aghast, not only at the attack itself, but also at its most inopportune timing. For, after considerable preparation, the ICU, in collaboration with the Joint Council of Natives and Europeans, the African National Congress, and the Trades Union Congress, was on the point of securing the reception by General Hertzog, as Minister of Native Affairs, of a deputation aiming at achieving some mitigation of the harsher and less reasonable aspects of the pass laws. In a letter to Hertzog Mrs Lewis dissociated herself from his 'outrageous speech'.[33] 'Each time recently,' she wrote, 'that he has spoken violently, it is nothing but brandy that has so fatally inspired him.'[34] She begged the Prime Minister not to judge by Kadalie's behaviour the 'good and decent men in the ICU office, chafing at this public flouting and ruination of all their laudable efforts to maintain a moderate native organisation . . .' As before, she reminded her correspondent that, unstable as he was, Kadalie was better than the Communists, and she urged him again to see Ballinger before it was too late.

On this occasion the General Secretary was brought to heel and induced to tender an apology,[35] bombarded as he was by admonitory letters from London and Lovedale[36] and, no doubt, by advice from closer quarters and perhaps by the urgings of his own colleagues.[37] In November he asked for six weeks' leave for domestic reasons, and he went off to Natal with some money that Ballinger had succeeded in borrowing for him as advance salary.[38] Returning in time to participate in the National Council meeting on 4 and 5 January at Bloemfontein, he submitted a written request for a year's leave of absence, during which, however, he offered his services for 'propaganda work'. The verbal explanation he then gave, so the Ballinger account ran, was that 'he anticipated trouble and legal proceedings against him by his wife; and it was his desire that, when such matters came up before the public eye, he should not be officially connected with the Organisation.' The National Council sanctioned his leave on half pay and accepted his offer to assist in the way he suggested. Theo Lujiza was appointed Acting General Secretary.[39]

'I see,' wrote Creech Jones to Ballinger, 'you have sent Kadalie off for a period,' and as late as the end of January he was expressing the hope that the worst was over.[40] Mrs Lewis, however, assessed the situation differently and, as it turned out, more shrewdly. In a letter reproaching General Smuts for failing, in a recently uttered criticism of the ICU in Natal, to recognize the value of Ballinger's work in the Transvaal, she made the point that not only was 'the native called Champion' no longer an ICU official, but that Kadalie also had virtually been thrown out. 'Kadalie, who has ruined himself with drink, has been forced by his colleague [*sic*] to take a year's leave which he knows very well is dismissal by his native colleagues, and he will do all the damage he can.'[41]

Kadalie's head was not the only one to roll. At the National Council meeting at Bloemfontein (at which incidentally Ballinger had spoken censoriously of 'the intemperate habits of almost every official'[42]) the General Secretary's old friend Tyamzashe was dismissed, apparently as the result of a petty squabble about money, though Tyamzashe himself complained of a plot concocted by the Administrative Secretary (a new appointment), Bennet Gwabini,[43] who seemed to be one of the officials most trusted by Ballinger[44] and most detested by the Kadalie group, disliked with justice perhaps, since he appears to have taken a spiteful pleasure in humiliating Kadalie.[45]

As Mrs Lewis predicted, Kadalie did not make a decorous withdrawal. A week after the Bloemfontein meeting he asked for money to go to Durban, which was refused. On 25 January, in a letter to the President of the ICU, which he issued to the press before his colleagues had seen it, he proffered his resignation, because he could not 'subscribe to its present policy of servitude, as conducted by those now at the head of affairs'.[46] In the course of an interview with a newspaper reporter he enlarged upon his repudiation of the Ballinger policy. A fighting policy was necessary, he said, a campaign against the pass laws and the Native Administration Act, as decided by the Bloemfontein Conference of April 1928. He went on to object to 'certain business' of the ICU 'being relegated to a coterie of Europeans and natives who assembled in the

Bantu Men's Social Centre', a reference to a meeting held there by the pass laws conference the previous year. Ballinger, invited to comment on Kadalie's outburst, declared, 'The resignation does not surprise me, but it is a damp squib.' Prophetically he continued, 'It is a wonder Kadalie did not go on to say that all the officials are "good boys" – his favourite term of reproach – that they are under the influence of the joint councils, have been bought by the Chamber of Mines . . .'[47]

Kadalie followed up his resignation with a series of attacks upon his former colleagues, in speeches at Johannesburg, Bloemfontein, where he was accompanied by trimmer Maduna, and elsewhere. At a meeting of the Reef branches on Sunday 10 February, as many as a thousand people heard him complain that he had received no pay since the previous November. In the course of his speech he composed the accusation that was to be the burden of the threnody of the succeeding months: 'Our present policy is dictated by the Joint Council of Europeans and Natives.' He then went on to inform the audience that he would resume his office as General Secretary on Wednesday 13 February and bring in a new executive. It was to include Mbeki, Maduna, and 'Mote, all unreliable and hardly an acquisition. In the event nothing came of it. Instead of storming the ICU offices, Kadalie got drunk and was arrested.[48]

Kadalie's gibe that Ballinger was the puppet of the Joint Council, it need hardly be said, was absurd. It was the General Secretary himself who had been instrumental in opening the door to its influence. Ballinger, on the other hand, found his relationship with the White liberals at times trying and exasperating, as he confided bitterly to Fenner Brockway some months later. 'They prate of "conciliation" ,"No Strikes" & "Industrial action only". They are well-meaning sentimentalists but they cannot realise that there is a racial and an economic problem in Africa. That they as well as the Mineowner and the industrialist are living on the back of the Black Man does not enter into their calculations. They want to remove the Color [*sic*] Bar to give the Native a chance and get *Cheaper Labour* . . . Anti-Communism is an obsession with the Lewis's.'[49] The truth of the matter was that Kadalie's resentment was not founded in policy at all. For he did not much care what ICU policy was, provided that it was bold and imaginative and, most important, under his own direction. Nor was his real grievance the patently untrue complaint that he had not been paid for three months, while the rest of Head Office had.

On 13 February three of the officials loyal to Ballinger circulated a letter to all the officers and members of the organization as a riposte to Kadalie's attacks, accusing him of habitual lying, neglect of duty, drunkenness, ingratitude, extravagance and selfishness, and even theft.[50] Ten days later a meeting of the members of the Reef branches, summoned by A. P. Maduna on behalf of Clements Kadalie, styled General Secretary in spite of his resignation, resolved to install the latter in the ICU Transvaal provincial and Johannesburg branch office and to instruct branches not to centralize their funds to Head Office.

The next day Kadalie, Tyamzashe, and Maduna moved in. Gwabini, Kadalie's *bête noire*, ordered them to move out again and, when they failed to comply, took legal action.[51]

A confrontation between the ex-General Secretary and his Adviser took place at a special meeting of the National Council Sub-Committee in Johannesburg on 28 February. Kadalie was accompanied by Tyamzashe. It was agreed to permit the attendance, in addition, of newspaper reporters, a number of minor ICU officials, and members of the public, mostly people belonging to the union. Its composition thus much enlarged beyond its normal size, the Sub-Committee proceeded with its first item of business, the reception of a deputation from the Reef branches. A memorandum submitted by the deputation complained that Kadalie had been contemptuously treated, attacked in the White press by Head Office, and arrested, together with Tyamzashe and Maduna, for trespassing on ICU property; and that Tyamzashe had been wrongfully dismissed from *The Workers' Herald*. In conclusion it demanded the removal of the Adviser, 'a stupid dictator and betrayer of this noble movement'. By way of a rejoinder, the 'stupid dictator' took advantage of the otherwise rambling discussion that followed to remind one of the members of the deputation, P. F. Sijadu, who it was that had stood bail for him when arrested under the Native Administration Act.[52]

In the course of the afternoon the Sub-Committee concluded its hearing of the deputation's case and took up the business on its agenda, firstly discussing the ex-General Secretary's resignation. Gwabini led the prosecution in what was virtually a trial. He accused Kadalie of violating the constitution and inciting others to do the same. Kadalie replied and in the course of a somewhat meandering defence claimed that he had used the Johannesburg branch office in the interests of the organization, 'sending out circulars instructing secretaries to continue centralising in terms of the constitution', and he alleged that Ballinger, Gwabini, and the Joint Council had conspired to oust him from the leadership by trapping him into taking what was really indefinite leave, a charge which Ballinger later emphatically denied. He disclaimed any intention of starting a rival organization. When his turn came, the Adviser spoke with some exaggeration – 'When I left Britain, the friends who sponsored my appointment, as well as myself, fully believed I was coming to a union of very strong financial standing' – and went on to accuse Kadalie, in plain terms or by implication, of lies, extravagance, and dishonesty. He defended the acceptance of help from the Joint Council and denied that he had ever acted dictatorially. It was Lujiza, however, who, leaving aside the generalities and the trivialities, stated with succinctness the gravamen: Kadalie had resigned through the press, withdrawn his resignation 'without reference to anybody', and 'had worked the branches against the Head Office'.

At length Gwabini moved Kadalie's dismissal, but it was not put to the vote. Instead Kadalie re-submitted his resignation, reserving his 'right to appeal to the Annual Congress'. Chairman: 'What are you going to appeal against, if you tender your resignation yourself?' Kadalie: 'Well, I withdraw my appeal and only tender my resignation.' Two members of the Sub-Committee having tried unsuccessfully to persuade him to continue his propaganda work, Lujiza regretfully moved the resignation be accepted. That was the motion carried. The ICU agreed to take responsibility for a debt that Kadalie had incurred in his official position and to withdraw the trespass charge. Thus ended an association that had lasted just over ten years.

Before dispersing the Sub-Committee suspended Keable 'Mote, who was plotting a Free State secession, and agreed upon a union conference at Kroonstad in June, 'if funds allowed'.[53]

It was not to be expected that the Reef supporters of Kadalie would be satisfied with the proceedings of the Sub-Committee, nor surprising that on 13 March the branch executives met to express their dissatisfaction, resolving to summon a special congress of dissident branches at Bloemfontein at Easter (1 April). As an immediate measure they decided to secede and form an Independent ICU under the leadership of Kadalie, supported by Mbeki, 'Mote, who had by then founded the Independent Coloured Workers' Union in the Orange Free State,[54] Elias, and Tyamzashe. In a letter, or manifesto, to officials and members of the ICU Kadalie gave his version of 'the true causes of the unhappy position of the present organisation'. Mistakes, he admitted, had been made by the ICU leaders, 'particularly in dealing with the financial side'. That was why he had sought an Adviser, who, however, had sold the ICU to the Chamber of Mines. The proceedings of the National Council Sub-Committee had been a travesty of justice. With an eye to an alliance with 'Mote and, more especially, Champion, he went on to promise provincial control of funds and property, and with an eye to rural support he promised a land scheme to be fully worked out at the proposed Easter conference.[55]

To discredit Kadalie the ICU issued, on 14 March, a statement of his expenditure on his European tour of 1927. This revealed no conspicuous scandals, simply indifference to the requirements of accountability and gross extravagance at a time when hundreds of ICU members whose subscriptions had paid for the trip were homeless and destitute. During seven months (28 April to 25 November 1927) the then National Secretary had gone through over £700, none of which was accounted for by receipts. A good deal of it, it is true, had been spent on union business, on such items as office rent, typing, postage and telegrams, and much travelling, and hotel accommodation.[56] Kadalie's rejoinder (of 15 March) was vague, evasive, and irrelevant.[57]

Champion greeted the news of the Kadalie-Ballinger split with some satisfaction, and the promise made by Kadalie of future provincial autonomy in money matters he regarded as a vindication of his own secession in 1928. A proposed constitution for an Industrial and Commercial Workers' Federation of Africa, to which autonomous provincial organizations would be affiliated and in which the General Secretary would have no executive power, was sketched out,[58] but, if it was promulgated, it had no sequel. 1929 was to prove a busy year for Champion in his own parish.

After issuing his manifesto of March Kadalie, accompanied by Maduna, made his way to the Orange Free State to team up with 'Mote and to capture the ICU branches there. At an open-air meeting at Heilbron, where he appeared with 'Mote and Maduna, he was reported as having had so hostile a reception from his audience that in the end he could not be heard. He left behind him a new Independent ICU branch and a legacy of factionalism.[59] However, he went ahead with his Bloemfontein conference, which fifty delegates attended, though it is impossible to tell whether these represented any substantial body of opinion.

Both sides in the dispute appealed to sympathizers in England. The arguments advanced were the familiar ones. Ballinger (thus ran the Independents' complaint) had ousted Kadalie and capitulated to the Chamber of Mines and the Joint Council.[60] But if the Kadalie faction thought it would win over British socialist support by attacking the Joint Council, it was gravely mistaken. Creech Jones for one was much in favour of collaboration with the White South African liberals.[61] In any case he and the others in Britain were much less likely to accept Kadalie's version of events than Ballinger's account of extravagance and resentment at the introduction of proper financial controls. Those in England were dismayed and disappointed. 'It is,' wrote Citrine to Ballinger, 'a heartless story of deception, the more heartless because of the trust and confidence reposed in him.'[62] 'The behaviour of Kadalie,' lamented Creech Jones, 'is disgraceful . . . Kadalie seems to be bringing discredit on everybody, and I hope the saner elements will be strong enough to stem his wild eloquence and get him put in his proper place.' Dr Leys commented: 'All movements towards liberation among Africans fall down flat because of moral failure, and there is no hope for future movements unless rapidly Africans realise that . . .'[63]

Kadalie, then, had no more credit to draw on in England. Rather desperately he turned again for help to the extreme left. Support, above all financial assistance, was sought from the League Against Imperialism in Paris. In a letter written in May 1929 to that body, Kadalie accused Ballinger of having 'fraternised with the boss class . . . desired us to worship at the shrine of capitalism'; and then went on in a similar strain in a subsequent letter, 'The Chamber of Mines got hold of him.'[64] Revolutionary socialism and moderate socialism alike turned a deaf ear, as indeed did most of his old supporters in South Africa. For some time he remained in Johannesburg, where he ran a newspaper, *New Africa*, edited by Tyamzashe and dedicated chiefly to attacking Ballinger, nicknamed 'Hubert'. Its arguments were hackneyed and absurd, its tone abusive.

New Africa was also a vehicle for promoting a land scheme. This appears to have been the brain child of a Johannesburg lawyer, Philip Morris, who was the ICU legal adviser at the beginning of 1929. At least, early that year he was trying to persuade Ballinger to help promote such a scheme. He himself was to put up

£2 000 and to make his profit from the transfer fees (apparently £22 for each sale), and he offered Ballinger a thousand shares in the company. Unlike Ballinger Kadalie was willing to listen to 'the "fairy tales" ' of this 'solicitor of doubtful antecedents' and Ballinger went so far as to suggest that Morris was behind the formation of the Independent ICU, not only intending to use it for pushing the land scheme, but also hoping for rich pickings from the litigation that was an inevitable part of ICU activity. The further allegation was made that this was where the IICU money was coming from, a charge that does not seem incredible. For how else could Kadalie, who incidentally used Morris's postal box number, have run an office, supported a large staff, and subsidized a newspaper? Since the ICU was bankrupt before Ballinger's arrival, there is no reason to suppose that Kadalie was drawing much revenue from what was only a fraction of the old membership.[65]

The Independent ICU launched its African Native Land Settlement Corporation Ltd with a nominal capital of £100 000, offered in £1 shares. '£1,' ran the *New Africa* advertisment, 'makes you a full member of the ICU, pays your contribution to the Land Settlement Fund and gives you the right to purchase land on terms. Buy it.' The land was to be sold in lots of three to six acres.[66] In August, 1929, Kadalie claimed that his organization had spent £1 000 on land purchases.[67] It is improbable, however, that the scheme ever evoked much response. The IICU's newspaper appears to have petered out towards the end of 1929, presumably because its revenue, whatever its provenance, ceased. Kadalie withdrew to East London.

Before leaving the Rand Kadalie participated in two events that involved Ballinger too. One occurred in August 1929, when the two of them publicly debated their differences outside the Workers' Hall under the chairmanship of Eddie Roux. Needless to say few new arguments emerged on either side. Although he added to his stock the charge that Kadalie, in leaving the ICU to escape domination by a White man, had done so only to fall into the clutches of another, Philip Morris, Ballinger concentrated mainly on financial shortcomings, including the extravagance of the European tour. The assertion of the Communists that their members were expelled from the union because they wanted proper financial controls, was revived, as well as the allegation that Kadalie was as guilty as Champion of the financial drain in Durban. In his reply Kadalie, while he could justly claim that the Communists had been ejected 'through pressure from Mrs Palmer and Mrs Ethelreda Lewis' because the Party had 'attempted to take the whole administration of the ICU into its hands', and, with less justice, disclaim all responsibility for the financial side of the organization, since he had rarely been in direct charge of the money affairs of the ICU from the very beginning, he could not, nor did he attempt to, explain away the strictures the Communists La Guma and Glass had uttered in their day upon the financial laxity of senior officials, and when he came to deal with the European tour expenses, he relied more upon vituperation than explanation, making much of his encounters with British racial prejudice and dealing with small items of expenditure without being able to escape from the fact that during seven months he had spent several hundred pounds. He repeated the claim that he had been the victim of a Joint Council conspiracy. The evidence he produced was an unidentified letter, rebuking him for disparaging the Joint Council and suggesting that that was no way to gain the confidence of those best able to help him – clearly Mrs Lewis's letter of the previous October. It contained no hint of a plot. There were, however, no bounds to Kadalie's credulity or malice. 'I don't denounce you,' he told Ballinger, 'because you are a white man. My main objection to you is that you are a traitor of the black workers, you cannot speak the truth, you have split up and sold the workers to the capitalist. Yes, he is like Judas Iscariot.'[68]

The second incident took place in November, when both men addressed a mass meeting in Johannesburg to protest against a proposed amendment to the Riotous Assemblies Act, which was to empower the Minister of Justice to banish from one part of the country to another any person thought to be threat to public order. The demonstration was organized by the Federation of Non-European Trade Unions; and another Communist-inspired body, the League of African Rights, also participated. It was dominated by the Communists, who, benefiting from the disintegration of the ICU and from their energy, determination, and willingness to make personal sacrifices, were entering upon a brief period of influence. To this meeting they had brought an effigy of the Minister of Justice, Oswald Pirow, which they had carried from their headquarters in a straggling procession. Kadalie, who, according to Ballinger, was 'not quite sober', acted as chairman and under his control the meeting became lively, reaching a climax with the burning of the effigy. An incensed Government afterwards demanded an explanation from Ballinger, who readily provided one and also obligingly passed on what information (or gossip) he had about the state of the Communist Party, evidently succeeding in allaying official suspicion.[69]

Effigy burning was not Ballinger's way of doing things, and he was at pains to dissociate as far as possible the ICU of Africa (as his section of the union was now called, to distinguish it from the Independent ICU) from the violence that the old leaders had threatened, though never carried out, and from their incompetent, even dishonest, administration. He wondered, at least for a time, whether it might not be best to start a brand new organization with a new name, but was persuaded that the old name had a magic that justified its retention, and this view was upheld by Citrine.[70] Apart from the name there were few assets at his disposal in his task of revitalizing the organization. The most hopeful avenue open to him was to complete the sectionalization of the union, get the various sections registered, and negotiate on their behalf with the Wage Board. In fact, this proved to be a disappointment, but hope persisted in it for a long time – and with some cause, since officials of the Board were sympathetic, even encouraging.[71] In the immediate post-Kadalie days Ballinger was not altogether despondent.[72] One sign of confidence was the revival once again of *The Workers' Herald*, which had not been published since December 1928. It continued for a few more issues before disappearing for ever.

The 1929 Conference was held at Kroonstad in June as arranged. The same month a promising contact was made at Nylstroom with the executive of the Waterberg farmers in the Transvaal. Wage Board applications were made in a number of towns, the most promising at Kroonstad, where a request for a minimum wage of £7.10s. a month for all Black and Coloured workers in commerce and industry, which was supported with written and oral evidence by the local Joint Council, seemed to have a fair chance of success after the Bloemfontein award in 1928. There followed a long delay. By the beginning of 1930 it became clear that no determination was to be made: Colonel Creswell, the Minister of Labour after Boydell, was not going to use the Wage Board for the purpose of uplifting Blacks, but only as an instrument for safeguarding the interests of Whites. The Bloemfontein award was an aberration.[73]

Despite the disappointments Ballinger was encouraged to carry on by the loyalty he commanded from the remaining officials, who had little to gain by way of material reward.[74] The most flamboyant and lively officials had gone, but some able men stayed on, some who had been in the movement for years, notably A. M. Jabavu (Senior Vice-President) and T. B. Lujiza (General Secretary); and the departure of Kadalie made possible the belated return of H. Selby Msimang as a 'national propagandist'. In March 1929 they issued a manifesto, pledging their continued support and paying tribute to the Adviser's selflessness and dedication.[75] Yet for all this, Ballinger enjoyed little support in the country. There was a marked drop in income from branches in February 1929, the month of Kadalie's resignation, and thereafter payments dwindled to the point that they could not balance administrative costs.[76] By September 1929, the total liquid assets of the ICU stood at just over ten pounds.[77] A sum of one hundred and twenty pounds was collected by Mrs Lewis on a visit to England that year, when she also endeavoured to arouse sympathy in non-socialist quarters[78] and to recruit idealistic young men for the settlement that she had always set her heart on. Sacrificing a trip to America planned by her husband and herself, she gave the money to the union for Ballinger's salary.[79] It was Trader Horn, she said – with some justice – in 1930, that kept the ICU going. His reminiscences 'directly paid for the last two years' work and the living of Mr Ballinger and before that paid ICU debts and rescued it from bankruptcy.'[80] Needless to say, the White labour movement in South Africa did not spring to Ballinger's assistance.[81]

Undoubtedly old ICU members were disenchanted with Kadalie, but they were equally unwilling to give support to the ICU of Africa.[82] Its very virtues were a liability. Patient endeavour, honesty, and integrity, together with modest success in achieving limited aims, were unexciting and not the way to gain widespread and enthusiastic support. Faith had to be aroused by convincing promises, however unrealistic and extravagant; and this is how the ICU enjoyed its moment of wealth and glory in 1927. How is it, asked the pro-Ballinger manifesto of 1930, 'that we hear of a bucket of half-crowns collected amongst Natives for the pocket of Dr Wellington and yet for the ICU officials and their adviser who make no promises but get things done there are no buckets, even of pennies to support them?' It was the promises that mattered.

In 1930 the financial position of the ICU of Africa improved somewhat with an increase in contributions from well-wishers in both South Africa and England. In February Josiah Wedgwood visited the country and displayed sufficient interest in the union to organize on his return home an appeal that raised £200. Other grants were made, through the efforts of Howard Pim and Charles Roden Buxton, by wealthy Quakers and the Noel Buxton Trust. These relatively small sums were paid into the 'Ballinger Fund', specially set up to provide the Adviser with a small (£100 a quarter in 1930), regular, though somewhat precarious, salary and administered by Howard Pim. Money from England was supplemented in South Africa by contributions from Dr F. O. Stohr, a rather eccentric psycho-analyst who had witnessed the Kadalie-Ballinger confrontation of 28 February 1929, and, more regularly, from his sister, Miss C. N. Stohr.[83] In March 1930, a gift of £25 from Dr Stohr financed a six week tour of the Orange Free State and Transvaal by four officials, 'to resuscitate our Union, which is on the verge of collapsing owing to lack of funds'.[84] A year later Miss Stohr provided the funds for a similar expedition. These somewhat forlorn attempts at revival enjoyed scant success.[85] 'Your headquarters has passed,' reported Ballinger to the Conference of 1932, 'through extremely trying times, and during the last eighteen months some white friends have several times, and at the last moment, relieved desperate financial difficulties that would have necessitated the closing of your headquarters, and the actual starvation of your officials. This state of affairs reveals that the Native people either cannot, or are unwilling to support your organisation in sufficient numbers to meet the ordinary financial requirements of your headquarters.'[86] It is true that the ICU of Africa still carried on in a small way, with a few officials in different parts of the country investigating grievances brought to their attention; while the hope persisted that it would yet be restored to its old glories.[87] However, quite early in 1931 Howard Pim was writing: 'There is very little left of the ICU and Ballinger becomes daily more of a general adviser to the natives here.'[88] Gradually the better known survivors from the old ICU disappeared. The biggest loss was Lujiza, whose place was taken in 1932 by an unknown, Daniel Budulwayo.[89]

Ballinger himself became less absorbed by the affairs of the ICU. This was partly because he fell victim to severe illness that afflicted him first in late 1930, then again in 1931, when he was laid low for more than a year. He was not sufficiently recovered to attend the 1932 Conference at Heilbron.[90] Moreover his interest was distracted to a variety of projects remote from the ICU. Between 1930 and 1933 he made tours to study labour conditions and the background of migrant labour in the Protectorates, Basutoland, Bechuanaland and Swaliland, and also Southern Rhodesia, accompanied by Miss Margaret Hodgson,[91] who taught History at the University of the Witwatersrand until she forfeited her appointment by marrying Ballinger in 1934. Another interest he developed was the establishment of a consumers' co-operative in the Western Native Township, Johannesburg and a projected producers' co-operative in Swaziland.[92] In 1935 and 1936 he attended the International Labour Conference as an adviser to the British workers' delegation.[93]

Mrs Lewis still clung to her hopes of recruiting a crop of John Chinns and to that end lodged appeals in various quarters, but in vain. In 1931, however, she withdrew from active intervention in the affairs of the ICU of Africa, following the death of her husband, though she continued to take an interest in Ballinger's activities. In a valedictory letter to Winifred Holtby she expressed no regrets at her participation in what she had constantly referred to as 'this work', but some disillusionment with the recipients of her assistance. 'No one who knows Natives intimately expects gratitude,' she confided in Miss Holtby. 'The negro is not yet, as a nation, sufficiently developed on the spiritual side to be aware of such a debt as gratitude, nor should we expect it at so early a stage in their race from the primitive life . . . No Native, however well educated, can systematically apply himself to a cause – if it entails self-sacrifice and not visible gain – for more than a few years, perhaps two or three. In this respect they are still, despite the opinion of many who know the Native intimately, children; easily wearied, easily led astray, easily depraved by civilisation . . .'[94]

Ballinger's English supporters continued doggedly to promote his cause – Winifred Holtby, by then smitten with a mortal disease and destined to die in 1935, Creech Jones, Leonard Barnes, and Livie-Noble, who had gone to live in London. In June 1932, at a time when the Ballinger Fund was exhausted, a band of assorted distinguished sympathizers that included Lord Olivier, Archbishop William Carter, Leonard Barnes, H. G. Wells, Constance Malleson, Mr and Mrs Pethwick-Lawrence, Josiah Wedgwood, Lord Sanderson, Bertrand Russell, Roden Buxton, Bernard Shaw, Arnold Plant and Winifred Holtby, was persuaded to sign a letter of urgent appeal that was published in *Time and Tide* and *The New Leader*. It had but a limited effect, for, a year later, the Ballinger Fund was again empty and Ballinger's salary reduced.[95] Fresh appeals were directed to the Noel Buxton Trust, the International Federation of Trade Unions, the Trades Union Congress, and the Co-operative Guilds, but the only regular income came from Winifred Holtby herself, who promised £100 a year.[96] Such efforts merely provided Ballinger with a meagre salary; they did not directly help the organization, which remained as poverty-stricken as ever.[97]

In 1934 the Society of the Friends of Africa, with members in Britain and South Africa, was founded through the efforts of Winifred Holtby, Arthur Creech Jones, and F. S. Livie-Noble. To some extent its formation was precipitated by the death that year in England of Howard Pim, who had unobtrusively and subject to constant criticism from Mrs Lewis done a great deal to permit the continuation of Ballinger's work.[98] The Society interested itself in pay and working conditions of Blacks in industry, Black land and agriculture, Black education, and the remuneration of Blacks in teaching and other professions; it pressed for the recognition of Black trade unions and the abolition of the pass laws, the industrial colour bar, and the poll tax; and it devoted itself to gathering information and attempting to influence public and official opinion.[99] Heavily dependent upon voluntary contributions in Britain, it lived from hand to mouth,[100] and there can be little doubt that Ballinger worked extremely hard for his modest salary and, as a rule, without complaint.

By 1934 the ICU of Africa was to all intents and purposes defunct. Ballinger himself put the date of its death at 1936.[101]

Notes

1. A. C. Jones to C. Kadalie 22 December 1927 (WH); G. Aitken to W. Holtby 10 February 1928 (B/UCT); Ballinger, W. G., Winifred Holtby – first contacts with South Africa, undated MS. (B/UCT).
2. W. Holtby to E. Lewis 11 April 1928 (B/Wits); C. Kadalie to W. Holtby 2 May 1928 (B/UCT); telegram E. Lewis to W. Holtby (May 1928) (B/Wits); A. C. Jones to W. G. Ballinger 25 May 1928 (B/UCT).
3. W. Holtby to W. G. Ballinger 18 April, 15, 25 and 29 May 1928 (B/UCT); Ballinger, W. G. 'Winifred Holtby – first contacts with South Africa.'
4. W. Holtby to E. Lewis 11 April and 26 November 1928 (B/Wits and B/UCT) and to W. G. Ballinger 30 May and 26 November 1928 (B/UCT).
5. C. Kadalie to A. C. Jones 21 March 1928 (WH); telegram C. Kadalie to A. C. Jones 4 May 1928 (B/Wits).
6. Agreement (with corrections in Mrs Lewis's hand) signed by C. Kadalie, headed Industrial and Commercial Workers' Union, and beginning, ' "A Friend" will give £300 to the ICU as follows . . .' (B/UCT). The balance of £70 was for Kadalie's legal defence. Cf. also W. G. Ballinger to W. Holtby 14 August 1928 (B/Wits and B/UCT).
7. The South African Government did seek information from the British Government (*The Star* 26 August 1950 – *sic*).
8. W. G. Ballinger to W. Holtby 12 September 1928 (B/UCT).
9. W. G. Ballinger to W. Holtby 14 August 1928 (B/Wits and B/UCT); R. P(hillips) and R(heinallt) J(ones) to J. M. B. Hertzog 19 October 1928 (B/Wits). When Ballinger was elected to the Senate as a representative of Black interests, an attempt was made, in 1950, to unseat him on the grounds of his not being a Union of South Africa national (*The Star* 26 August 1950).
10. Ballinger, W. G., The rise and fall of the ICU, undated MS. (B/UCT); Champion, A. W. G., ICU Federation and Independent ICU, n.d., (F/MSS/25) draft letter from W. G. Ballinger to W. Holtby 22 July 1928 (B/Wits); W. G. Ballinger to W. Holtby 8 and 14 August 1928 (B/Wits and B/UCT); W. G. Ballinger to A. C. Jones 22 August 1928 (B/Wits). The final estimate of ICU debts at the time of Ballinger's arrival was £1 500 (ICU of Africa, ICU Adviser's Report 22 June 1929, B/Wits).

11. President and General Secretaries to Secretaries and Members of the ICU Branches 26 July 1928 (B/Wits; *The Workers' Herald* 18 August 1928).
12. For the last cf. Jameson Coka to C. Kadalie 13 August 1928 (B/Wits).
13. ICU News Letter (*Weekly News*) 19 October 1928.
14. Webber, Wentzel, Solomon, and Friel to W. G. Ballinger 13 August 1928 (B/Wits).
15. E. Lewis to W. G. Ballinger 25 September 1928 (B/Wits).
16. W. Holtby to W. G. Ballinger 24 July 1928 (B/Wits); W. G. Ballinger to W. Holtby 14 August 1928 (B/Wits and B/UCT); W. Holtby to E. Lewis and W. G. Ballinger 13 November 1928 (B/UCT); A. S. Cripps to C. Kadalie 14 November 1928 (B/Wits); W. Holtby to E. Lewis 26 November 1928 (B/UCT); W. Holtby to W. G. Ballinger 26 November 1928 (B/UCT); A. C. Jones to W. G. Ballinger 28 December 1928 (B/Wits); W. G. Ballinger to A. C. Jones 23 January 1929 (B/UCT); W. G. Ballinger to W. Citrine 8 May 1929 (B/UCT); ICU Appeal (1928) (B/Wits and B/UCT); Administration Report (*c.* January 1929) (B/UCT); The manifesto of the ICU of Africa to the Native People 31 March 1930 (B/Wits); W. G. Ballinger to E. Lewis n.d. (B/Wits).
17. ICU News Letter (*Weekly News*) 19 October 1928; Administration Report (*c.* January 1929) (B/UCT); W. G. Ballinger to W. Holtby 8 and 14 August and 3 October 1928 (B/Wits and B/UCT); W. G. Ballinger to W. Citrine 8 May 1929 (B/UCT).
18. W. G. Ballinger to W. Holtby 14 August 1928 (B/Wits and B/UCT); J. Harrison to E. Lewis 4 December 1928 (B/UCT).
19. E. R. Roux to N. Leys 16 September 1928 (B/Wits); E. R. Roux to W. G. Ballinger 19 March 1929 (B/UCT).
20. E. Lewis to H. Pim 16 July 1928 (B/Wits and B/UCT); C. Kadalie to W. Holtby 3 October 1928 (B/UCT); *The Star* 22 October 1928.
21. W. G. Ballinger to A. C. Jones 22 August, 3 and 24 October 1928 and 23 January 1929 (B/Wits and B/UCT); C. Kadalie to W. Holtby 3 October 1928 (B/UCT); W. G. Ballinger to W. Holtby 3 October 1928 (B/UCT); E. Lewis to J. M. B. Hertzog 15 October 1928 (B/Wits); R. P(hillips) and J. D. R(heinallt) J(ones) to J. M. B. Hertzog 19 October 1928 (B/Wits); ICU New Letter (*Weekly News*) 19 October and 5 December 1928; Findlay and Niemeyer to C. Kadalie 19 October 1928 (B/Wits); A. J. Phoofolo to *Weekly News* 26 November 1928; Ballinger, W. G. General Observations, n.d. (B/Wits).
22. Ballinger, W. G., Winifred Holtby – first contacts with South Africa; *idem*, Mr Madeley and the ICU, n.d. (B/UCT).
23. A. S. Cripps to C. Kadalie 14 November 1928 (B/Wits).
24. Cf. *The Natal Advertiser* 18 June 1931; W. G. Ballinger to *Rand Daily Mail* 9 August 1946 (B/Wits).
25. Ballinger, W. G., Winifred Holtby – first contacts with South Africa.
26. *The Star* 20 November 1928.
27. ICU News Letter (*Weekly News*) 5 December 1928.
28. A.W. G. Champion to W. G. Ballinger 21 and 28 July, 1 and 9 August, 27 September and 23 October 1928 (B/Wits); W. G. Ballinger to A. W. G. Champion 3 and 13 August and 25 October 1928 (B/Wits); W. G. Ballinger to W. Holtby 14 August 1928 (B/Wits).
29. W. G. Ballinger to W. Holtby 3 October and 19 December 1928 (B/UCT); P. Ka I. Seme to A. W. G. Champion 9 November 1928 (B/Wits); W. G. Ballinger to T. B. Lujiza 10 November 1928 (B/UCT); *The Natal Advertiser* 28 November 1928; W. G. Ballinger to A. C. Jones 23 January 1929 (B/UCT); ICU of Africa, ICU Adviser's Report 22 June 1929 (B/Wits).
30. W. G. Ballinger to W. Holtby 14 August and 3 October 1928 (B/Wits and B/UCT) and to A. C. Jones 22 August 1928 (B/Wits); ICU News Letter (*Weekly News*) 19 October 1928 W. G. Ballinger to A. W. G. Champion 25 October 1928 (B/Wits); *The Star* 15 November 1928.

31. E. Lewis to C. Kadalie 17 October 1928 (B/Wits).
32. W. G. Ballinger to A. C. Jones 24 October 1928 (B/UCT).
33. E. Lewis to General Hertzog 1 November 1928 (B/UCT).
34. There is abundant evidence that Kadalie was drinking heavily and continued to do so for the next ten years (Kadalie, C., *My Life*, 193; *African Drum*, June 1952, 33).
35. *The Times* 27 December 1928.
36. E. Lewis to General Hertzog 1 November 1928 (B/UCT); J. Harrison to E. Lewis 4 December 1928 (B/UCT). Miss Holtby thought the news about Kadalie was 'sickening' (W. Holtby to E. Lewis 3 December (1928), (B/Wits).
37. The Administrative, Organizing and Financial Secretaries, ICU to the Presidents, Provincial Secretaries, Branch Secretaries and Committees, and all Members of the Industrial and Commercial Workers' Union of Africa 13 February 1929 – Mr Clements Kadalie and his Resignation (B/UCT).
38. 'Later we learned that he went to Natal and took with him a colored [*sic*] woman, with whom he is still living. During his absence his wife and family were evicted from their home. His wife came to me for assistance. On his return Kadalie complained that by helping his wife I was interfering between them . . .' (W. G. Ballinger to W. Citrine 8 May 1929, B/UCT) Kadalie married his first wife, Molly (also a Coloured woman), in Cape Town in his early years in South Africa. His second wife, Eva, he met at Greytown in Natal in 1926 when she was still a schoolgirl (*African Drum* June 1952).
39. Mr Clements Kadalie and his Resignation; B. Gwabini and J. Kokozela to W. Citrine 30 January 1929 (B/Wits); W. G. Ballinger to T. B. Lujiza 10 November 1928 (B/UCT).
40. A. C. Jones to W. G. Ballinger 10 January 1929 (B/Wits) and 30 January 1929 (B/UCT).
41. E. Lewis to General Smuts 15 January 1929 (B/Wits) Ballinger also thought that Kadalie might 'yet undo all the re-construction work' (W. G. Ballinger to A. C. Jones 23 January 1929, B/UCT).
42. H. D. Tyamzashe to E. Lewis 10 January 1929 (B/Wits).
43. H. D. Tyamzashe to A. W. G. Champion 13 February 1929 (F 1929/1).
44. W. G. Ballinger to W. Holtby 8 August 1928 (B/UCT).
45. Cf. an interchange of letters between them in March 1929, about furniture (B/Wits).
46. B. Gwabini and J. Kokozela to W. Citrine 30 January 1929 (B/Wits).
47. *The Star* 25 January 1929.
48. Mr Clements Kadalie and his Resignation; Minutes of meeting of the Sub-Committee of the National Council of the Industrial and Commercial Workers' Union, held in the ICU Workers' Hall, 14 Market Street, in Johannesburg, on Thursday 28 February 1929 (F 1929/2).
49. W. G. Ballinger to A. Fenner Brockway 15 May 1929 (B/Wits).
50. Mr Clements Kadalie and his Resignation.
51. Minutes of meeting of the Sub-Committee of the National Council 28 February 1929.
52. He later, when Sijadu was sentenced, with some generosity paid his £25 fine (ICU of Africa, ICU Adviser's Report 22 June 1929, B/Wits).
53. Minutes of meeting of the Sub-Committee of the National Council 28 February 1929 (F 1929/2); ICU Adviser's Report 22 June 1929.
54. B. Gwabini to A. W. G. Champion 13 March 1929 (F 1929/3).
55. T. Mbeki, Provincial Secretary, Transvaal, IICU to Executives and Members of the ICU, 13 March 1929 (B/UCT); C. Kadalie to Executives and Members of the ICU, 13 March 1929 (B/UCT).
56. Financial statement on European tour of Clements Kadalie, 14 March 1929 (F 1929/5).
57. C. Kadalie to Executives and Members of the ICU, 15 March 1929 (B/UCT).
58. A. W. G. Champion, ICU Federation and Independent ICU, undated MS (*c.* March 1929) (F/MSS/25).

59. *The Friend* 26 March 1929.
60. T. Mbeki, Provisional Secretary, Transvaal, Independent ICU to A. C. Jones 19 March 1929 (B/UCT).
61. A. C. Jones to W. G. Ballinger 20 February 1929 (B/Wits.)
62. W. G. Ballinger to W. Citrine 8 May 1929 (B/UCT); W. Citrine to W. G. Ballinger 4 June 1929 (B/UCT).
63. A. C. Jones to W. G. Ballinger 13 March 1929 (B/UCT); N. Leys to W. Holtby 16 February 1929 (B/UCT).
64. Roux, E. R., *Time Longer than Rope*, 187–8.
65. G. T. Nolutshungu, Financial Secretary, ICU to President and Members, National Council, ICU 3 January 1929 (B/UCT); W. G. Ballinger, undated memorandum (B/Wits); W. G. Ballinger to W. Citrine 8 May 1929 (B/UCT); Holtby, W., Kadalie's resignation, n.d. (B/UCT); W. G. Ballinger to Members of ICU 7 August 1929 (B/UCT); Dorothy Woodman to W. Holtby 12 August 1929 (B/UCT); *New Africa* 14 September 1929; W. G. Ballinger to W. Holtby 1 October 1929; Champion, A. W. G., ICU Federation and Independent ICU (F/MSS/25).
66. *New Africa* 29 June 1929; Hunter, M., 1936, *Reaction to Conquest; Effects of Contact with Europeans on the Pondo of South Africa*, London, 568.
67. *New Africa* 14 September 1929.
68. Ibid.; W. G. Ballinger to W. Holtby 1 October 1929 (B/UCT).
69. W. G. Ballinger, Joint Meeting ICU of Africa; African Congress; Non-European Federation of Trade Unions; Communist Party; League of African Rights; Independent ICU Sunday 10 November 1929 (B/Wits and B/UCT).
70. W. G. Ballinger to A. C. Jones 3 April 1929 (B/Wits) and to W. Citrine 8 May 1929 (B/UCT); W. Citrine to W. G. Ballinger 4 June 1929 (B/UCT) Norman Leys, however, disagreed (N. Leys to W. Holtby 16 February 1929, B/UCT; A. C. Jones to W. G. Ballinger 20 February 1929, B/Wits).
71. Draft letter W. G. Ballinger to W. Holtby 31 July 1929 (B/UCT).
72. W. G. Ballinger to W. Citrine 8 May 1929 (B/UCT).
73. Draft letter W. G. Ballinger to W. Holtby 31 July 1929 (B/UCT); ICU of Africa, ICU Adviser's Report 22 June 1929 (B/Wits); W. G. Ballinger to W. Holtby n.d. (B/UCT); Ballinger, W. G., Incitement or procrastination – which? n.d. (B/UCT).
74. E. Lewis to Hon. H. Wyndham 16 June 1929 (B/Wits).
75. Manifesto of the ICU of Africa (ICU) to the Native People 31 March 1930 (B/Wits).
76. Statement of Income and Expenditure sent to the President and National Councillors, Kroonstad 21 June 1929 (B/Wits).
77. H. Pim to W. G. Ballinger 20 September 1929 (B/Wits).
78. Including Sir Abe Bailey (E. Lewis to Hon. H. Wyndham 16 June 1929 (B/Wits).
79. Apparently the money was used, to Mrs Lewis's annoyance, for other ICU purposes. Cf. E. Lewis to H. Pim 14 September 1929 (B/Wits and UCT), H. Pim to E. Lewis 17 September 1929 (B/Wits), and E. Lewis to W. Holtby 15 October 1929 (Wits ICU).
80. E. Lewis to F. Keppel 19 May 1930 (B/UCT). She contributed some £388 between November 1928 and May 1929 (Statement of Income and Expenditure 21 June 1929, B/Wits).
81. W. G. Ballinger to A. C. Jones 3 April 1929 (B/Wits). In April that year, however, the SATUC conference passed a guarded resolution in favour of Black unions (Leubuscher, C., 1931, *Der südafrikanische Eingeborene als Industriearbeiter und als Stadtbewohner*, Jena, 189).
82. Cf. T. B. Lujiza to E. Lewis 28 November 1930 (B/Wits) and H. Binda to H. Pim 18 September 1929 (B/Wits).
83. C. N. Stohr to E. Lewis 11 May 1930 (B/UCT) Miss Stohr appears to have been subscribing £25 a month in 1930 (T. B. Lujiza to E. Lewis 2 September 1930, B/Wits).

84. B. Gwabini, A. Phoofolo and others to F. O. Stohr 26 March 1930 (B/Wits).
85. Cf. W. Holtby to W. G. Ballinger 20 July (1931) (B/UCT).
86. W. G. Ballinger to Secretary, Chairman and Delegates, ICU of Africa Conference 14 June 1932 (B/UCT).
87. Ibid.; J. Mancoe to W. G. Ballinger 1 December 1930, 10 March 1931, and 12 December 1932 (B/Wits); S. H. Mbulawa to W. G. Ballinger n.d. (1934) (B/Wits); Private Secretary to the Minister of Justice (General Smuts) to Acting General Secretary, ICU of Africa 10 January 1934 (B/Wits). In 1931 Jameson Coka offered Ballinger two columns each week in the ANC paper, *Ikwezi le Afrika* (J. G. Coka to W. G. Ballinger 25 July 1931, B/Wits).
88. H. Pim to C. R. Buxton 20 January 1931 (B/Wits).
89. At that time Gwabini was still with the ICU (W. G. Ballinger to Secretary, Chairman, and Delegates, ICU of Africa Conference 14 June 1932, B/UCT).
90. T. B. Lujiza to E. Lewis 28 October 1930 (B/Wits); N. Leys to M. Hodgson 13 November 1930 (B/UCT); H. Pim to C. R. Buxton 20 January 1931 (B/Wits); W. Holtby to M. Hodgson 16 August (1931) (B/UCT); A. C. Jones to W. G. Ballinger 25 November 1931 (B/UCT); W. G. Ballinger to Secretary, Chairman and Delegates, ICU of Africa Conference, 14 June 1932 (B/UCT).
91. M. Hodgson to N. Leys 14 January 1931 (B/UCT), H. Pim to C. R. Buxton 20 January 1931 (B/Wits); E. Lewis to W. Holtby 22 June 1931 (B/Wits).
92. *Time and Tide* 25 June 1932; Holtby, W., Suggested draft of appeal to co-operative guilds (1932) (B/UCT); W. Holtby to M. Hodgson and W. G. Ballinger 28 August 1933 (B/UCT); W. Holtby to Lord Lothian 27 November 1933 (B/UCT); The Beginnings of Co-operative Retail Trading and Production in the Union of South Africa and the British Protectorates (1933) (B/UCT); W. Holtby to M. Hodgson 6 December 1933 (B/UCT); M. Perham to H. Matheson 28 November 1933 (B/UCT).
93. W. Holtby to M. Ballinger 4 June 1935 and 15 July (1935) (B/UCT); telegrams from W. Citrine to W. G. Ballinger 3 and 22 April 1936 (B/UCT); A. C. Jones to W. G. Ballinger 15 April 1936 (B/UCT); W. G. Ballinger to W. Citrine 22 June 1936 (B/UCT).
94. E. Lewis to W. Holtby 22 June 1931 (B/Wits).
95. W. Holtby to M. Hodgson 29 May 1933 (B/UCT) and to M. Hodgson and W. G. Ballinger 28 August 1933 (B/UCT).
96. W. Holtby to W. G. Ballinger and M. Hodgson 10 August (1933) (B/UCT). A further £12 a year was promised by Dr Leys.
97. Cf. D. Budulwayo to W. G. Ballinger 8 August 1934 (B/Wits).
98. W. Holtby to W. G. Ballinger and M. Hodgson 11 May 1934 (B/UCT).
99. Ballinger, W. G., Society of Friends of Africa – Memorandum to Industrial Laws Legislation Commission 15 February 1949 (B/UCT); W. Holtby to M. Hodgson and W. G. Ballinger 17 January 1933 and 29 May 1933 (B/UCT); W. Holtby to M. Ballinger 27 May 1935 (B/UCT).
100. Cf. W. Holtby to M. Ballinger 27 May 1935 (B/UCT) and A. C. Jones to M. Ballinger 27 June 1938 (B/Wits).
101. Ballinger, W. G., Society of Friends of Africa.

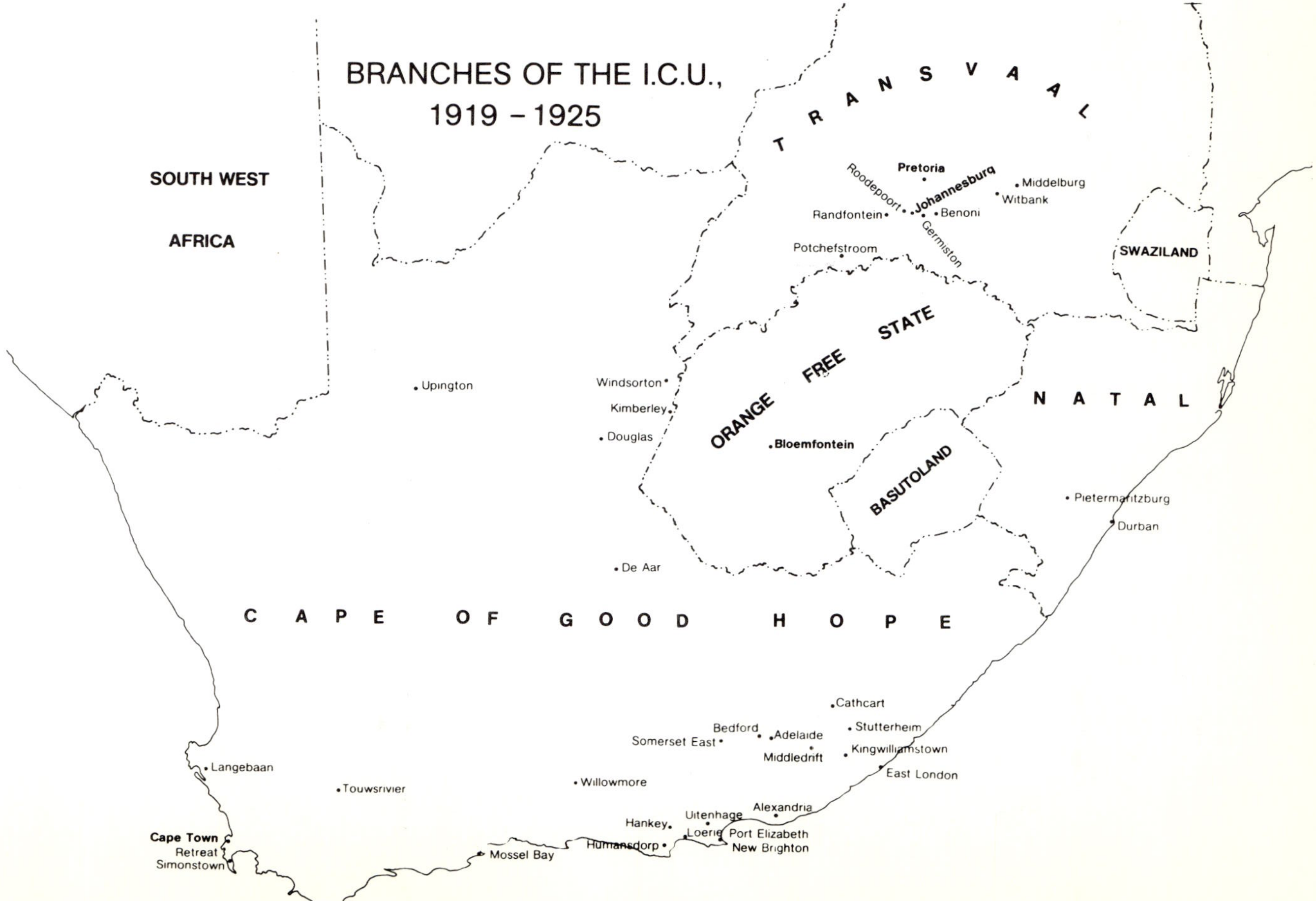
BRANCHES OF THE I.C.U.,
1919 – 1925
SOUTH WEST
AFRICA
TRANSVAAL
Pretoria
Johannesburg
Roodepoort
Randfontein
Benoni
Germiston
Middelburg
Witbank
Potchefstroom
SWAZILAND
ORANGE FREE STATE
Bloemfontein
BASUTOLAND
NATAL
Pietermaritzburg
Durban
Upington
Windsorton
Kimberley
Douglas
De Aar
CAPE OF GOOD HOPE
Cathcart
Stutterheim
Bedford
Adelaide
Somerset East
Middledrift
Kingwilliamstown
East London
Langebaan
Touwsrivier
Willowmore
Alexandria
Uitenhage
Hankey
Loerie
Port Elizabeth
New Brighton
Humansdorp
Mossel Bay
Cape Town
Retreat
Simonstown

BRANCHES OF THE I.C.U., 1927 – 1929

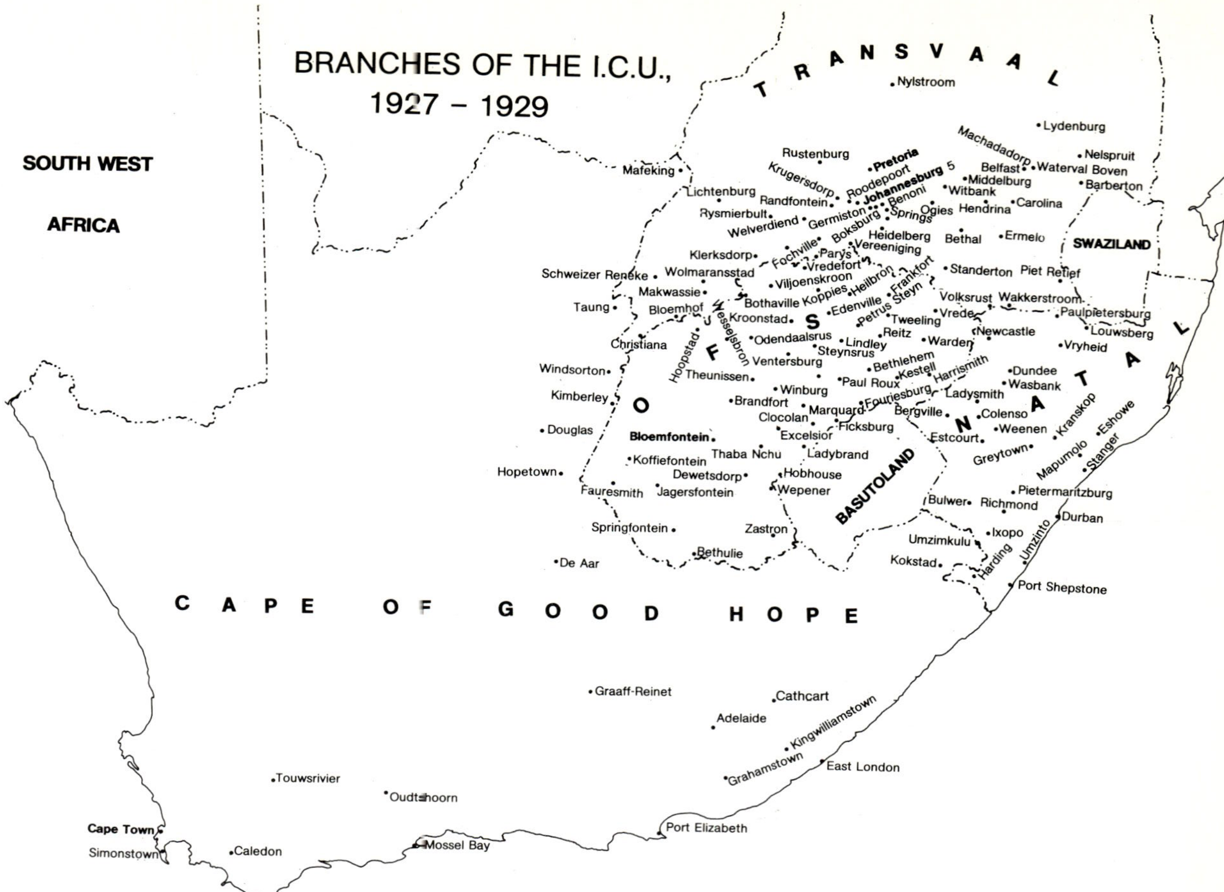

CHAPTER 12

All the King's Horses

'I plead with you to look and see how, who eradicated the ICU to such irrecoverable inefficiency and recklessness? Is it not the lulling sweet mouths of white friends, the political chameleons? . . . Where are the Batty's, Ballingers, Glasses and a host of other sweet crookes [sic], *who stood on their hindlegs, bums and chins, insidiously showering, towering the ICU?'*

S. J. Sitebe, 1930

When Durban seceded from the ICU at the end of May 1928, most of the Natal branches seem to have thrown in their lot with the ICU yase Natal,[1] as did some of the better known leaders, such as Maduna (for a short time) and William Smith, the latter absconding with Ballinger's ICU money.[2] To many the Natal ICU seemed to have a better chance of survival than did the parent body. For some months in 1929 the Ballinger ICU maintained a presence in Natal, but by the middle of the year this had disappeared.[3] The fortunes of the Champion ICU, too, were soon at a low ebb.[4] In December 1928 a subcommittee of the Governing Body of the ICU yase Natal was forced into a policy of retrenchment in Durban. All the employees of the branch were to be dismissed 'owing to the Financial position of the Branch, which continues to decline'. Champion proposed to act as Branch Secretary himself, as well as continuing as General Secretary. This gave rise to one of those bitter squabbles that are endemic in small ineffectual organizations. There was a struggle for possession of the union's premises in Durban. Later events indicate that there was a compromise providing for shared premises, but separate organizations.[5]

It seems all too likely that the Natal leader in 1929 was casting around for a suitable grievance to exploit in the interests of reviving the ICU's following in Durban. Such a grievance came to hand in April of that year, when in one of the suburbs of the city, Sydenham, the Local Administration and Health Board acquired the right under the 1923 Natives Urban Areas Act of manufacturing its own African beer (Kaffir beer) and the exclusive right of sale within the area under its control. This arrangement was long familiar in Durban itself, which had first assumed its sole manufacture and sale, in municipal beer halls, under the Native Beer Act of 1908,[6] and for many years exercised its monopoly, which was confirmed by the 1923 Act. Champion in a protest to the Native Commissioner at Durban objected to the very principle of raising revenue through municipal beer sales, which he considered 'not a proper and honest way of maintaining the western civilisation in this land'. A protest in similar terms was addressed to the Secretary of the Sydenham Health Board.[7]

On successive Sundays in May (5, 12, 19 and 26) a column of Blacks, armed with sticks and headed by brass bands, marched from the ICU Hall in Durban to Sydenham to hold protest meetings. On the 19th two White motorists were assaulted and on the 26th some of the marchers wore red tunics. Then, towards the end of May, the disturbances spread to the barracks at the Point in Durban, where the Acting Compound Manager forbade the making (though this was not in fact against the law) and storing of *mahewu*, a non-intoxicating beverage derived from maize. The objection to this prohibition by a resident at the barracks, one Mcijelwa, resulted in the forfeiture of his togt badge – and therefore of his right to reside at the barracks and to seek employment as a day labourer – on the ground that he had advocated, in retaliation, a boycott of the municipal beer hall at the Point. When the man applied for renewal of his badge on 12 June and was refused, the ICU took up his case and at the same time came out in support of a boycott. The following day the boycott was enforced by pickets, and an attack by a crowd one thousand strong on the Point beer hall under the impression that an induna from the railway works had flouted the boycott, brought the local Durban police, the Borough Police, on the scene and resulted in a number of injuries among police and rioters. Champion, who was accompanied by Batty, urged moderation and reiterated this advice in the evening at a big meeting. Although on this occasion considerable damage was done, there were to be no further assaults on property by the Blacks.[8]

On Saturday 15 June five thousand leaflets were distributed by the ICU threatening those who did not observe the boycott and attacking the municipal authorities in Durban. African beer, it was alleged, had 'enriched the Corporation', which had used the proceeds to build 'barracks where natives were badly treated'. 'Native spendthrifts', 'tempted with kaffir beer', had no money left to go home, which meant 'many supportless people at the kraals'. Next day, Sunday, a gathering of 5 000 on Cartwright's Flats was addressed by Champion and J. T. Gumede of the African National Congress. Champion's speech was an attack upon the Durban Corporation, Black police constables, and the Government. 'All those present,' ran a report, 'were warned to join the ICU as members, failing which they would be dealt with by a society called the Unity League.'

On Monday 17 June events reached a climax. In the early afternoon a deputation headed by J. H. London of the ICU made known to the Corporation's Native Affairs Department the grievances of the city's Blacks, the most important being the case of the man who had lost his togt badge, and, of somewhat less importance, the Sydenham beer monopoly and Durban's lack of a proper location with a location advisory board. Meanwhile a group of ICU men, armed with sticks, was making the rounds of the beer halls and enforcing the boycott. When the Borough Police, armed with pick handles, attempted to arrest them for contravening the by-laws relating to carrying sticks, they resisted and there were casualties on both sides. Champion, evidently alarmed at the turn of events, although he himself was in large measure responsible for what was happening, was persuaded by Captain Baston of the South African Police to use his influence in the interests of peace. After inducing a crowd at the Point barracks to disperse, he agreed to call off the pickets on the understanding, given by Captain Alexander of the Borough Police, that grievances would be brought before the proper authorities. He was then accorded an interview by two members of the Borough Council. The police authorities were satisfied that the disturbances were at an end. They were not.

As in Port Elizabeth in October 1920 and in Bloemfontein in April 1925, there ensued the intervention of a White mob that the police would not or could not control. During the afternoon of the 17th, Whites who had seen or heard of the clash between the police and the ICU patrol earlier in the day began to gather outside the ICU Hall in Prince Edward Street, and their numbers were greatly swollen in the late afternoon as the first edition of the evening paper appeared on the streets. By five o'clock there were, at the very least, five hundred people besieging the Hall. The beleaguered Blacks, who included two dozen or so women and a couple of children, barricaded the windows against flying bottles and stones and telephoned the South African Police. The toll inflicted by an armed sortie from the Hall – four men (led to the scene by curiosity more than anything else) either dead or badly injured – roused the White mob to a frenzied shriek: 'Blood for blood.' Sometime during the fracas Champion arrived, only to leave at once when he saw how things were. Fortunately, before an assault could be effected, a combined force of Borough and South African Police, accompanied by the Mayor and Chief Magistrate, came to the rescue, forcing the crowd back. In the meanwhile, however, a relief column of some 2 000 ICU supporters was approaching. The Port Elizabeth/Bloemfontein formula produced the same reaction: unruly, uncontrollable armed White civilians fired on the oncoming column and, when it broke, pursued the fleeing Blacks on foot and by car. As it grew dark the ICU Hall was evacuated and the police guard withdrawn. The following morning the mob returned and played havoc. The total known casualties were ninety-one. Three people were killed (one White, two Black), four died of wounds (one White, three Blacks), and eighty-four wounded (13 Whites, 65 Blacks, of whom 14 had gunshot wounds, 3 Indians, and 3 Coloured).

A Commission of Enquiry was appointed on 28 June 1929, with a single Commissioner, Mr Justice de Waal, who took evidence over a period of eight days at the beginning of July. Sixty-one witnesses were heard, and they included the Mayor and Chief Magistrate of Durban, W. G. Ballinger, A. F. Batty, Rev. J. L. Dube, A. W. G. Champion, and J. T. Gumede. The ICU yase Natal was represented by Cecil Cowley. In his report de Waal was unsparing in his condemnation of the behaviour of the White vigilantes, whose inhumanity, he said, more than matched the savagery with which the victims of the sortie from the Hall were treated. The police were commended for their restraint, and absolved from any charge of negligence in their failure to disperse the crowd of Whites and protect the ICU premises from being ransacked. Champion came in for some severe criticism. The Commissioner, though not denying the existence of well-founded cause for complaint, regarded him as a trouble-maker who exploited grievances of a trifling nature. He was convinced that Champion's references during his speech of Sunday 16 June to Communists and Communism revealed his sympathy towards them, and this sympathy was further betrayed by his acquiescence in the use of the ICU Hall for speeches by 'notorious communists' and in the sale of *The South African Worker* at ICU meetings. 'Communistic agitation,' he declared, 'although not directly being a cause of the riot, certainly contributed to the general unrest.'

De Waal concluded his report by recommending the continuation of the existing arrangement for the brewing and sale of beer, which he thought was in the interests of moderation and order; the establishment of a township where men could have their families and have a small piece of land; the provision of recreation facilities; the setting up of an advisory board which would replace the ICU as the means of laying grievances before the municipal authorities; the restoration of Mcijelwa's togt badge 'as an act of grace'; and clemency 'in generous measure' to Blacks convicted of offences committed during the riots.

Durban continued to smoulder after the June riots. The beer hall boycott was maintained and the Chief Magistrate of the city refused to allow the ICU to re-open its offices or to resume public meetings, with the result that in August the Natal ICU President, J. J. Macebo, and five others were arrested for addressing a meeting in defiance of the magisterial ruling and convicted in the magistrate's court. Resentment was not confined to the Black population, and there was some agitation among Whites for strengthening the curfew law that Champion had successfully challenged in 1926.[9] As a punitive measure the Minister of Justice drafted heavily armed police into Durban and opened a stern campaign to run tax-defaulters to earth.[10] The climax of the operation was the flight of Oswald Pirow himself to the city, determined to forestall an alleged Communist plot and to teach the Zulus a lesson; and this was made more instructive by an experimental and unjustified use of tear gas.[11] Champion was dealt with under the newly amended Riotous Assemblies Act. Though anxious to make his peace with the Government, he was ordered to leave Natal in September 1930. Intervention on his behalf by the Mayor of Durban, the Rev. A. Lamont, failed to move the Minister, who certainly had the support of most White Durban opinion. The exiled leader spent the next three years, while the ban was in force, mostly in Johannesburg,[12] where he worked for a bank.[13] In his absence the ICU yase Natal continued its briefly interrupted decline. The ill-feeling between the headquarters of the union and its Durban branch (eventually the only branch) that had broken out as early as December 1928, recurred.[14]

While Champion was taking all the limelight in Durban Kadalie was still hoping to repair his damaged fortunes. Invitations were issued to a conference at East London, called the Second Annual Conference of the Independent ICU, the second annual conference within ten months, as Ballinger, who declined an invitation to attend, sarcastically observed. In the Orange Free State 'Mote and Elias received invitations, but did not attend, Elias because his car broke down, 'Mote probably because he had no money. It may safely be presumed that, with the possible exception of some Johannesburg adherents, the delegates to the conference came from the few Independent ICU branches in the Eastern Province, the only known ones being East London, Port Elizabeth, King William's Town, Mooiplats, and, perhaps, Grahamstown. In the absence of outside delegations the conference was preoccupied with parochial issues, above all the grievances of the East London employees of the Railways and Harbours Administration. The delegates decided to approach the Administration with a demand for a minimum wage of six shillings and six pence a day, which, if granted, would have been a marked advance on the prevailing rate of three and six. It was agreed to call a strike on 16 January if the demand were not met, and this decision was endorsed by a mass meeting in one of the locations. An ultimatum was passed to the Administration, which responded with threats of dismissal or loss of privileges.[15]

Since the union had not amassed any funds to sustain a strike, Kadalie sent telegrams impartially to the League Against Imperialism in Berlin and the International Transport Workers' Federation in Amsterdam asking for money. He also telegraphed the South African Trades Union Congress, the Cape Federation of Labour Unions, and the National Union of Railway and Harbour Servants soliciting help in preventing scabbing by White workers. Two members of the Legislative Assembly, Madeley and Krige, were asked to take up the cause of the Black railway employees in Parliament. In the meantime preparations went ahead for a strike. A committee was formed that included Kadalie and his brother Robert, Tyamzashe and Maduna, and a belated attempt was made to build up a strike fund from local contributions. Strike rules were issued, imposing a code of discipline – no alcohol and no carrying of sticks or other weapons.

When the strike began on Thursday 16 January only three hundred men stopped work, but it affected the stevedores of the Union Castle Company as well as the labourers of the Railways and Harbours. As was to be expected, there were allegations of intimidation. A daily routine was established of prayers, hymns, and abusive and hortatory speeches, replete with vague promises of external assistance. Although there were no threats of violence, the authorities enrolled special constables and sent police patrols into the location. The stoppage never became complete. Not only was White casual labour taken on, but there was also little solidarity among the Black tribal groups. The Union Castle Company brought in labour from Durban, while the Basuto workers, who had their own organization, the Basuto Workers' Association, carried on working.

On Monday 20 January an attempt made to extend the strike to the town had some success at first, but after a few days it became difficult to keep the town workers away from their jobs. No assistance came from far-off, and it is clear that the ICU had only very limited means of feeding the strikers. The International Transport Workers' Federation sent an evasive reply by telegraph, and all Kadalie got was a message of solidarity from the African National Congress in Johannesburg. Although the hard core of strikers among the dock workers (rather fewer than 500 men) remained resolute, in the harbour, which had filled since the beginning of the strike, all the ships were being worked within the week. On the evening of the Friday Kadalie and Maduna announced that on the following Monday the IICU would put out pickets to make the strike more effective. 'Today,' said Maduna, 'we have arrived at our decision. By the blood of their fathers shall the children get their freedom.' Consequently on Saturday afternoon the Chief Magistrate, addressing a meeting in the location, warned the crowd that picketing was unlawful and that the police would take action to prevent it. On Sunday the entire strike committee was arrested, by means of a trick that Kadalie thought most dishonest. Complying with a polite request to go to the police station, the members of the committee fell into a trap. 'This,' wrote Kadalie in his autobiography, 'was my darkest hour, but I strove to behave like an African warrior.'[16] It appears that the location residents heard the news without much sign of emotion. The special constables were disbanded, though regular police remained in the location.

When they appeared in court the next day, the IICU leaders were remanded in custody on a charge of incitement to public violence. After his remand Kadalie, allowed or induced to address the people who had gathered outside the courthouse, told them that the strike was over, following this up with a letter of confirmation to the Executive Committee of the union. Although his instruction to the strikers to return to work was repudiated by two members of the Executive Committee who had not been on the strike committee and therefore had not been arrested, the strike did not continue much longer. On 10 February the arrested men appeared before the Resident Magistrate, who accepted Kadalie's application for bail but fixed it at an impossibly high figure – £200 for Kadalie and Maduna and £100 for each of the others. They were committed on 26 February for trial on eleven counts of incitement to public violence or, alternatively, of a contravention of section 29, the hostility clause, of the Native Administration Act. At Grahamstown, whither the accused were taken, a more reasonable bail was obtained on the application of Advocate W. Stuart, whose wife paid Kadalie's. He and Tyamzashe made their way home to Johannesburg, where they awaited the opening of the trial in May.[17] Though acquitted on the alternative charge, Kadalie was found guilty of incitement and fined £25, which was paid immediately. The others were acquitted. Having been released the IICU leaders returned to East London to a hero's welcome, at least according to Kadalie.[18]

The Independent ICU continued to enjoy considerable support in East London, where, until well into 1931, subscriptions were running at something like £100 a month, indicating a membership in the order of a thousand.[19] Nevertheless, the strike of 1930 can only be reckoned a failure. Though perhaps for a day or two as much as 86 per cent of the Black labour force of the city stayed away from work and though great determination was displayed by a number of men working for the Railways and Harbours, the stoppage was short-lived and partial and there was never any sign that the employers were prepared to compromise. One firm increased its daily wage from three shillings to three and six. The Railways and Harbours Administration rewarded with a bonus the men who had remained at work and punished with a loss of seniority and, in some cases, dismissal those who had joined in the strike. This undoubtedly had been ill-conceived and hastily executed without preparation, as was admitted, in a letter to Mrs Lewis, by H. D. Tyamzashe, who put the blame on Kadalie.[20] The impression is created that Kadalie, desperately anxious to recover his standing, was consciously or unconsciously influenced by a desire to repeat the success that the Cape Town dock strike of ten years earlier had had in establishing his position. The East London strike showed how ineffective strikes are – however spectacular – that are not backed by organization, planning, and experience and are met with an adamant refusal by employers to admit the need for generosity, combined with an implacable determination to concede nothing. The public authorities in East London acted with decided coolness, skill, and lack of scruple.

Since East London was no doubt a backwater for Kadalie, he returned to Johannesburg as soon as possible with Tyamzashe and Maduna, where, however, he was not permitted to remain long. After holding a meeting in Pretoria he was served with an order from the Minister of Justice, prohibiting his attending or addressing public meetings on the Rand and in Pretoria. Thus muzzled there was little point in his remaining in Johannesburg, and so, leaving behind Tyamzashe, at least for a time, to act as a one-man headquarters, he made his way back to East London, where he was based for the rest of his life. The City Council viewed his choice of residence with distaste, but, although after a long and costly legal battle it succeeded in ousting him from the East Bank Location, he was, as a parliamentary voter, able to resist eviction from the city itself, where he bought a house in 1936. His last significant action before retiring to the Cape was to use his influence in Bloemfontein against a pass law defiance campaign organized by the Communist Party, which was supposed to culminate in public pass burning on Dingaan's Day, 16 December 1930. Henceforth Kadalie had only local importance. The authorities kept a close watch on his movements and, until it became apparent that his influence was gone for good, subjected him to a degree of harassment. In 1931 he was foiled in an attempt to visit the Transkei, where the IICU claimed to have two branches, and in 1932 he was arrested twice, firstly for failing to pay his poll-tax, secondly for failing to keep a proper record of the financial transactions of his organization. The second case, which resulted in his being fined, revealed the persistence of that laxity in money matters which had bedevilled the original ICU. For a time he was suspected, not without cause perhaps, of illicit diamond buying.[21]

In the 1930s there were sporadic attempts at reunification of the several ICUs. In 1931 the initiative came from Keable 'Mote, then Acting General Secretary of the Federated Free State Industrial and Commercial Workers' Union in Kroonstad, who tried to get Champion to participate in a reunification conference.[22] The latter, no doubt unwilling to attract official attention and so prolong his 'exile', made excuses. It was he, feeling that he had been shabbily treated by his former colleagues in his martyrdom,[23] who poured cold water on a more determined effort in 1933, when Kadalie was the moving spirit. A reunification conference held in Bloemfontein in June of that year accepted reunification in principle and decided to take steps to reconcile the constitutional differences amongst the three surviving sections, the Ballinger ICU, the Natal ICU, and the Independent ICU,[24] and to hold a further conference in October at Durban to ratify an agreed constitution for a united ICU. The Bloemfontein conference was attended by Kadalie and Tyamzashe of the Independents, John Mancoe of the ICU of Africa, and James Ngcobo, General Secretary in Champion's absence of the ICU yase Natal, but no one else of note, apart from J. T. Gumede of the ANC, who acted as chairman.[25] The poverty of the three fragments is shown by the difficulty Kadalie experienced in extracting £1 for expenses from the Natal and Ballinger organizations.[26] Not only were they poor, but they were also subject to schisms. When Kadalie went to Durban after the Bloemfontein conference in order to arrange for the projected Durban gathering, he found the ICU yase Natal in two sections, though both apparently recognizing the authority of the General Secretary-in-exile. By trying to bring the warring factions together, he incurred Champion's reproach that he was interfering in the domestic affairs of Natal.[27] Not that Kadalie's own position was so secure. For there was also a split in the Independent ICU.[28]

Champion returned to Durban in October 1933, and tried, apparently without much success, to put new life into the ICU yase Natal.[29] His old union was then in such straits that it could not pay him enough to live on and he was compelled to get a job as a clerk.[30] Reduced circumstances, however, did not kindle in him any spark of enthusiasm for reunification and, by boycotting it, he successfully sabotaged the conference, originally planned for October and eventually held in Durban in December.[31] After the abortive conference Kadalie appeared in Port Elizabeth, where, however, he attracted – at least according to his enemies in the dividend Independent ICU – but tiny audiences.[32]

There was some further negotiation in 1936 for reunion and Kadalie still cherished hopes of regaining his position of influence.[33] He – now called the General Secretary of the United ICU, the name given to the supposedly reunited body of 1933 – and Champion appeared at a meeting in Durban. 'Workers of Durban,' urged the public notice, 'come and hear the two leaders speaking from one platform. Roll up in your thousands.'[34] It is unlikely that they did.

The failure of the Black trade union movement in the 1920s gave Black aspirations once again a political direction. Disillusioned by the ICU, people turned to the ANC and the All-African Convention, a protest movement against the Hertzog Native Bills. In this post-ICU situation Champion was more successful than Kadalie in accommodating himself to the change. Kadalie, who had never been a Congress man, remained to his dying day associated only with the ICU, a relic of the past. Champion, on the other hand, entered upon a political career which brought him quite as much prominence as his work with the ICU had done. They both attended the All-African Convention in Bloemfontein in December 1935. The removal of Black voters from the common electoral roll went ahead despite Black protest, but they were allowed to elect three members – White – to the House of Assembly. Four Senate seats were set aside for White representatives of Blacks throughout the entire Union, to be indirectly elected by chiefs, headmen, district councils, and location advisory boards. A Native Representative Council, composed of a Black elected majority and a White nominated minority, was set up to advise the Government on matters of interest to the Black people. The question was now whether the Blacks were to co-operate in putting the new arrangements into operation; and to discuss this a second All-African Convention was held in July 1936, also attended by Kadalie and Champion. The former submitted a motion calling for non-co-operation that was never put to the vote. A majority of the delegates decided in favour of co-operation.[35]

Although Kadalie had advocated a boycott of the new electoral arrangements established by Parliament in 1936, he made use of the services of the Member of the Legislative Assembly chosen to represent the interests of Blacks in the Eastern Province, Mrs Margaret Ballinger. In fact, he became respectable, securing election to the Location Advisory Board and, by his own account, being accepted by the authorities as the voice of the Black railway and harbour workers. During the war, in 1942, he even sought election to the Native Representative Council, but, after he had started his election campaign, it turned out that he was ineligible to stand because he had been born outside the Union of South Africa. Somewhat abject appeals to authority personally and through Mrs Ballinger achieved nothing then or in 1946, when he was hoping to stand in the 1947 election. A long letter at the beginning of 1947 to Smuts was his last, unsuccessful attempt.[36] Champion was more successful. He did become a member of the Native Representative Council in 1942. Like Kadalie he became a leading light of the local Advisory Board. His appetite for litigation and business enterprise remained and it is apparent that he found opportunities to indulge it.[37]

One more strike must be mentioned, again at Buffalo Harbour, East London, in May and June 1946. Although it seems unlikely that Kadalie had much to do with it, the authorities suspected him. Their suspicions were based on the flimsy evidence proffered by the Railways and Harbours Administration's Inspector of Non-European Labour, who spoke of clandestine meetings and ICU agitation. The evidence seems to be just as strong that Kadalie tried to take over the conduct of the strike, but was rebuffed. The same Inspector suggested that the principal source of Kadalie's influence was his 'system of agents who contact Natives arriving from the Reserves and arrange lodging and employment, where possible. For these services the "raw native" is duly made to pay and he is kept under the influence of Kadalie.'[38]

Kadalie, who had once led a nation-wide union, spent his declining days preoccupied with the affairs of the East Bank Location, renamed Duncan Village, ruling his tiny kingdom, a Napoleon on St Helena, like a mighty empire. He lived 'in the "North End" – in a most unprepossessing suburb of East London populated by a mixture of races – in a reasonable dwelling house for that area, but one which is most beautifully furnished'.[39] The latter-day triumphs of the ICU were a growing membership running into four figures, the capture of all six seats on the Location Advisory Board, and memoranda to government departments and commissions. 'Notwithstanding,' he wrote late in life, 'the fact that the ICU is not functioning in many parts of Africa . . . at East London the work of the Union goes on smoothly every day, rendering yeoman service to its members.'[40]

In October 1951, Clements Kadalie, accompanied by his wife, paid a visit to the land of his birth. Shortly afterwards, he died of diabetes, diagnosed too late for effective treatment.[41] Allison Champion outlived him by more than twenty years, dying in 1975.

Notes

1. Cf. *The Natal Advertiser* 9 July 1928.
2. Ibid.; W. G. Ballinger to Winifred Holtby 8 August 1928 (B/UCT); Batty remained faithful to Champion until his death in 1930.
3. L. H. Greene to W. G. Ballinger 1 March 1929 (B/Wits); ICU of Africa, Administration Report 20 June 1929 (B/Wits).
4. W. G. Ballinger to Winifred Holtby 8 August 1928 (B/UCT) and to A. C. Jones 3 October 1928 (B/UCT).
5. A. W. G. Champion to Branch Secretary, Durban 4 December 1928 (F 1928/62a); Branch Secretary to A. W. G. Champion 12 and 14 December 1928 (F 1928/62c and e).
6. For the disreputable aspects of the Act see M. W. Swanson, "The Durban System": roots of urban apartheid in colonial Natal (*African Studies*, XXXV, 159–176).
7. Commission of Enquiry – Native Riots at Durban, 29 July 1929 (Forman Collection). The account given here of ensuing events is drawn largely from this report.
8. *The Natal Advertiser* 14 June 1929.
9. A. W. G. Champion to Chief Magistrate, Durban 24 August 1929 (F 1929/30); Chief Magistrate to A. W. G. Champion 26 August 1929 (F 1929/31); Account of Cowley and Cowley to ICU yase Natal 28 August and 17 October 1929 (F 1929/28); A. W. G. Champion

to Chairman, Native Affairs Commission 4 October 1929 (F 1929/38).
10. A. W. G. Champion to District Commandant, South African Police, 28 October 1929 (F 1929/42).
11. Roux, E. R., *Time Longer than Rope*, 192.
12. Ibid., 192–3.
13. The Colonial Banking and Trust Company (A. W. G. Champion to the Chairman and Members of the Committee of Inquiry into the Conditions of Natives in Urban Areas, n.d., F/MSS/40).
14. Cf. D. L. Bopela to T. J. Macebo 13 March and 22 April 1931 (F 1931/8, 17).
15. For an account of the strike see H. H. Smith, loc. cit., 162–188; Kadalie, C., *My Life*, Chapter XIII; and H. D. Tyamzashe, loc. cit., 30–5.
16. Op cit., 188.
17. Ibid., 195; H. D. Tyamzashe to E. Lewis 29 March 1930 (B/Wits).
18. Kadalie, C., *My Life*, 199.
19. *The Daily Dispatch* 27 April 1932.
20. H. D. Tyamzashe to E. Lewis 29 March 1930 (B/Wits).
21. Kadalie, C., *My Life*, 201–6; Roux, E. R., *Time Longer than Rope*, 196, 246–7; *The Daily Dispatch* 27 April 1932; D. Budulwayo to W. G. Ballinger 19 June 1930 (B/UCT); T. B. Lujiza to W. G. Ballinger 4 June 1931 (B/UCT); C. Kadalie to M. Ballinger 5 January 1943 (B/Wits).
22. K. 'Mote to A. W. G. Champion 25 March 1931 (F 1931/11).
23. A. W. G. Champion to C. Kadalie 31 May 1933 (F. 1933/5).
24. Nothing is heard of 'Mote.
25. C. Kadalie to Chairman and Secretary, ICU yase Natal 7 April 1933 (F 1933/19); ICU Reunion Conference; unanimous agreement to unification [*sic*] (F 1933/16c); *The Star* 17 July 1933; D. L. Bopela to A. W. G. Champion 14 July 1933 (F 1933/2).
26. C. Kadalie to A. W. G. Champion 1 November 1933 (F 1933/17).
27. J. Ngcobo to C. Kadalie 3 July 1933 (F 1933/23); General Secretary, ICU yase Natal to Branches 21 July 1933 (F 1933/4); C. Kadalie to A. W. G. Champion 25 and 30 July and 15 August 1933 (F 1933/8, 10 and 15).
28. J. J. Magade to A. W. G. Champion 1 August and 1 November 1933 (F 1933/12).
29. *Natal Mercury* 18 December 1933.
30. A. W. G. Champion to Manager, Colonial Banking and Trust Co. Ltd 20 December 1933 (F 1933/31).
31. A. W. G. Champion to C. Kadalie 27 July, 24 October, 15 and 30 November 1933; C. Kadalie to A. W. G. Champion 31 July, 23 November, 4 and 8 December (telegrams), 16 and 17 December 1933; C. Kadalie to General Secretary, ICU yase Natal 23 November 1933 and to H. Msomi 14 October 1933; A. W. G. Champion to J. J. Magade 7 December 1933 (F 1933/9, 10, 14, 17, 19, 22, 23, 24, 27 and 28).
32. J. J. Magade to A. W. G. Champion 8 January 1934 (F 1934/1).
33. Kadalie, C., *My Life*, 213–4.
34. F 1936/1.
35. Kadalie, C., *My Life*, 208-11.
36. Ibid., 214–7; C. Kadalie to M. Ballinger 5 January 1943 (B/Wits).
37. A. W. G. Champion to Chairman and Members of the Committee of Inquiry into Conditions of Natives in Urban Areas, n.d. (F/MSS/40); Chief Assistant Editor, *Natal Mercury* to A. W. G. Champion 22 May 1936 (F/General Letters 147).
38. H. H. Smith, loc. cit., 194, 200.
39. Ibid., 142.
40. For the last years see Kadalie, C., *My life*, 217–9.
41. *African Drum* June 1952, 32–3.

CHAPTER 13

The Achievement

Natives can be taxed as in the case of Europeans without having to be subjected to the indignity of having to produce, under compulsion and a pain of imprisonment, on demand by any policeman, any receipt of payments made or papers of identification.

Resolution of the Bloemfontein Conference, July 1920

Our union would humbly request the commission to consider the methods usually employed by the South African Police, who round up Africans in our locations in the early hours daily. In East London one finds that a state of martial law exists; for raids are carried out by the police early in the mornings for passes and poll-tax receipts.

Memorandum of the ICU, East London, to the Natives Law Commission of Inquiry, October 1946

A great deal of obscurity surrounds the actual size of the ICU's following. At the end of 1921 it had a claimed membership of 10 004. Early in 1924, before the movement into Natal and the Transvaal, Kadalie was claiming 20 000, in September 1925, 30 400. By June 1927, the claim had risen to 80 000 members; by November that year, when the union applied for affiliation to the South African Trades Union Congress, to 100 000; and early in 1928 'very nigh to 200 000'.[1] It is, however, improbable that Head Office ever knew the exact state of the membership at any one time, in spite of the constitutional obligation imposed on the General Secretary by the 1925 Constitution and on the Financial Secretary by the 1927 constitution to keep a members' statistical register. Towards the end of 1928, finding itself a defendant in a number of civil actions, the ICU was required to draw up a list of members, for, although an unincorporated body, it could, under the provisions of the Magistrates' Court Act, be called upon by a creditor to produce a statement of the names and addresses of the members within three days.[2] In the magistrate's court in Johannesburg the Administrative Secretary was able to offer a list of only 819 names and, when pressed, said, 'I can produce about a thousand or two more names if you give me time; but I shall want about two weeks, because some of the handwriting is indecipherable.'[3] Since central records were so inchoate, it seems unlikely that the branches, where there was less administrative talent than at headquarters, kept more complete or more accurate records.

What one knows of the finances of the ICU makes it impossible to view membership claims without scepticism. It is difficult to accept a claimed membership, for example, of twenty thousand in 1924, when one recollects that Kadalie on his 1924 tour was stranded at Upington without enough money to buy himself a meal.[4] 'In the earlier days of the ICU,' he declared in December 1927, 'he had starved his family and worked without a salary for two years.'[5] Allowance must be made for exaggeration, but there are few signs of affluence in the union before late 1926. The spasmodic appearance of *The Workers' Herald* is another piece of evidence. Although the intention was apparently to publish this fortnightly,[6] at its most regular and most frequent it was never more than a monthly, and indeed, up to 1925 it appeared only irregularly. There were only ten issues between May 1923, and December 1924, and only four of these came out in 1924. One of the members of the Economic and Wage Commission in 1925 pointed out that, even if only half the claimed 30 000-odd membership were in financial compliance and if as many as one third of the paid-up members were women paying three pence a week instead of the usual six pence and one sixth of the male members were farm labourers paying three pence a week too, that would still give an income of about £15 000 a year, which is most unlikely. What the subscriptions collected really amounted to, the ICU witnesses were unwilling to divulge – or perhaps simply did not know.[7]

The most reliable statistics come from Durban,[8] but even these must be treated with some reserve, not because they deliberately misled, rather because they were imperfectly kept and never revised. While the nominal membership at the end of 1927 stood at 45 487, there is little evidence to show how accurately this figure reflected real or 'financial' membership. Perhaps a more reliable guide is the income from subscriptions. This reached its highest point in May 1927, and it would not be unreasonable to take the nominal membership at that date (27 000) as the greatest effective membership attained, after which new membership was offset by wastage. Giving evidence to the de Waal Commission in July 1929, Detective-Sergeant Arnold of the CID stated that up to May 1928, 88 000 Natal Blacks had joined the ICU.[9] He did not say where he got his information,[10] but he was certainly not exaggerating the strength of the union in an attempt to prejudice opinion against it, since he went on to say that the current membership was only 2 342. The fact, however, that 88 000 people joined the ICU in Natal at some time or other before May 1928, is no evidence that there was ever that number of members in the province at one time.

It is no use trying to arrive at an estimate from the total income to Head Office. In 1927 this was £11 695.2s.0d.,[11] and this represents only ten to fifteen thousand members, according to the estimated ratio of female and rural workers to male urban workers (that is, 'three-penny members' to 'six-penny members'). The difficulty is that Head Office income represented only a fraction of the total revenue of the ICU. In spite of the strict procedures enjoined by the constitution, failure of branches to centralize funds is attested by ample evidence. Durban itself, sent in only £1 684.17s.11d. out of a total income from enrolment fees and subscriptions of £6 606.15s.11d., in 1927.[12] Durban was not untypical. Even with the stricter methods introduced by Ballinger it is apparent that local officials were lax in sending in subscriptions.[13]

It would, however, be excessively pedantic and sterile to stress unduly upon paid-up membership, since the support enjoyed by the ICU extended beyond it. Subscriptions were high in relation to wages and undoubtedly many members were constrained by poverty, not indifference, from paying their dues.[14] There must, therefore, have been a great deal of informal and spasmodic support. Subscriptions were in fact haphazardly collected, sometimes only when a rally was held. Some joined, paid two or three subscriptions, joined again after a lapse, then perhaps repeated the performance. Buckets were passed round at meetings and often filled to overflowing, and it is unlikely that the money collected was properly checked and accounted for.

To arrive at a rough estimate of ICU support is it helpful to consider the number of branches established. When, towards the end of 1927, the union was claiming a membership of 100 000, there were some hundred branches. A total claimed membership of 100 000 would require an average branch membership of a thousand. This is by no means improbable, even though numbers were inflated by the issue of two or three membership cards to each subscriber. Some branches had a far larger membership. In Natal, for example, apart from Durban, there were Port Shepstone, Estcourt, and Vryheid, the last named claiming a membership of 9 081.[15] In the Orange Free State an enrolment of 10 813 was claimed for Kroonstad during 1927–8.[16] It seems by no means unlikely then that, at its most influential, the ICU did command the support of not fewer than the hundred thousand members it claimed. The maximum membership, however, was maintained for only a few months, Natal beginning its climb towards the end of 1926 and starting its descent in the middle of 1927 and the Orange Free State and the Transvaal reaching their peak towards the end of 1927. If one were to add together all those who at one time or another supported the movement, they would probably number more than 150 000. Its influence was felt throughout a very large part of the Union of South Africa and even beyond its borders. External branches were certainly formed in Southern Rhodesia, South-West Africa, and Basutoland, while in South Africa itself, though in the Cape it moved little outside its early sphere of influence (only to Graaff-Reinet, Griqualand East, and the Mafeking area), the ICU covered with its branches most parts of the remaining provinces.

A variety of discontents lay behind the protest that membership – staunch or transitory – of the ICU represented. It began its career as an offshoot of the South African industrial labour movement, itself an offshoot of the British. Its early membership included agricultural labourers in the Eastern Province of the Cape, but essentially it was a town-based general trade union, though one prone to a preoccupation with political issues that, added to, among other things, a low level of administrative competence, impaired the efficient performance of conventional trade union functions. From 1926, more particularly in 1927–8, the rural component of the membership predominated. The movement became a peasants' revolt. In that revolt there appears to have been a mixture of the rising expectations of the landless – the hope of a more generous land settlement hinted at by the Hertzog programme of segregation – and the despair of labour tenants, already subject to a harsh servitude, now threatened with a deterioration of their situation. To the extent that despair was the spur, the movement was a resistance to a deprivation of grazing and cultivating rights which induced either emigration to industrial employment or the total loss of all independence on White-owned land. Despite the quasi-feudal conditions under which many squatters and labour tenants lived, membership of the ICU was a protest not against a feudal relationship, but rather against the loss of such advantages as that relationship gave. It was enforced 'proletarianization' that aroused the hostility. Whether the motives that actuated the legislators were a conscious or sub-conscious desire to solve the labour problem of White farmers or mine magnates and industrialists, or to facilitate the extraction of surplus value by actual or aspirant capitalists, made little difference in practice.

The ICU leaders talked a great deal about the class struggle, but for all the jargon they affected, they were not revolutionaries. Many – notably Champion – were thwarted entrepreneurs; most, like Kadalie, wanted to prosecute their ambitions within the system, not overthrow it. Their struggle was a racial, not a class, one. It was not that they were preoccupied with concepts of racial purity or dedicated to racial exclusivism. What they wanted was not dominance, but acceptance into White society and unimpeded progress of Blacks into full civil rights. Realizing like the Economic and Wage Commissioners of 1925 that the South African omelette could not be unscrambled, they sought an extension of the franchise and the opening of skilled employment to Blacks, or, rather, protested against the whittling away of privileges and the closing of doors.

It would not be difficult to assemble evidence that would appear to show quite the contrary. Occasionally Black prejudice against the Coloured community and Asians was expressed, as well as some support for the ideas of Marcus Garvey and some anti-White feeling.[17] Yet ICU propagandists rarely spoke in unison and they betrayed a lamentable lack of consistency. On the whole the expression of intolerant and threatening opinions was untypical and, when it occurrred, an understandable response to the White oligarchy's commitment to a policy that was, if less relentless and less merciless in the more civilized days of the 1920s, nonetheless compounded of racial intransigence and political obduracy. It would have been surprising had the ICU escaped the influence of a contemporary movement so powerful and exciting as the Universal Negro Improvement Society, but there is no evidence that any of the leading figures of the ICU, except perhaps J. G. Gumbs,[18] was deeply influenced by Garvey.

White people were shocked by sentiments, now commonplace in the world, then unfamiliar. 'Let the white people in general forget,' wrote Clements Kadalie, 'once and for all the blasphemous lie that it is a law of God that some nations shall rule over others continuously . . . The lie has never worked and never will. Those who believe it have always perished.'[19] There were complaints among Whites that Blacks were treating them with less respect than in the past. The situation was changing. D. D. T. Jabavu confessed to the Select Committee on the 'Native Bills' in 1927 'We instinctively take off our hats to the white man even where we know he is distinctly inferior to us in educational and economic attainments. In my own case, I unconsciously say "boss" to the white man who mends my fences, just because of my natural respect for the white colour which has behind it a history of 2 000 years of development, a respect which in these exceptional cases I do not regard as being derogatory.' In contrast, the younger generation of Black leaders felt itself sufficiently versed in the ways of European civilization to demand equality of opportunity and reward. More important, however, was that the supposed guardians of the civilization that bestowed honour and respect were embarking upon a policy of racial tyranny which they dignified with such euphemisms as 'civilized labour policy', thus degrading the civilization they claimed to be defending. 'Natives of the type of Mr Kadalie,' continued Professor Jabavu, 'are produced by the abnormal development of natives due to abnormally bad laws and conditions . . . The Kadalies are simply the natural and inevitable result of the persecution of natives.'[20]

'These Kadalies', this first generation of the new-style Black nationalist leaders, had a significance beyond their immediate achievement, which was but meagre. There was a view current at the time that, had Clements Kadalie acted in some different way, that achievement would have been more effective and lasting. Such a view was expressed by W. G. Ballinger: 'If Kadalie could have accepted guidance and advice, he would have changed the whole history of Native policy in South Africa.'[21] The advice and guidance that Ballinger had in mind, of course, were his own. His enemies argued that what the ICU suffered from was an excess of those commodities from that quarter, that, in fact, Ballinger killed the ICU. The obvious weakness of that argument is that the ICU was already bankrupt and disintegrating when he took over as Adviser. Perhaps, if the circumstances of the union had been different, he might have proved an admirable choice and enjoyed a fruitful collaboration with Kadalie, as indeed for a short time he did. He was eminently capable of introducing into the organization that stiffening which its administration so clearly needed. Financial integrity is what he valued above all else and he himself was transparently honest, dedicated, and unsparing of his time and energies. It must be considered doubtful, however, whether he and Kadalie could have maintained an unruffled relationship for long; whether the volatile and impetuous Kadalie could have endured for long the stern demands of financial accountability. What to Ballinger were guidance and advice were to Kadalie intolerable intrusion and insufferable patronage.

From the left came the criticism that the ICU did not pursue a policy that was militant enough. It never called a strike and discouraged those that spontaneously occurred. Despite, however, the widespread membership of the union at its greatest, it never disposed of effective power. Without influence in the labour force of the mining industry, it could never have mounted a general strike. The capacity of the employers to lock out and dismiss was immensely greater than the ability of the ICU members to strike. It is unlikely, moreover, that the ICU leaders had either the organizational ability or, much more to the point, any funds to prosecute a strike, as the 1930 East London strike, a rather insignificant local affair, amply demonstrated. The ICU failed to built up any reserves apart from a fixed deposit in the bank that was inviolate chiefly because it was not readily accessible. As for violent resistance to the regime, that was inconceivable. All the power lay with a governing class armoured in self-confidence and self-righteousness.

It might be thought that the ICU died from White hostility, scorned by employers and suffocated by oppressive legislation. This, too, is a view difficult to argue. The obstacles to the development of Black trade unionism were indeed formidable and in the 1920s the South African situation became increasingly inimical to them. Starting off in an unfavourable economic and social environment, the ICU saw during its brief existence the passage of further inhibitory laws. Nevertheless, the climate of the period was far more propitious than it was to become. The South Africa of the 1920s may have been a country where a Black trade union had difficulty in surviving. It was not a country where a Black trade union could not function because of the antagonism of the Government. Next to the Industrial Conciliation Act stood the Wage Act. Seen in retrospect, the punitive legislation and bureaucratic controls seem incredibly mild. Very little restraint was placed upon the movements of the ICU leaders and even the Native Administration Act could not bridle Kadalie's tongue. Magistrates were often lenient and disposed to give the benefit of the doubt. The police were sometimes capable of showing sympathy and understanding. Most important of all, within the ranks of the ruling class, there was a faction that lent some support to the Black proletariat in its struggle. The White labour movement, both in its industrial and its political guise, may have been selfish and narrow-minded, but it was not completely deaf to the voice of conscience and the demands of class solidarity. The Wage Board was used on behalf of Black workers; the White trade unionists did kill the Prevention of Disorders Bill and did modify the Native Administration Bill; Madeley did receive the ICU deputation. Other support, albeit cautious, came from the civil servants. Clearly the trend in Department of Labour policy was in the direction of acceptance of Blacks on equal terms in the White economy. Towards the end of 1928 the Secretary for Labour wrote, 'I believe that the Native has been told and come to believe that the White man regards him as a menace and fears him and that a policy of repression has been dictated by fear. The counter for an attitude of this kind – in regard to industrial matters *with which alone my remarks are concerned* – is by administrative methods to accept the Native – who *de facto* takes so large a share in our industries – as being there *de jure* and entitled to participate according to his standing and abilities in the protection and opportunities afforded by law to other workers'.[22] It is true that the future lay with the dogmatists and the segregationists and that the fall of Madeley and Pirow's foray into Durban were symptoms of growing harshness in other official quarters. Whatever moderating influence the White labour movement could exercise was greatly reduced by the success of the National Party in 1929 in gaining an overall majority in the House of Assembly. Nevertheless, the argument that the ICU would never have survived in the wintry climate that was being ushered in is irrelevant.

Nor is it true that employers were all aloof and unbending. While farmers' associations were usually, though not always, incapable of seeing good in the ICU, some urban employers, including South African Railways and Harbours on occasion, were approachable, and there is reason to believe that the union itself was neglectful of opportunities for influencing them.[23] The conclusion is inescapable that the ICU was not done to death by the assassins of capitalism, but died of its own fatal flaws. One wonders what sort of Black general labour union could have survived. The austere ICU of Ballinger failed as completely as the spendthrift ICU of Kadalie and the pettifogging ICU of Champion. The militant and presumably incorruptible and democratic South African Federation of Non-European Trade Unions, run under the aegis of the Communist Party with J. A. La Guma as General Secretary, also did not last.[24] It is difficult to suppress the conclusion that Black trade unionism is simply an anomaly in a multiracial society.

It is all too easy to show the deficiencies of the ICU's administration and policy. Money was poured out as fast as it came in on costly litigation, unwise business ventures, needless use of cars, telephones, and telegrams, expensive premises, ostentatious conferences, and a newspaper that never paid. It was a rake's progress. The officials were frequently inept, sometimes barely literate in English, the language of administration, and mostly ignorant about the methods and objects of trade unionism. Disgraced officials were regularly taken back into senior positions. The whole administration was top-heavy, with far too many paid officials. If each of the hundred branches of the ICU at its peak had a Secretary paid six pounds a week, this alone meant an expenditure of £7 200 a year. Add to that the salaries of half a dozen Provincial Secretaries and of the ten or so Head Office officials, another £1 500 or £2 000. Even Ballinger's truncated ICU of Africa, with a modest estimate of needs, aimed at a budget of more than £4 000 a year.[25]

Its very improvidence would have killed the ICU whatever else happened. The goose laid only one golden egg before its neck was wrung, and that was squandered in a profitless splurge. All too often the ICU did not seem to know what to do. The inexperience of its leadership and the disparate and geographically dispersed character of its membership inhibited its welfare and negotiating functions, and consequently there was a tendency to be bemused by mere size of membership. Organization – by which was meant expanding membership – seemed often to be an end in itself. If Champion had a policy, it was recourse to the courts. In the short run it brought results, but in the long run it was easy enough to thwart by simple changes in the law, and it all ended with the Tatham judgment and the sale of ICU property for the benefit of lawyers. If Kadalie had a policy, it was appeal to the international labour movement, and the only outcome of that appeal was the support of a small group of English socialists whose enthusiastic and high-minded interest and concern were matched by an almost total impotence.

The obvious achievements of the ICU did not amount to much: the Cape Town wage increase of 1920 (and it is doubtful how far that can be attributed to the union); Champion's legal victories in 1926–7; Kadalie's successful defiance of the Government's ban in 1926 and his appearance at Geneva in 1927; the Bloemfontein wage award (once again scarcely attributable to the ICU); and the fall of Madeley in 1928 (a Pyrrhic victory, if one at all). Otherwise there was nothing but bloodshed, bickering, and extravagance, all ending in bitterness, recrimination, and disillusionment. It is difficult to forget the betrayal, not less poignant for being unintentional, of the wretched farm labourers in 1927–8. Yet, perhaps, such an assessment would be unduly pessimistic. One cannot but marvel at the size and complexity of an organization built up by half-educated men in a strange and hostile environment; at the high level of debate at the great conferences; and at the essential moderation and unanswerable justice of the demands that were made. It is arguable, moreover, that the achievement of the ICU was the welding together – however transiently and partially – of the Black and Coloured workers into a single movement, something the African National Congress and the African People's Organization failed to achieve. It did something else novel, too. It penetrated for the first time beneath the crust of the articulate and educated class and initiated the first genuinely popular movement among Blacks in South Africa. While it was the chief representative of Black opinion, the ICU explored what avenues were open to it, and if those turned out to be blind alleys, this does not mean that the exploring was not worth doing.

Notes

1. Sources for membership – Union of South Africa, *Social Statistics No. 4 of 1922*, 88; *Umteteli wa Bantu* 5 April 1924; ICU, *Evidence of the ICU to the Economic and Wage Commission*, 2; Facts for the International Labour Conference (B/Wits); Kadalie, C., Development of the African Labour Movement (B/UCT).

2. Findlay and Niemeyer to W. G. Ballinger 23 October 1928 (B/Wits).
3. Unidentified newspaper cutting (B/UCT).
4. Kadalie, C., *My Life*, 69–70.
5. *The Workers' Herald* 18 January 1928.
6. *The Workers' Herald* 21 July 1923.
7. ICU, *Evidence of the ICU to the Economic and Wage Commission*, 40–1.
8. Investigation and Report; the Natal Provincial and Durban Offices of the ICU 4 April 1928, Annexure F (F 1928/24).
9. *Natal Mercury* 19 July 1929.
10. Perhaps Champion – cf. W. G. Ballinger to A. C. Jones 23 January 1929 (B/UCT).
11. Statement showing branch transfers (F 1927/107).
12. Ibid.; Investigation and Report . . . Annexure F.
13. Circular letter of President and General Secretary 26 July 1928 (B/Wits); ICU News Letters 19 October 1928 and 18 January 1929.
14. 'Quite a number of the country members pay their subs in kind' (W. G. Ballinger to A. C. Jones 24 October 1928 B/UCT).
15. Branch Secretary, Vryheid to W. G. Ballinger 21 August 1928 (B/Wits).
16. H. Binda to H. Pim 16 September 1929 (B/Wits).
17. Cf. for example, *The Workers' Herald* 15 August 1925 and 15 January and 20 February 1926.
18. Kadalie, C., *My Life*, 99.
19. *The Workers' Herald* 20 July 1925.
20. Union of South Africa, *The Select Committee on the Subject of Native Bills*, 282.
21. Ballinger, W. G., The rise and fall of the ICU, n.d. (B/UCT).
22. Central Archives: Department of Labour 4002/1103/2 Secretary for Labour to Minister of Labour 15 November 1928. The italics are original.
23. *The Workers' Herald* 20 February and 28 July 1926.
24. Central Archives: Department of Labour 4003/1103/2 Report on the Federation of Non-European Trade Unions, Johannesburg 7 February 1929.
25. ICU of Africa, Administrative Report 20 June 1929 (B/Wits).

Sources

MANUSCRIPTS

Ballinger Papers, University of Cape Town (B/UCT) and University of the Witwatersrand (B/Wits)

Correspondence of W. G. Ballinger, C. Kadalie, A. W. G. Champion, A. Creech Jones, Mrs Ethelreda Lewis, Winifred Holtby, and others; newspaper cuttings; ICU reports; and stray copies of *The Workers' Herald*, the ICU Newsletter, and *New Africa*. All the material is dated 1926 or later. A considerable proportion of it relates to W. G. Ballinger's career after the virtual disappearance of the ICU. The collection is divided between the two universities on no obvious principle and some items are found in both parts.

Cape Archives, Cape Town

Agendas, Reports and Résumés Books of the City of Cape Town Council and Minutes of Meetings of the City's Native Affairs Committee. Apart from rare – but useful – references this source throws little light on the ICU, but is invaluable for information about the Black locations in Cape Town, especially the construction of Langa and the movement of Blacks into the Western Cape.

Central Archives, Pretoria

Department of the Interior A/1787 – information respecting the proposed deportation of Clements Kadalie in 1920 and subsequent references to it.

Department of Justice 3/527/17, 3/1064/18, 3/127/20 – police reports with few direct references to the ICU, but indispensable for the study of post-war African unrest, especially on the Witwatersrand.

Department of Labour 4002/1103 – official attitudes to the ICU in the Departments of Labour and Native Affairs, throwing light, in particular, on the Wage Act of 1925.

Forman Papers, University of Cape Town (F)

The Forman and Ballinger Collections make up the major manuscript holdings relating to the ICU. The former is composed of letters to ICU officials, other organizations, public authorities etc.; accounts and receipts; reports; leaflets and other printed matter; newspaper cuttings; minutes of meetings, especially of the ICU National Council; autobiographical pieces of A. W. G. Champion; photographs, etc. The Papers are arranged partly chronologically (yearly files 1925 to 1935, one file for the period 1936–1944) and partly topically (in some twenty files). Originally they were the personal archives of A. W. G. Champion, and those relating to the ICU cover the period of his own involvement in the union, that is from 1925. There is a good deal of information on his activities both before and, more particularly, after the main ICU period. In all there are some two thousand items.

Winifred Holtby Collection, Kingston-upon-Hull Central Library (WH)

Letters from Clements Kadalie to A. Creech Jones and copies of replies, about forty items.

South African Institute of Race Relations, Braamfontein

1. Minutes of the Joint Council of Europeans and Natives, Johannesburg – of slight value for ICU studies, but a useful source of information about the 'Native problem'.

2. The Saffery Papers – B Papers on the Industrial and Commercial Workers' Union of Africa (ICU) – Forty or so items dating from 1927, but overwhelmingly from 1929, and mostly duplicating printed material in other collections. They include, however, the brief history of the ICU by H. D. Tyamzashe.

Papers of the Trade Union Council of South Africa, University of the Witwatersrand (TUCSA Papers)

This collection contains minutes of meetings and some correspondence of the Cape Federation of Labour Unions. The references to the ICU are scanty, but much can be learnt about the labour movement in Cape Town during and after the First World War. Any research into the White industrial labour movement in South Africa would have to include a careful study of the entire collection.

University of the Witwatersrand Champion Papers (Wits CP)

A 1925/6 letter-book of A. W. G. Champion, covering an earlier period than the similar letter-book in the Forman Collection. It is valuable for the light thrown on his early days as ICU organizer in Durban.

University of the Witwatersrand ICU Collection (Wits ICU)

This is composed of six files, with some items going back to 1926, but with most dating from the later years of the organization. Letters from Mrs Lewis, A. Creech Jones, and W. G. Ballinger predominate. The miscellaneous material is of marginal significance.

NEWSPAPERS

1. Of major importance –

The Workers' Herald

A thorough study of this, the ICU's own newspaper, is essential. The main files (both imperfect) are in the Library of Congress and the South African Library, Cape Town. Scattered issues are to be found in the Ballinger Collection and in the Cory Library, Grahamstown, the latter belonging originally to Professor E. R. Roux.

New Africa

Clements Kadalie's short-lived newspaper of 1929, extant copies of which are rare.

Cape Times (Cape Town), *The Friend* (Bloemfontein), and *The Eastern Province Herald*

Essential for piecing together the very early history of the ICU.

The Natal Advertiser (Durban) and *The Star* (Johannesburg)

Very useful for the later period of the ICU, when, however, the manuscript collections are the main sources of information.

2. Of less importance –

APO

The newspaper of the Coloured African People's Organization (APO), from which bits of information about the ICU's early years can be gleaned.

Abantu-Batho

The paper of the African National Congress (ANC), this is difficult to come by, but is of limited value for a study of the ICU.

Ilanga lase Natal

Rev J. L. Dube's Natal paper has fairly sparse references to the ICU.

Imvo Zabantsundu

A paper edited firstly by John Tengo Jabavu and then by his son, A. M. Jabavu, the Senior Vice-President of the ICU. The references to the ICU are surprisingly meagre, but worth hunting for.

The International

The organ of the International Socialist League, this is also difficult to come by in South Africa, but in any case is of limited value.

Umteteli wa Bantu

Published by the Chamber of Mines and, being hostile to the ICU, perhaps the most informative of the vernacular newspapers.

The Churchman
A mission paper with occasional references to the ICU.
The Cape Argus (Cape Town), *The Cape Mercury* (King William's Town), *The East London Daily Dispatch*, *The Frankforter* (Frankfort, Orange Free State), *Natal Mercury* (Durban), *The Natal Witness* (Pietermaritzburg), *Port Elizabeth Advertiser*, *The Queenstown Daily Representative and Free Press*, and *Rand Daily Mail* (Johannesburg)
Newspapers that can profitably be consulted for local or supplementary national information.
The Times (London)
There are scattered reports that are not without value.

GOVERNMENT PUBLICATIONS (UNION OF SOUTH AFRICA)

1. Of major importance –
Debates of the House of Assembly
Indispensable for recapturing the controversies surrounding contemporary legislation and useful for occasional references to Clements Kadalie and his union.
Report of the Commissioners Appointed to Enquire into the Causes of, and Occurrences at, the Native Disturbances at Port Elizabeth on the 23rd October, 1920, and the General Economic Conditions as they Affect the Native and Coloured Population (Annexure 143 – 1921) and *Letter Addressed to the Acting Prime Minister by the Members of the Commission Appointed to Enquire into the Native Riots at Port Elizabeth on the 23 October, 1920* (Annexure 656 – 1921)
Report of the Economic and Wage Commission (U.G. 14 – 1926)
Very useful for general information about the African labour question and for contemporary attitudes to industrial legislation for Africans.
Report of the Native Economic Commission 1930–1932 (U.G. 22 – 1934)
Essential source of information about conditions amongst Blacks in town and country during the ICU period.
Report of the Select Committee on the Subject of the Union Native Council Bill, Coloured Persons Rights Bill, Representation of Natives in Parliament Bill, and Natives Land (Amendment) Bill (S.C. 10 – 1927)
A mine of information, especially of value for the study of land and agricultural questions.

2. Of less importance –
Annual Departmental Reports No. 6 Covering the Period 1925–1926 (U.G. 6 – 1927)
Annual Report of the Department of Justice for the Calendar Year 1919 (U.G. 35 – 1920)
Annual Report of the Factories Division, Department of Mines and Industries, for the Period 1 May 1919 to 31 December 1919 (U.G. 42 – 1920)
Census of Population, Part VIII – Statistics Regarding Non-Europeans (U.G. 40 – 1924)
Native Affairs Act (Act to provide for the constitution of a commission and of native councils and for convening native conferences, with a view to facilitating the administration of native affairs) (Act No. 23 of 1920)
Native Labour Regulation Act (Act No. 15 of 1911)
Official Year Books of the Union of South Africa
Report of the Administrator of South-West Africa for the Year 1924 (U.G. 33 – 1925)
Report of the Commissioner of Police for the Year 1928–1929 (U.G. 13 – 1930)
Report of the Department of Justice for the Calendar Year 1918 (U.G. 36 – 1919)
Report of the Economic Commission, January 1914 (U.G. 12 – 1914)
Report of the General Manager of Railways and Harbours for the Year Ended 31st March, 1924 (U.G. 43 – 1924)
Report of the Native Affairs Commission for the Year 1921 (U.G. 15 – 1922)

Report of the Native Churches Commission (U.G. 39 – 1925)
Report of the Select Committee on the Wage Bill (S.C. 14 – 1925)
Report of the Third Census of the Population 3 May, 1921 (U. G. 37 – 1924)
Social Statistics No. 2 – 1920 (Statistics of Retail and Wholesale Prices, Rents and Cost of Living)
Social Statistics No. 3 – 1921 (Statistics of Wages and Industrial Matters and of Retail and Wholesale Prices, Rents, and Cost of Living 1895–1921)
Social Statistics No. 4 – 1922 (Statistics of Wages and Industrial Matters and of Retail and Wholesale Prices, Rents, and Cost of Living, 1895–1922)

CONTEMPORARY PRINTED SOURCES, ALL OF DIRECT SIGNIFICANCE FOR A STUDY OF THE ICU

Ballinger, W. G., 1930, Industrialisation and the Bantu, in Student Christian Association, *Christian Students and Modern South Africa*, Alice
Ballinger, W. G., 'Iseeyou', *The Nusas*, I, 10, November 1928
Barnes, L., 1930, *Caliban in Africa, an Impression of Colour-Madness*, London
Brittain, V. and G. Handley-Taylor, 1960, (eds.), *Selected Letters of Winifred Holtby and Vera Brittain, 1920–1935*, London
Champion, A. W. G., *c.* 1929, *Mehlomadala, My Experiences in the ICU*, Durban
Champion, A. W. G., 1927, *The Truth about the ICU*, Durban
Gitsham, E., and Trembath, F. F., 1926, *A First Account of Labour Organisation in South Africa*, Durban
Hunter, M., 1936, *Reaction to Conquest, Effects of Contact with Europeans on the Pondo of South Africa*, London
Industrial and Commerical Workers' Union of Africa, 1925, *Evidence of Industrial and Commercial Workers' Union of Africa, Submitted at Johannesburg on September 19th, 1925*, Johannesburg
Industrial and Commercial Workers' Union of Africa, *Revised Constitution as Amended by Conference at Johannesburg, 1925* Cape Town, 1925
Industrial and Commercial Workers' Union of Africa, *Constitution and Rules, Revised and Adopted by Special Congress at Kimberley 16th to 21st December, 1927* Johannesburg, 1928
International Labour Office, *International Labour Conference Tenth Session* Geneva, 1927
Kadalie, C., The aims and motives of the ICU, in Seventh General Missionary Conference of South Africa, *The Realignment of Native Life on a Christian Basis, Being the Report of the Proceedings of the Seventh General Missionary Conference of South Africa*, Lovedale, 1928
Kadalie, C., 1927, *The Relation between White and Black Workers in South Africa, A Brief Account of the Labour Movement*, Johannesburg and London
Lenono, G., 1927, *The ICU Funds: Mr Allison Champion, Provincial Secretary, ICU (Natal) and the ICU Funds*, Durban
R. Leslie, 1930, Coloured labour and trade unionism in Cape Town, *The Journal of the Economic Society of South Africa*, III, Part 2, 6
Leubuscher, C., 1931, *Der südafrikanische Eingeborene als Industriearbeiter und als Stadtbewohner*, Jena
Lucas, F. A. W., The determination of wages in South Africa, *South African Journal of Economics*, I, 1 March 1933
Mahabane, Z. R. n.d., *The Good Fight, Selected Speeches*, Evanston
S. M. Makgatho, *Presidential Address Delivered at the Ninth Annual Congress of the South African Native National Congress Held at Queenstown, Cape Province on the 24th May, 1920* Pretoria, 1920

Mweli Skota, T. D., *The African Yearly Register, Being an Illustrated National Biographical Dictionary (Who's Who) of Black Folks in Africa*, Johannesburg, n.d.
Nicholls, G. H., 1923, *Bayete. 'Hail to the King'*, London
Robertson, H. M., The economic condition of the rural natives, in Schapera, "I 1934, ed., *Western Civilisation and the Natives of South Africa, Studies in Culture Contact*, London
F. A. Saunders, 1920, *Municipal Control of Locations, a Paper Read at the 13th Session of the Association of Municipal Corporations of the Cape Province*, Grahamstown
Silburn, P. A., 1927, *South Africa; White and Black – or Brown?* London
South African Law Reports; Decisions of the Supreme Court of South Africa
South African Native Races Committee (ed.), 1908, *The South African Natives; their Progress and Present Conditions* London

SUBSEQUENT ACCOUNTS AND REMINISCENCES

Burger, J. (pseudonym of L. Marquard), 1943, *The Black Man's Burden*, London
Coka, G., 1936, The story of Gilbert Coka of the Zulu tribe of Natal, South Africa, in M. Perham (ed.), *Ten Africans*, London
Msimang, H. Selby, South Africa's freedom struggle in focus, *Contact*, III, 30 July 1960
Perry, J. A. G. & C., 1975, (eds.), *A Chief is a Chief by the People: The Autobiography of Stimela Jason Jingoes*, London
Roux, E. R., 1944, *S. P. Bunting, a Political Biography*, Cape Town
Roux, E. R. and W., 1970, *Rebel Pity, the Life of Eddie Roux*, London
Smith, H. H., 1949, The development of labour organization in East London, 1900–1948, M. Econ. thesis, Rhodes University
Tyamzashe, H. D., 1941, Summarised history of the Industrial and Commercial Workers' Union of Africa (typescript), East London

Index